Freud and Monotheism

Berkeley Forum in the Humanities

Freud and Monotheism
Moses and the Violent Origins of Religion

Gilad Sharvit
and Karen S. Feldman, editors

Townsend Center for the Humanities
University of California, Berkeley

Fordham University Press
New York

Copyright © 2018 The Regents of the University of California

The publishers have no responsibility for the persistence or accuracy of URLs for external or third-party Internet websites referred to in this publication and do not guarantee that any content on such websites is, or will remain, accurate or appropriate.

The publishers also produce their books in a variety of electronic formats. Some content that appears in print may not be available in electronic books.

Library of Congress Cataloging-in-Publication Data available online at http://catalog.loc.gov.

Printed in the United States of America

20 19 18   5 4 3 2 1

First edition

Contents

Freud and Monotheism

Gilad Sharvit and Karen S. Feldman

Introduction

THERE ARE MANY points of entry to Sigmund Freud's monumental *Moses and Monotheism* (1939). Freud's last work presented a remarkable contribution to a wide array of topics. The book revisited neo-Lamarckian theories of heredity, offered a theory of the formation of religions, mounted radical criticism against modern historiography, and presented a new psychoanalytic theory of the collective mind and of trauma. The historical context of the book, and Freud's personal motivations, however, fed the book's sense of urgency. Freud began to work on his new book on "The Man Moses" in Vienna in the summer of 1934. It was only a year after his works were added to the Nazi list of blacklisted books and burnt in the great fire that portended the dark times to come. In *Moses and Monotheism*, Freud addressed that upheaval. His book originated out of a desire to shed light on the anti-Semitism that would come to motivate the horrors awaiting Europe. As he revealed to his close friend the Austrian author Arnold Zweig, Freud would use his psychoanalysis to explain the long history of the hatred of his people.

For being somewhat at a loss what to do in a period of comparative leisure I have written something myself and this, contrary to my original intention, took up so much of my time that everything else was neglected. . . . The starting point of my work is familiar to you—it was the same as that of your *Bilanz*. Faced with the new persecutions, one asks oneself again how the Jews come to be what they are and why they have attracted this undying hatred. I soon discovered the formula: Moses created the Jews. So I gave the work this title: *The Man Moses, a Historical Novel* [*Der Mann Moses, ein historischer Roman*].[1]

Freud's nod to happenstance need not mislead us. Although he supposedly undertook this investigation only because he was "at a loss of what to do," Freud, an experienced public figure, had clear understanding of the turmoil ahead. His letter detailed his apprehension over the increased danger that anti-Semites like the Austrian ethnologist Pater Wilhelm Schmidt and others in the Catholic orthodoxy had posed to himself, his family, but also, and perhaps even most worryingly, to psychoanalysis in Vienna. It was not only Freud's life but his life's work that was in danger.

The book's unconventional publication process reflected the gravity of this problem. Written over several years amid increasing concern about anti-Semitism, *Moses and Monotheism* was completed and published only at the heels of Freud's escape from the Nazi occupation of Austria. All the while, Freud had to "remain silent," as he confessed in an early letter on his new Moses project to Lou Andreas-Salomé.[2] The first two of the book's three essays appeared in 1937 in *Imago*. Freud delayed the publication of the third essay until after he was able to escape Vienna in the spring of 1938. Only in the safety of London did Freud feel confident enough to publish this work on the psychological roots of anti-Semitism.[3] In the prefatory note to the third essay, Freud gave voice to his anxieties about the anti-Semitic establishment that had hitherto prevented him from publishing the book. These were exactly the same fears he expressed in secret to Arnold Zweig half a decade earlier: "At the earlier date I was living under the protection of the Catholic Church, and was afraid that the publication of my work would result in the loss of that protection and would conjure up a prohibition upon the work of the adherents and students of psycho-analysis in Austria. . . . [In London,] I can breathe a sigh of relief now that the weight has been taken off me and that I am once more able to speak and write—I had almost said 'and think'—as I wish or as I must."[4]

Nevertheless, if Freud meant to explain anti-Semitism, he had a curious way of doing so, as the opening remarks of the book acknowledged:

> To deprive a people of the man whom they take pride in as the greatest of their sons is not a thing to be gladly or carelessly undertaken, least of all by someone who is himself one of them. But we cannot allow any such reflection to induce us to put the truth aside in favor of what are supposed to be national interests; and, moreover, the clarification of a set of facts may be expected to bring us a gain in knowledge.[5]

Freud's book about anti-Semitism, written and published during a most difficult time of his people, would indeed take away the "greatest of their sons." The book did not merely hint at this dispossession but directly argued for it. In Freud's retelling of Jewish history, Moses was an Egyptian nobleman. Freud's last denouement was to uncover and establish that the Jewish hero and lawgiver was after all a Gentile.

To support this claim, the first essay of the book examined the etymology of the name Moses, which, Freud argued, had an Egyptian origin—a claim that had appeared in biblical exegesis since Goethe, Schiller, and Heine. Freud added to this argument by alluding to Otto Rank's 1909 *The Myth of the Birth of the Hero*. Rank's study of ancient myth suggested that many hero legends in the archaic world had "a literal conformity"[6] in their narrative plot. These legends depicted a hero born to aristocratic parents but condemned to death. In this classic plot, the hero was rescued as a child by people of humble origins, only to rediscover his aristocratic lineage as an adult. The biblical story of Moses, claimed Freud, mirrored the pattern of the ancient hero legend but at the same time also inverted it, insofar as the powerful adult Moses discovers his true origins as a child of slaves. Freud thus concluded that while the story of Moses's humble origins served the Jewish tradition well, both Moses's name and the structure of his myth revealed a different story than that of the Bible. They indicated that Moses did actually descend from the royal Egyptian dynasty.

The first essay of *Moses and Monotheism* was modest in its length and its theoretical novelty. It mostly repeated known facts about Moses and earlier speculations of other biblical scholars in order to examine the possibility that Moses was an Egyptian. In the second essay of the book, Freud made an even more drastic move. He reread the story of Moses in light of his own work on the origins of religion in *Totem and Taboo* (1913). In this essay, it was not only the ascription to Moses of an Egyptian identity that would unnerve the Jewish community around Freud but Freud's recasting of the end of Moses's life.

THE SECOND ESSAY opened with Freud's growing appreciation of the apparent similarities between Jewish monotheism and the brief monotheistic episode in Egyptian history during the reign of Akhenaten. This analogy provoked Freud to suggest that Moses was an Egyptian nobleman who adopted the Israelite slaves after the collapse of Egyptian monotheism and instructed them in his monotheistic religion of Aten. The Israelites, in other words, were put to use by a noble Egyptian Moses in order to save the dying Egyptian religion. The Israelites' conversion to the Egyptian monotheism, however, was not effortless. In Freud's recounting, the Israelites were now forced to obey "the harsh prohibitions" of their new religion, for instance, the taboo "against making an image of any living or imagined creature."[7] Moses's version of monotheism demanded a radical restriction of the drives of a people who were accustomed to the sensual gratification of a polytheistic religion. This tension, argued Freud, was very soon to erupt. The Israelites could not have "[tolerated] such a highly spiritualized religion," and in accord with the plot of *Totem and Taboo*, "the savage Semites took fate into their own hands and rid themselves of their tyrant."[8]

Freud's scandalous claim about the murder of Moses was not the first attempt to uncover the violent end of the first Jewish leader. Freud, in fact, was extremely impressed with a similar claim by Ernst Sellin in his 1922 *Mose und seine Bedeutung für die israelitisch-jüdische Religionsgeschichte*. In this controversial work, the German theologian based his argument about the death of Moses in the desert on several ambiguous sentences in Hosea. Freud, however, aimed at much more than a project of biblical exegesis. *Moses and Monotheism* was a study of the violent origins of religion in general. Building on his work on the first totem religion, Freud assumed that the Israelites, like the brothers in the primal tribe, repented for the murder of Moses and were crushed by their own guilt. Their struggle with their guilt was, however, different from that of the murderous brothers. The brothers in *Totem and Taboo* went on to replace their dead father with the totem animal and thus created the first religion in history. The Israelites found solace in the image of another, second Moses, a priest of the pagan god Yahweh in Kadesh. This second Moses and his "volcano God, . . . an uncanny, bloodthirsty demon,"[9] allowed the Israelites to enjoy a religious sensuality whose renunciation the Egyptian Moses and his abstract God had demanded.

Yet this pagan priest of the desert was able to offer his new followers only temporary comfort. After a short period under his command, their trauma over the murder of Moses reappeared. As a result, the Israelites accepted the monotheism of the father they had killed. The first Moses and his religion won over the hearts of the Israelites, following a latency period at the service of the second Moses, signaling the "final victory of the Mosaic god."[10] The same spiritual characteristics of the first, Egyptian Moses that were rejected under the second Moses of Kadesh were now imprinted on the Jews. Rationality and the denunciation of sensual enjoyment, Freud suggests, define them ever since. *Totem and Taboo* described how the first murder of the primal father introduced the first religious prohibition; Freud's last book argued that the murder of Moses established a new kind of religion: the monotheistic religion.

The second essay presented an analogy between the murder of the primal father and Freud's myth of a twofold Moses but lacked theoretical force. It was a fascinating historical novel—to echo the first title Freud had selected for the book—but not much more. The third and last essay of *Moses and Monotheism* was to provide the conceptual ground for Freud's radical argument. Indeed, the history of the Jewish people, Freud's own people, required that Freud reassess the basic tenets of his psychoanalysis. Published only a few months prior to Freud's death in London, *Moses and Monotheism* presented Freud with a final opportunity for reflection and reconsideration of his life work. Edward Said noted this aspect of the book in *Freud and the Non-European* (2004), claiming that the book was a formative example of a so-called late style (*Spätstil*). According to Said, *Moses and Monotheism*, similar to other last great works—of Theodor Adorno, Thomas Mann, and Mozart—was not meant to achieve a "resolution and reconciliation" but to evoke "more complexity and a willingness to let irreconcilable elements of the work remain as they are: episodic, fragmentary, unfinished (i.e., unpolished)."[11] Freud's last work, written over half a decade, famously suffered from unnecessary repetitions and inconsistencies and multiple contradictions. With Said, the idiosyncratic nature of the book became its most valuable asset: it was here that Freud finally allowed his psychoanalytic theory to open up the kinds of discrepancies and inconsistencies that characterize great works of the humanities. It was here that *Moses and Monotheism* amounted to much more than a book on the origins of Judaism but a masterpiece of psychoanalysis and a groundbreaking work in the history of secular and postsecular thought.

FREUD'S THIRD AND last essay of the book, "Moses, His People and Monotheistic Religion," proposed first and foremost an alternative to modern theories of history and historiography. Freud, let us note, went against all that is sacred and known in Jewish history. His work purported to uncover a devastating *historical truth* that was missing from the official Jewish historical record. It openly declared the shortcomings of modern historical science, which according to Freud failed to recount the true history of the ancient Israelites. Freud discovered a locus of truth that historical science neglected. The third essay opened with Freud's explanation of this scandalous fact.

> The people who had come from Egypt had brought writing and the desire to write history along with them; but it was to be a long time before historical writing realized that it was pledged to unswerving truthfulness. . . . As a result of these circumstances a discrepancy was able to grow up between the written record and the oral transmission of the same material—*tradition*. What had been omitted or changed in the written record might very well have been preserved intact in tradition. . . . A tradition of such a kind might meet with various sorts of fate. What we should most expect would be that it would be crushed by the written account, would be unable to stand up against it, would become more and more shadowy and would finally pass into oblivion. But it might meet with other fates: one of these would be that the tradition itself would end in a written record, and we shall have to deal with yet others as we proceed.[12]

History, claimed Freud, was for too long concerned with the written record, with the organized and controlled information that previous generations consciously wanted to report to the next. Freud, a master of the hermeneutics of suspicion, approached history otherwise. While history told much but revealed little on the formative events that shaped the present, Freud looked for unconscious archival "evidence." He was interested in the oral tradition—instead of the written history—that preserved rumors of the past. In tradition, Jewish tradition, he was able to uncover a truth to which modern historiography, relying on formal historical records, was blind. This Jewish tradition was, for Freud, more reliable than history books. In essence, Freud called for a new, psychoanalytic study of the past. In the same way that Freud uncovered the past of his patients, he now searched for clues of "something [that] occurred in the life of the human species [that is] similar to what occurs in the life of individuals."[13] In his eyes, it was time to replace the old forms of historiography with a new and improved research of the past. His science presented a corrective model for such an endeavor.[14]

Freud's attack on historical science exemplified the limitations of modern historiography. The main body of the third essay of *Moses and Monotheism* aimed to justify an alternative procedure: the application of psychoanalysis to history. To a 1939 reader of the book, this was perhaps somewhat strange, since Freud already applied psychoanalysis to the history of religion in *Totem and Taboo*. Freud had shown that history obeys the same mechanism that forms the individual mind. "It is probable," Freud famously claimed in *Totem and Taboo*, "that the totemic system was a product of the conditions involved in the Oedipus complex."[15] Yet, in *Moses and Monotheism*, Freud suggested some important differences, despite his own continual insistence that his Moses project merely reiterated the conclusions of *Totem and Taboo*.[16] One crucial addition was Freud's theory of the return of the repressed.

Early trauma—defence—latency—outbreak of neurotic illness—partial return of the repressed. Such is the formula which we have laid down for the development of a neurosis. . . . The reader is now invited to take the next step . . . of supposing that events occurred of a sexually aggressive nature, which left behind them permanent consequences but were for the most part fended off and forgotten, and which after a long latency came into effect and created phenomena similar to symptoms in their structure and purpose.[17]

In *Moses and Monotheism*, historical traumas structure and restructure the history of peoples in the same way that traumas structure and restructure an individual life. The murder of Moses was such a trauma—it was the event that formed the Jewish people. In Freud's story, the Israelite slaves first defended against the trauma of the killing of Moses by accepting the second Moses. They distanced their guilt, repressed it, in the same way that an individual represses a personal trauma. However, after a period of latency, the trauma had to reappear, as happens in individual traumas, and the Jewish people returned to the laws of the Moses they had murdered. The trauma of the murder was the fundamental force of their history. Latency was a key concept in Freud's new vision of history. There was no latency in the totem myth: the sons resurrected the father in the totem figure as an immediate response to their guilt. In contrast, the Israelites had, according to Freud, a period of latency in which their guilt was temporarily expunged. History was now following the new model of return of the repressed: in analogy to the latency period in an individual's trauma, in which the trauma is forgotten, the Israelites enjoyed a relative ease under the second Moses. But in the same way that the trauma retains its hold on the individual, the first Moses retained his hold on his people. This addition of latency to Freud's theory of history also subverted the quasi-positivistic claims of *Totem and Taboo*. In *Moses and Monotheism*, there was no linear connection between historical events. History was informed by missing signs: events that were supposedly forgotten proved more powerful than recent events that were retained in memory.

Together with Freud's previous theoretical analysis of the return of the repressed in *Beyond the Pleasure Principle* (1921), *Moses and Monotheism* presented a radical theory of trauma. *Beyond the Pleasure Principle* uncovered the deep mechanisms of the undesirable return of trauma in the individual; *Moses and Monotheism* provided a theory of the social and historical effects of communal traumas. In *Beyond the Pleasure Principle*, written in the aftermath of World War I, Freud explained the traumas of the soldiers returning from the battlefields. The horrific experiences that the soldiers relived back home led to his conclusion that "there really does exist in the mind a compulsion to repeat which overrides the pleasure principle."[18] This assertion led to a revision of Freud's theory of instincts and to his speculation about the death-instinct, but it also set the stage for Freud's later vision of history. In essence, these early observations explained the insurmountable power of the murder over the Jewish people, as Freud summarized in his letter to Andreas-Salomé: "Religions owe their compulsive power to the *return of the repressed*; they are reawakened memories of very ancient, forgotten, highly emotional episodes of human history."[19] In the Freudian recounting of Jewish history, the murder promised the success of the Mosaic project. The return of the repressed explained the powerful hold of the murder: why the Jews will always be Moses's people. This insight would inform a new psychoanalytic theory of religion. Freud's theory of the return of the repressed emphasized the irresistible power of religions on our lives: the same way that a trauma maintains a hold on the individual, it possessed a whole people. Religions were a complicated and nuanced response to a collective trauma. Their compelling force was grounded in their violent origins.[20]

FREUD'S ANALOGY BETWEEN individual and collective formed the basis of his theory of history and religion. And yet, effective as it was, it was still missing one important ingredient. In Freud's psychoanalysis, it was well established that childhood traumas affect a person even into adulthood, but it was not at all clear how traumas of past generations affected future generations. Freud proved in his clinical practice and theoretical work that traumas imprint the individual psyche. He had yet to explain the deep mechanism of communal trauma. Freud still needed to show how the effects of trauma are transmitted through history: if a people was not only to remember the traumas but also to be forever changed by them, there had to be something that continually influenced the collective existence. Freud's answer to this problem exhibited his long-standing interest in neo-Lamarckism:

> On further reflection I must admit that I have behaved for a
> long time as though the inheritance of memory-traces of the
> experience of our ancestors, independently of direct com-
> munication and of the influence of education by the setting of
> an example, were established beyond question. . . . My posi-
> tion, no doubt, is made more difficult by the present attitude
> of biological science, which refuses to hear of the inheritance
> of acquired characters by succeeding generations. I must,
> however, in all modesty confess that nevertheless I cannot do
> without this factor in biological evolution. The same thing is
> not in question, indeed, in the two cases: in the one it is a mat-
> ter of acquired characters which are hard to grasp, in the other
> of memory-traces of external events—something tangible, as
> it were. But it may well be that at bottom we cannot imagine
> one without the other. If we assume the survival of these
> memory-traces in the archaic heritage, we have bridged the
> gulf between individual and group psychology: we can deal
> with peoples as we do with an individual neurotic.[21]

Freud, it appears, resorted to a "strong" theory of inheritance of memory traces to explain the effects of traumas on future generations. He proposed that humankind "inherits" acquired characteristics and, in the context of his last work, that the psychological effects of traumas had a substantive, organic effect that was transmissible to future generations. The first generation murdered Moses, and as a result, something was changed in their character. The next generations inherited that change. The Jewish people were marked by spirituality, reason, and renunciation, and these character traits were transmitted from generation to generation for thousands of years.

Freud's theory of transgenerational transmission of psychical characteristics received much attention in the literature on *Moses and Monotheism*. As we detail below, the debate that this theory generated over the years reflects the fundamental role of *Moses and Monotheism* in the legacy of Freud and psychoanalysis.

FREUD'S BOOK ON the contorted beginning of the Jewish people suffered from a problematic beginning of its own. Harshly criticized at the time of its publication, the book seemed doomed to pass into oblivion.[22] A book disrupted by repetitions, inaccuracies, and apologies, *Moses and Monotheism* was dismissed as an anxious reaction of an old man to his impending death in exile in London. It was perceived as sad evidence of the complicated relations of Freud—weakened in his struggle with throat cancer—toward his Jewish identity and heritage, far from the scientific work of the brave and honest scientist. Martin Buber's *Moses* (1946) clearly shared those sentiments as it dedicated only a short, dismissive footnote to Freud's own work on Moses from half a decade earlier. Buber had only disappointment with Freud's idea to rewrite the history of Moses: "That a scholar of so much importance in his own field as Sigmund Freud could permit himself to issue so unscientific a work, based on groundless hypotheses, as his *Moses and Monotheism*, is regrettable."[23] A generation later, Freud and his Moses were finally awarded their prominent place in the history of modern thought. That renewed interest proved *Moses and Monotheism* to be a fertile ground for discussions of history and tradition, religion and Judaism, political theory and identity theory, ethics, racism, and anti-Semitism.[24]

The debate on Freud's theory of transgenerational transmission is an important example of the diverse and often conflicting ways *Moses and Monotheism* has been understood in recent decades. Freud's theory of the return of the repressed seemed to suggest discontinuities and ruptures within the constitution of the Jewish tradition. And yet the theory of transgenerational transmission seemed to ascribe to Freud a certain positivism; there was a concrete, identifiable, and unchanging content to the Jewish character that was passed on from generation to generation. This debate was sparked by Yosef Hayim Yerushalmi in *Freud's Moses* (1991), who framed Freud's theory of transgenerational transmission within the context of modern Jewish life. According to Yerushalmi, the book presented a radical attempt to reformulate modern Jewish identity, indeed all religious identities, on new and psychoanalytically enhanced foundations. *Moses and Monotheism* was meant to solve an urgent problem of modern secular Judaism: faced with the growing assimilation to German-speaking society, Freud sought to develop a new positive psychological definition of Judaism that would secure the Jewish identity of Freud, himself an assimilated Jew. Freud achieved this definition of identity by identifying an archaic heritage that is common to all Jews, religious and nonreligious alike.[25] In Freud's book, Jews were Jews not because of their religious faith, practices, or culture but because they shared a set of basic qualities that were imprinted on their forebears following the murder of Moses. Jews were truly the "Chosen People"[26] but not *God's* chosen: it was *Moses* who chose his people and eternally marked them with his demand for spiritual and intellectual life.[27]

Yerushalmi's positivistic approach to *Moses and Monotheism* and his overemphasis of Freud's "Lamarckian schemas" was criticized in Richard Bernstein's *Freud and the Legacy of Moses* (1998) and Jacques Derrida's *Archive Fever* (1996).[28] While Yerushalmi was all too happy to commit Freud to a biological framework, in order to secure a positive meaning to the psychologically transmitted

Jewish tradition, Bernstein and Derrida found Freud's description of tradition and history more nuanced and complicated.[29] In contrast to Yerushalmi's focus on the powerful effects of the trauma of the murder of Moses, Bernstein concentrated on its nonlinear manifestation in history. Freud, according to Bernstein, postulated a "gap" in Jewish tradition—a latency period after the murder—during which the murder of Moses was "suppressed and repressed, before it eventually proved triumphant." This gap presented a different model of tradition: if Yerushalmi identified consistency and accessibility in the Jewish tradition, in Bernstein's version tradition was not "simply continuous, [but involved] ruptures and reversal,"[30] conscious *and* unconscious processes, and an interplay of hidden and accessible social forms and historical trajectories that invite a critical project of the hermeneutics of culture.

For Derrida, the stakes were even higher. In *Archive Fever*, Derrida built on Freud's theory of tradition to deconstruct modern notions of knowledge. Derrida was interested specifically in the conventional conceptions of knowledge as the accumulation of facts. Considering the function of archives as stagnant containers of historical data, Derrida found that Freud's denunciation of official history, and his insistence on the importance of irregular forms of information, presented a different model of historical archive. Against Yerushalmi's "facts" of identity that history preserved intact, Derrida's Freud showed that archives are inconsistent, ruptured, and even contaminated. Freud granted Derrida the opportunity to put into practice his essential claim that "archivization produces as much as it records an event."[31] Contrary to a completed notion of knowledge, Freud's ruptured tradition offered a subversive archive that "produces more archive, and that is why the archive is never closed. It opens out of the future."[32]

Edward Said added to this criticism from a different perspective. Focusing on Yerushalmi's reading of Freud's theory of identity as positive and exclusive, Said insisted on the relevance of the Egyptian Moses to Freud's new theory of identity. While Yerushalmi disregarded the Egyptian roots of Judaism, for Said the possibility that Moses was a "stranger" to the Israelites was decisive. Moses's otherness was a constitutive element in the construction of Jewish identity and of Western identity in general: he was the non-European who formed the Western tradition and as such proved that "identity cannot be thought or worked through itself alone; it cannot constitute or even imagine itself without that radical originary break or flaw."[33] Said's message offered critical political implications to postcolonial consciousness, in which the relation to the other is defined, at best, in terms of empathy or compassion. Freud's Egyptian Moses illustrated a different form of communication, one marked by the mutual recognition of identity itself as "a troubling, disabling, destabilizing secular wound."[34]

FREUD'S DECISION TO focus on the figure of Moses in order to explain anti-Semitism was not random. Since the seventeenth century, Moses was at the focus of an ongoing debate regarding the essence of Judaism in particular and monotheism in general. Jan Assmann in *Moses the Egyptian* (1997) famously read Freud's book against the background of earlier interest in Moses by John Spencer, Friedrich Schiller, and other modern Bible scholars. His work illustrated the critical place of *Moses and Monotheism* in the context of the reemergence of the ancient "Mosaic distinction." In Assmann's history of religions, monotheism is identified as counterreligion, that is, as a special kind of religion that "rejects and repudiates everything that went before and what is outside itself as 'paganism.'"[35] This distinction was foreign to the ancient pagan world of translatable religious identities and practices. It both highlighted the violence of early monotheism toward neighboring religions and registered the violent core of Western civilization. By insisting on the Egyptian source for Jewish monotheism, Freud, according to Assmann, was "the one who restored the suppressed evidence [of counterhistory]." His revelation of the Egyptian origins of Moses aided modern efforts "to deconstruct 'counter-religion . . .' by blurring the basic distinctions as they were symbolized by the antagonistic constellation of Israel and Egypt."[36]

Freud, however, had ulterior motives for choosing the protagonist of his last work. Moses, he revealed to Andreas-Salomé in his 1935 letter, "has pursued [him] throughout the whole of [his] life." This lifelong fascination with the biblical figure of Moses was present already in September 1913, when Freud dedicated weeks of daily long visits to the famous sculpture of Moses by Michelangelo in the Basilica di San Pietro. He expressed his understanding of the sculpture in a work that was published anonymously. This "non-analytical child,"[37] as Freud characterized his analysis of the sculpture to a friend years later, manifested—in his image of Moses—the intricate place of religious and Jewish themes in Freud's life and work.

Freud's admiration of the figure of Moses encouraged some people to read *Moses and Monotheism* as a biographical work. The tale of a leader, a prophet, who was betrayed by his people; the heroic quest for eternal truths; Moses's imminent death—all of these are easily projected on Freud.[38] In that context, it has become, as Yerushalmi well noted, "something of a commonplace . . . to regard both the content of *Moses and Monotheism* and its convoluted gestation as symptoms of Freud's deep 'ambivalence' (that tired and evasive cliché) about his own Jewishness."[39] Marthe Robert, Freud's biographer, further noted in her *From Oedipus to Moses* (1976) that *Moses and Monotheism* provided the conditions under which Freud could say (as could Moses) "that he was neither a Jew, nor a German, nor anything that still bore a name; for he wished to be the son not of any man or country, but like the murdered prophet only of his life work."[40]

The personal aspect of the book, however, related to more than questions of identity. For Bluma Goldstein in *Reinscribing*

Moses (1992), Freud's lifelong attraction to the figure of Moses was founded on his fears concerning anti-Semitic violence. Faced with Nazi violence during the composition of the book, Freud was fascinated with Moses as an ideal hero of antiquity, a violent patriarchal ruler who was able to lure and coerce the masses and to fight the Gentiles. Moses was Freud's model for the Great Man:

> There is no doubt that it was a mighty prototype of a father which, in the person of Moses, stooped to the poor Jewish bondsmen to assure them that they were his dear children. And no less overwhelming must have been the effect upon them of the idea of an only, eternal, almighty God, to whom they were not too mean for him to make a covenant with them and who promised to care for them if they remained loyal to his worship. It was probably not easy for them to distinguish the image of the man Moses from that of his God; and their feeling was right in this, for Moses may have introduced traits of his own personality into the character of his God—such as his wrathful temper and his relentlessness.[41]

Moses was truly a great man: he had the "ability to influence others profoundly and therewith determine the course of history."[42] And Freud needed such a Moses to protect him from the horrors of anti-Semitism and to save his people.[43]

Daniel Boyarin's reconstruction of Freud's "colonial mimicry" in *Unheroic Conduct* (1997) portrayed a deeper, darker meaning of Freud's attraction to Moses.[44] This work, along with others, proved fertile to the ongoing discussion on the conflation of sexuality, circumcision, and racism in *Moses and Monotheism*. They highlighted the critical edge of Freud's psychoanalytic theory.[45] As with Goldstein's interpretation, for Boyarin, *Moses and Monotheism* registered a fascination of Freud with Moses as a figure of masculinity. In Boyarin's reading, however, this fascination was a perverse reaction to racist accusations: it represented Freud's admiration of ideals of masculinity that were alien, according to Boyarin, to Jewish history. In *Moses and Monotheism*, Freud accepted and to a large extent incorporated into his theories an anti-Semitic configuration of the Jew as feminine, homosexual, and weak. Moses expressed Freud's wish to distance himself from these charges. He had such a hold on Freud exactly because he granted Freud an opportunity for an "imaginary and desirable" conversion of the Jews to masculine Gentiles.[46] Moses was an Egyptian figure: he presented an Aryan form of masculinity that Freud adopted to defend himself and his people from the racist portrayal of Jews as feminine.

Sander Gilman, while arguing with Boyarin that "race is a category vitiated by the new science of psychoanalysis," suggested in a different vein that Freud's Moses in fact guaranteed the final victory of Freud against the anti-Semitic construction of the Jewish male as circumcised/castrated.[47] In *Moses and Monotheism*, Gilman claimed, Freud defined "who is diseased."[48] Freud portrayed circumcision, the source of the racist disgust with the Jews (and the root of racist representations of the Jew as feminine), as Moses's own invention, that is, as originating in Egypt or with the Gentiles, such that "anti-Semitic response to the nature of the Jews was not at all a response to the Jews themselves, but to the world of the anti-Semites."[49]

Moses and Monotheism was since its publication approached from a range of historical, biographical, religious, anthropological, and literary-critical angles. Wildly speculative but groundbreaking, its claims about the violent origins of religion and about the centrality of trauma and repression to the course of history make for invigorating and unresolvable controversies. It provided the opening for a series of debates, the Freud/Moses debates, that motivated the reframing of the psychoanalytical work of Freud in the humanities writ large and inspired the present volume.

Freud and Monotheism: Moses and the Violent Origins of Religion comprises nine chapters based on presentations that were originally given at the conference "Revisiting Freud and Moses: Heroism,

History and Religion," which took place at the University of California, Berkeley, in October 2015. The book highlights the broad impact of *Moses and Monotheism* across the humanities, drawing on the disciplines of philosophy, comparative literature, cultural studies, German literature, religious and Jewish studies, history, and psychoanalysis.

Richard J. Bernstein, whose contribution to the Freud/Moses debates was highlighted earlier, opens the collection. His chapter, "'Why [the Jews] Have Attracted This Undying Hatred,'" returns to his *Freud and the Legacy of Moses*, indeed to Freud's own motivation for writing *Moses and Monotheism*, in order to explain recent anti-Semitism. As he considers the implications of Jewish exceptionalism for growing anti-Semitic tendencies, Bernstein adds to ongoing discussions of the cultural implications of ethical iconoclastic monotheism, with respect to the philosophical import of Freud's theory of *Fortschritt in der Geistigkeit*. In a similar vein, Joel Whitebook offers a critical reappraisal of Freud's formulation of the advance in *Geistigkeit*. In his *"Geistigkeit*: A Problematic Concept," Whitebook finds Freud's concept to be too uncritical and even unanalytic. Whitebook is critical of Freud's celebration of *Geistigkeit* as an "unabashedly androcentric and patriarchal" concept, but more importantly, the term suggested an unambiguous progress in psychic life or cultural history, while psychoanalytic theory insists that all points of progress or advance "exact their price."

Willi Goetschel's "Heine and Freud: Deferred Action and the Concept of History" focuses on Freud's theory of tradition. Reading Freud's project through Heine's work on history and messianism, Goetschel finds *Moses and Monotheism* to be a pointed intervention in a larger discourse on the multiple origins of tradition. Goetschel's survey of Heine's writing proves that Freud's Moses did not originate from "Egypt" but from a notion of tradition that already viewed origins in "a multiple, differential, and open form." Gabriele Schwab targets a different aspect of Freud's attraction to Moses. Her "Freud's Moses: Murder, Exile, and the Question of Belonging" unearths a dialectics of belonging and exile in Freud's story of Moses. Schwab claims that Freud's interest in Moses was complicated by its historical context, especially the Nazi persecution of Jews and the dangers it posed to psychoanalysis as a Jewish science. The relationship between "writing, violence, forgetting," and transference that Freud highlights in the book becomes, in her reading, something more than a mere topic he pursues. It has a historical and personal presence that reflected back to Freud's own text. In "A Leap of Faith into *Moses*: Freud's Invitation to Evenly Suspended Attention," Yael Segalovitz addresses the relations between therapeutics and hermeneutics in *Moses and Monotheism*. While most readers focus on the arguments of *Moses and Monotheism* concerning religion and history, Segalovitz is interested in excavating a theory of reading from Freud's most contradictory and idiosyncratic work. Her essay focuses on Freud's radical conceptualization of "evenly suspended attention," which differs, according to her account, from both conventional modern literary practices of attention and from the practice of "distraction" proposed by Walter Benjamin.

Jan Assmann, whose own contribution to the Freud/Moses debates is featured in this introduction, offers a critical review of Freud's narrative in *Moses and Monotheism*. In "Freud, Sellin, and the Murder of Moses," Assmann directs his attention to Sellin's theory of the murder of Moses, aiming to resurrect Sellin from the long shadows of Freudian mythology. Sellin, Assmann argues, was much more successful in pointing to evidence directly conveyed by the biblical narrative for the mutiny of the Israelites and the violent tradition of prophets. Equally important, Sellin, with Goethe, redirected the feeling of guilt from Freud's Mosaic trauma to the historical traumas that were inflicted at the time of the establishment of the biblical canon. It is not the ambivalence of the father-son relationship that shaped Jewish history, Assmann argues, but the inherent ambivalence of the Jewish people toward their covenant with God. Ronald Hendel in "Creating the Jews: Mosaic Discourse in Freud and Hosea" pursues Assmann's argument in another direction. Looking for the historical truth from within the biblical text, Hendel aims to find in Hosea a "generative text" that sheds new light on Freud's basic claim in *Moses and Monotheism* for the role of Moses in the creation of the Jewish people. Dismissing Freud's and Sellin's unwarranted thesis of the murder of Moses, Hendel locates in Hosea a theo-political project that alludes to Moses—not to the man but to the discourse of Moses. For Hendel, Hosea speaks in the conceptual space of "the authoritative prophet" that Moses generated. Hosea thus participated, as a pedagogue—or as a superego in Freud's terms—in the larger mission of Moses: the creation of the Jewish people.

Catherine Malabou's "Is Psychic Phylogenesis Only a Phantasy? New Biological Developments in Trauma Inheritance" engages with Freud's theory of the return of the repressed from the perspective of modern science. Addressing Freud's neo-Lamarckism, Malabou investigates Freud's ongoing search in *Moses and Monotheism* for a model of transgenerational inheritance between biology and history and between determinism and contingency. For Malabou, this complicated position echoes new findings in epigenetic research. Gilad Sharvit's contribution addresses the book from the perspective of biopolitical theory. His "Moses and the Burning Bush: Leadership and Potentiality in the Bible" revisits the despotic essence of Freud's Moses. Sharvit argues that Freud's one-dimensional depiction of Moses misrepresents the image of the biblical Moses at the scene of the Burning Bush. In that scene, Moses was not a leader concerned with imposing restrictions but, rather, an isolated person who fought to negate God's command. By way of comparison with Agamben's theory of impotentiality, Sharvit argues that the biblical Moses's indecision illuminates his struggle for his position as a leader and to uphold biopolitical power.

WE WOULD LIKE to extend our sincere thanks to Alan Tansman, director of the Doreen B. Townsend Center for the Humanities at UC Berkeley; Rebecca Egger, associate director of the Townsend Center; and Thomas Lay, of Fordham University Press, for their generous help and support in facilitating the publication of this volume. We are also grateful to the programs and departments at UC Berkeley that sponsored the conference out of which this collection originated: the Center for Jewish Studies; the departments of English, German, and History; the Doreen B. Townsend Center for the Humanities; the Program in Critical Theory; the Berkeley Center for the Study of Religion; the Institute of European Studies; and the San Francisco Center for Psychoanalysis.

Notes

[1] Sigmund Freud to Arnold Zweig, Sept. 30, 1934, *The Letters of Sigmund Freud and Arnold Zweig*, ed. Ernst L. Freud, trans. Elaine Robson-Scott and William Robson-Scott (New York: Harcourt, 1970), 91, letter 47. Arnold Zweig's *Bilanz der deutschen Judenheit* was published the same year as an attempt to offer a semipsychoanalytic explanation of anti-Semitism in Germany.

[2] Sigmund Freud to Lou Andreas-Salomé, Jan. 6, 1935, *Letters*, ed. Ernst Pfeiffer, trans. Elaine Robson-Scott and William Robson-Scott (New York: Norton, 1972), 205.

[3] The third essay was first read by Anna Freud at the Paris International Psycho-Analytical Congress on August 1938 and was published in the following year in the *Internationale Zeitschrift für Psychoanalyse*. The three essays were published together in 1939 with a Dutch publishing house.

[4] Sigmund Freud, *Moses and Monotheism: Three Essays*, in *The Standard Edition of the Complete Psychological Works of Sigmund Freud*, vol. 23, trans. and ed. James Strachey (London: Hogarth, 1953 [1939]), 57. Hereafter the *Standard Edition* is abbreviated *SE*, followed by volume number.

[5] Ibid., 7. For *Moses and Monotheism*'s place in the history of Jewish thought, see David Bakan, *Sigmund Freud and the Jewish Mystical Tradition* (Princeton, NJ: Van Nostrand, 1958); and Eliane Amado Levy-Valensi, *Le Moïse de Freud ou la Référence Occultée* (Monaco: Editions du Rocher, 1984).

[6] Freud, *Moses and Monotheism*, 10.

[7] Ibid., 18.

8 Ibid., 47.

9 Ibid., 34.

10 Ibid., 51.

11 Edward W. Said, *Freud and the Non-European* (New York: Verso, 2004), 28. For an analysis of *Moses* as Freud's last opportunity to reflect back onto his psychoanalytic project, see Ilse Grubrich-Simitis, *Early Freud and Late Freud: Reading Anew Studies on Hysteria and Moses and Monotheism*, trans. Philip Slotkin (New York: Routledge, 1997).

12 Freud, *Moses and Monotheism*, 68–69.

13 Ibid., 80.

14 For an example of the implications of *Moses and Monotheism* for a modern theory of history, see Michel de Certeau, *The Writing of History*, trans. Tom Conley (New York: Columbia University Press, 1988).

15 Sigmund Freud, *Totem and Taboo*, in *SE* 13, 132.

16 See already in an early remark in Freud's letter to Lou Andreas-Salomé: "I have already said this in *Totem and Taboo*." Jan. 6, 1935, *Letters*, 205. And in his second prefatory note to the third essay: "I acquired that a quarter of a century ago when in 1912 I wrote my book about Totem and Taboo, and it has only grown firmer since." Freud, *Moses and Monotheism*, 58.

17 Freud, *Moses and Monotheism*, 80.

18 Sigmund Freud, *Beyond the Pleasure Principle*, in *SE* 18, 22.

19 Freud to Andreas-Salomé, Jan. 6, 1935, *Letters*, 205.

20 Cathy Caruth in *Unclaimed Experience* famously took on Freud's theory of the return of the repressed as an entry point to a new theory of history that, against a perceived postmodern danger of disconnection and lack of interpersonal reference, offers trauma as a way to reconnect to the other. In her words, "through the notion of trauma . . . we can understand that a rethinking of reference is aimed not at eliminating history but at resituating it in our understanding, that is, at precisely permitting *history* to arise where *immediate understanding* may not." Cathy Caruth, *Unclaimed Experience* (Baltimore: Johns Hopkins University Press, 1996), 11.

21 Freud, *Moses and Monotheism*, 99–100.

22 See for example Trude Weiss Rosmarin, *The Hebrew Moses: An Answer to Sigmund Freud* (New York: Jewish Book Club, 1939).

23 Martin Buber, *Moses: The Revelation and the Covenant* (New York: Harper, 1958), 7n1. In a rare exception, *Moses and Monotheism* received some attention in *Monotheism and Moses: The Genesis of Judaism*, ed. Robert J. Christen and Harold E. Hazelton (Lexington, MA: Heath, 1969). However, here as well, the tone is predominantly critical, as noted in Salo Baron's conclu-

sion: "In short, the cause of psychoanalytical interpretation of the history of religion . . . seems to the present reviewer to have received a setback rather than to have made further progress through its present application to the historical career of Moses." Salo W. Baron, "A Review of Freud," in Christen and Hazelton, *Monotheism and Moses*, 43.

[24] Two recently published volumes on *Moses and Monotheism* reflect these interests: Ruth Ginsburg and Ilana Pardes, eds., *New Perspectives on Freud's "Moses and Monotheism"* (Tübingen, Germany: Niemeyer, 2006); and Eveline List, ed., *Der Mann Moses und die Stimme des Intellekts: Geschichte, Gesetz und Denken in Sigmund Freuds historischem Roman* (Innsbruck, Austria: Studien Verlag, 2008).

[25] As Freud famously described it in his preface to the Hebrew translation of *Totem and Taboo*, "If the question were put to him [that is, to Freud]: 'Since you have abandoned all these common characteristics of your countrymen, what is there left to you that is Jewish?' he would reply: 'A very great deal, and probably its very essence.'" Freud, *Totem and Taboo*, xv.

[26] Yosef H. Yerushalmi, *Freud's Moses: Judaism Terminable and Interminable* (New Haven, CT: Yale University Press, 1991), 33.

[27] For a work on the Protestant origins of Freud's identification of the Jews as spiritual/intellectual, see Peter Schäfer, *Der Triumph der reinen Geistigkeit: Sigmund Freuds "Der Mann Moses und die monotheistische Religion"* (Berlin: Philo Verlag, 2003).

[28] Richard J. Bernstein, *Freud and the Legacy of Moses* (Cambridge: Cambridge University Press, 1998); Jacques Derrida, *Archive Fever: A Freudian Impression*, trans. Eric Prenowitz (Chicago: University of Chicago Press, 1996), 34. For a recent discussion of Yerushalmi's position in those lines, see Eliza Slavet, *Racial Fever: Freud and the Jewish Question* (New York: Fordham University Press, 2009).

[29] Derrida at this point rightly cited Yerushalmi's own words: "Deconstructed into Jewish terms, what is Lamarckism if not the powerful feeling that, for better or worse, one cannot really cease being Jewish, and this is not merely because of the chain of tradition, but because one's fate in being Jewish was determined long ago by the fathers, and that often what one feels most deeply and obscurely is a *trilling wire in the blood*." Yerushalmi, *Freud's Moses*, 31; Derrida, *Archive Fever*, 35n5 (emphasis added).

[30] Bernstein, *Freud and the Legacy of Moses*, 50.

[31] Derrida, *Archive Fever*, 17.

[32] Ibid., 68.

[33] Said, *Freud and the Non-European*, 54.

[34] Ibid.

35 Jan Assmann, *Moses the Egyptian: The Memory of Egypt in Western Monotheism* (Cambridge, MA: Harvard University Press, 1997), 3.

36 Ibid., 147. In a later work, *The Price of Monotheism* (Stanford, CA: Stanford University Press, 2010), Assmann's position changed, as he shifted his focus toward the violence that monotheism inflicted on its believers. In line with Freud's insight concerning the excessive demands made by monotheistic religion, the violence was now constructed as part of the commitment of the believer to the one and only God. In recent decades, a second round of works has taken a special interest in Freud's theory of the murder of Moses and the repressive essence of monotheism in *Moses and Monotheism*. Howard Eilberg-Schwartz's *God's Phallus and Other Problems for Men and Monotheism* (Boston: Beacon, 1994), Eric Santner's *On the Psychotheology of Everyday Life* (Chicago: University of Chicago Press, 2001), and more recently Gil Anidjar's *Blood: A Critique of Christianity* (New York: Columbia University Press, 2014), to name a few, invoked the book in recent interrogations of monotheism and its violent nature.

37 Sigmund Freud, *The Moses of Michelangelo*, in *SE* 13, 209.

38 Ilse Grubrich-Simitis elaborated on the unconscious attraction of Freud with the figure of Moses in *Freud's Moses-Studie Als Tagtraum* (Frankfurt: Verlag Internationale Psychoanalyse, 1991). While the Moses story is easily associated to Freud's relations with his father—as in Marianne Krüll, *Freud and His Father*, trans. Arnold J. Pomerans (New York: Norton, 1986)—Franz Maciejewski tells the story of Moses through a recollection of Freud's memories of his younger brother Julius Freud, who died in infancy. Franz Maciejewski, *Der Moses des Sigmund Freud: Ein unheimlicher Bruder* (Göttingen, Germany: Vandenhoeck and Ruprecht, 2006).

39 Yerushalmi, *Freud's Moses*, 6. Yerushalmi, we noted above, went against the emphasis on ambivalence in *Moses and Monotheism* to claim that the book offered a new foundation for modern Jewish identity.

40 Marthe Robert, *From Oedipus to Moses: Freud's Jewish Identity*, trans. Ralph Manheim (Garden City, NJ: Anchor Books, 1976), 167. For a similar reading, see Michael Steinberg's claims about Freud's role in attempts by secular Judaism to dislocate the connections of modern society with its religious origins, in order to advance secular cosmopolitan consciousness. Michael P. Steinberg, *Judaism Musical and Unmusical* (Chicago: University of Chicago Press, 2007). Emmanuel Rice in *Freud and Moses*, in opposition to Robert, aimed to retrieve Freud for Jews and Judaism. Rice dismissed Freud's theses about the importance of the Egyptian origins of Judaism, which he took as evidence of Freud's honest pursuit of truth, and focused instead on Freud's redefinition of Judaism as the religion of reason. For Rice, "Freud's religious roots, deep in ethical monotheism, led him to Moses," and the normative fissure that *Moses and Monotheism* promoted between Judaism and paganism (standing for violent and primitive religion) only proved that Freud was "a true prophet in the Jewish

prophetic tradition." Emmanuel Rice, *Freud and Moses: The Long Journey Home* (Albany: State University of New York Press, 1990), 143, 142. For *Moses and Monotheism* and Freud's Jewish identity, see also Martin S. Bergmann, "Moses and the Evolution of Freud's Jewish Identity," *Israel Annals of Psychiatry and Related Disciplines* 14, 3–26 (1976); Moshe Gresser, *Dual Allegiance: Freud as a Modern Jew* (Albany: State University of New York Press, 1994); and Jacques Le Rider, "Jewish Identity in *Moses and Monotheism*," *Psychiatry Review* 25 (1997): 245–254.

[41] Freud, *Moses and Monotheism*, 110.

[42] Bluma Goldstein, *Reinscribing Moses: Heine, Kafka, Freud, and Schoenberg in a European Wilderness* (Cambridge, MA: Harvard University Press, 1992), 111. See also in Gilad Sharvit, "Conscious Inhibitions: Freud, Anti-Semitism, and Hobbesian Imagination," *Journal of Modern Jewish Studies* 15.3 (2016): 349–365.

[43] On the harmful effects of Freud's politics of the hero, see Mark Edmundson, *The Death of Sigmund Freud: The Legacy of His Last Days* (New York: Bloomsbury, 2007).

[44] Daniel Boyarin, *Unheroic Conduct: The Rise of Heterosexuality and the Invention of the Jewish Man* (Berkeley: University of California Press, 1997), 248.

[45] For more on the castration/circumcision core of anti-Semitic ideology, see Jay Howard Geller, "The Godfather of Psychoanalysis: Circumcision, Antisemitism, Homosexuality, and Freud's 'Fighting Jew,'" *Journal of the American Academy of Religion* 67.2 (1992): 355–385; and Eric Santner, *My Own Private Germany: Daniel Paul Schreber's Secret History of Modernity* (Princeton, NJ: Princeton University Press, 1996).

[46] Boyarin, *Unheroic Conduct*, 245.

[47] Sander Gilman, *Freud, Race, and Gender* (Princeton, NJ: Princeton University Press, 1993), 42.

[48] Ibid., 189.

[49] Ibid., 191.

Richard J. Bernstein

1 "Why [the Jews] Have Attracted This Undying Hatred"

THE TITLE OF this chapter is a phrase from a letter that Freud wrote to Arnold Zweig on September 30, 1934. Here is the full passage:

> Faced with new persecutions, one asks oneself again how the Jews have come to be what they are and why they have attracted this undying hatred [*diesen unsterblichen Hass*]. I soon discovered the formula: Moses created the Jews. So I gave my work the title: *The Man Moses, a historical novel.* . . . The material fits into three sections. The first part is like an interesting novel; the second is laborious and boring; the third is full of content and makes exacting reading. The whole enterprise broke down on this third section for it involved a theory of religion—certainly nothing new for me after *Totem and Taboo*, but something new and fundamental for the uninitiated. It is the thought of these uninitiated readers that makes me hold over the finished work.[1]

Initially Freud's claims are perplexing. How are we to interpret his claim that Moses created the Jews? What does this have to do with why the Jews attracted such "undying hatred"? And, finally, what does Freud mean when he speaks about the "uninitiated"? These are the questions I will attempt to answer in this chapter. Freud continues the preceding passage by explaining what makes him "hold over the finished book." He tells Zweig, "we live here [in Vienna] in an atmosphere of Catholic orthodoxy." He mentions that Pater Schmidt, a confidant of the Pope, who presumably has had a great influence on Austrian politics, abhors psychoanalysis and vehemently rejects the theory of religion that Freud advanced in *Totem and Taboo*. Freud then declares,

> Now, any publication of mine will be sure to attract a certain amount of attention, which will not escape the notice of this inimical priest. Thus we might be risking a ban on psychoanalysis in Vienna and the suspension of all our publications here. If this danger involved me alone, I would be but little concerned, but to deprive all our members in Vienna of their livelihood is too great a responsibility.
>
> And in addition there is the fact that this work does not seem to me sufficiently substantiated, nor does it altogether please me. It is therefore not the occasion for martyrdom.[2]

Consider the date of this letter: September 30, 1934. Freud had good reason to be concerned. Although the letter was written almost four years before the *Anschluss*, Freud's books had already been burned in Germany. There is an even more significant reason why the date is important. The first two parts of *The Man Moses and Monotheistic Religion* (the literal translation of *Der Mann Moses und die Monotheistische Religion*) were published in 1938 in *Imago*. The entire book, including the crucial third part, was published only in 1939, after Freud had left Vienna and moved to London. At the conclusion of the second section of the book, "If Moses Was an Egyptian . . ." (in which Freud presents his narrative reconstruction of the fate of Moses and his Egyptian monotheistic religion), he tells us that there "would be a very great deal to discuss, explain and to assert" (23:52).[3] He then, in effect, outlines the topics that he will discuss in the crucial third part of the book. He concludes by saying, "To continue my work on such lines as these would be to find a link with the statements I put forward twenty-five years ago in *Totem and Taboo* [1912–13]. *But I no longer feel that I have the strength to do so*" (23:53; emphasis added).[4] But we *now* know that this last claim *masks* the fact that Freud had already virtually worked out his entire theory by 1934. Moses, an aristocratic Egyptian in Akhenaten's court, "created" the Jewish people (the Hebrews) from a "crowd of immigrant foreigners at a backward level of civilization" (23:18). After the death of Akhenaten, Moses imposed a new strict monotheism (derived from the Egyptian Aten religion) on a people that came to resent this iconoclastic monotheism. They eventually murdered Moses. The trauma of the murder was repressed, and there was a return to an older form of polytheistic idolatry. After a significant period of latency (centuries), there was a return of the repressed—the strict and pure ethical mono-theism of Moses reasserted itself and shaped the character of the Jewish people. The pattern that Freud developed for under-standing neurotic illness—trauma, defense, latency, return of the repressed—has its analogue in the development of patriar-chal religions. When Freud outlined his theory in a 1935 letter to Lou Andreas-Salomé, as Yosef Hayim Yerushalmi points out, she was one of the first "to intuitively grasp an essential aspect of *Moses and Monotheism*."[5] She responded,

> What particularly fascinated *me* in your present view of things
> is a specific characteristic of the "return of the repressed,"
> namely, the way in which noble and precious elements return
> despite long intermixture with every conceivable kind of
> material. . . . Hitherto we have usually understood the term
> "return of the repressed" in the context of neurotic processes:
> all kinds of material which had been wrongly repressed

afflicted the neurotic mysteriously with phantoms out of the
past, . . . which he felt bound to ward off. But in this case
we are presented with examples of the survival of the most
triumphantly vital elements of the past as the truest possession
in the present, despite all the destructive elements and coun-
terforces they endured.[6]

In *Freud and the Legacy of Moses*, I showed just how insightful
Lou Andreas-Salomé had been. Specifically, I argued that *Moses
and Monotheism* can be read as providing an answer to a question that Freud posed in the preface to the Hebrew translation of
Totem and Taboo. In that short preface, he asked how he, who was
estranged from the religion of his fathers as well as every other
religion, would answer the question, what is there left to you that
is Jewish? And Freud replies to his question, "A very great deal,
and probably its very essence [*Wesen*]."[7] He does not tell us what
that essence is, but he indicates that "someday, no doubt, it will
become accessible to the scientific mind" (23:xv). My primary
thesis is that this essence is epitomized in the title of one of the
sections of the third part of *Moses and Monotheism*, namely, "Der
Fortschritt in der Geistigkeit." In the first English translation of
Moses and Monotheism, Katherine Jones translated this key phrase
as "the progress in spirituality." Strachey—in the *Standard English*
translation—translates the phrase as "the advance of intellectuality." Neither translation quite captures the rich semantic resonances of the German *Geist*. When Freud was too old and feeble to
attend the 1938 meeting of the International Psychoanalytic Congress in Paris, he asked his daughter Anna to read this section on
his behalf at the Congress. In *Freud and the Legacy of Moses*, I wrote,

This is the brief section where Freud presents a summary of his
analysis of the cultural significance of the Mosaic monotheistic
religion and its profound effect on the character of the Jewish
people. It is here that Freud insists that there is no precept of
greater importance in the Mosaic religion than "the prohibition against making an image of God—the compulsion to wor-

ship a God whom one cannot see" (23:112–13). It is here too that Freud tells the story about the founding of the "first Torah school" by Rabbi Jochanan ben Zakkai, a story that serves as a parable about what enabled the Jewish people to survive through the long history of their persecutions. "From that time on, the Holy Writ and the intellectual concern with it were what held the scattered people together" (23:115).[8]

Jan Assmann has given a beautiful summary of this reading of *Moses and Monotheism* (which we share) when he writes, "I now think that Freud was trying . . . to present the Mosaic distinction (in the form of the ban on graven images) as a seminal, immensely valuable, and profoundly Jewish achievement, which ought on no account to be relinquished and that his own psychoanalysis could credit itself precisely with taking this specifically Jewish type of progress a step further."[9]

By the "Mosaic distinction," Assmann is referring to the sharp dichotomy between the one and only true God and all other false gods. The absolute ban on graven images in Judaism is a ban on all false idols. The Mosaic distinction underscores the pure spiritual character of Judaism. For Freud, psychoanalysis is a further progress in spirituality or intellectuality (*Geist*). But consider again what Freud wrote in his letter to Zweig. "Faced with new persecutions one asks oneself again how the Jews have come to be what they are and why they have attracted this undying hatred. I soon discovered the formula: Moses created the Jews." Note that Freud does not ask what characterizes anti-Semitism but rather what it is about the *Jews* that has attracted such hatred. Freud closely links this analysis of how the Jews have come to be what they are with why they have attracted this undying hatred. Both are related to his key claim that Moses created the Jews. Most of the extensive commentary on *Moses and Monotheism* has focused its attention on the controversial claims that Moses was an Egyptian, that he imposed a strict iconoclastic monotheism on the Jewish people, that the Jews murdered Moses, and that with the return of the repressed, the original Mosaic religion shaped the character of the Jewish people. But in the remainder of this chapter, I want to focus on how this is related to Freud's account of why the Jews have attracted undying hatred. I think that for all the strangeness and the seeming outrageousness of Freud's claims, it is relevant to the recent disturbing outbreaks of anti-Semitic incidents, especially in Europe. For Freud, at least, there is an intimate relationship between *Fortschritt in der Geistigkeit* and the "undying hatred" that the Jews have attracted.

To understand Freud's account of this "undying hatred," we need to emphasize the centrality of the Oedipal Complex in Freud's theory of psychoanalysis and especially his understanding of the origin of patriarchal religion. Religion has its origin in the myth of the primal horde, the tyrannical father, and the killing of the father by the brothers—the myth that Freud elaborates in *Totem and Taboo*. This killing of the primal father is central to Freud's account of the murder of Moses by the Jewish people. This murder "becomes an indispensable part of our construction, an important link between the forgotten event of primaeval times and its later emergence in the form of monotheist religions" (23:89).

> It is plausible to conjecture that remorse for the murder of Moses provided the stimulus for the wishful phantasy of the Messiah, who was to return and lead his people to redemption and the promised world-dominion. If Moses was the first Messiah, Christ became his substitute and successor, and Paul could exclaim to the peoples with some historical justification: "Look! The Messiah has really come: he has been murdered before your eyes!" (23:89–90)

There is a pattern of repetition of the murder of the father: the primal father of the primitive horde; Moses; and finally Christ.[10] It is against this background that Freud seeks to account for the undying hatred of the Jews. He concedes that "a phenomenon of such intensity and permanence as the people's hatred of the Jews must of course have more than one ground" (23:90). He then lists several reasons why the Jews have attracted "undying hatred." Because of their habitual stubbornness, they have continued to disavow the father's murder. They have been reproached by Christians, "You have killed our God!" and this accusation is justified, if it is correctly translated. If it is brought into relation with the history of religions, it runs, "You will not *admit* that you murdered God (the primal picture of God, the primal father, and his later reincarnations)" (23:90). According to Freud, there is a repetition—literally or symbolically—of the killing of the primal father. The murder of Moses by the Jews is a repetition of the murder of the primal father, but the Jews refuse to admit that they have killed God (the father figure).

Freud suggests other explanations of the undying hatred. He tells us that the Jews have been taken to be an alien people. He thinks this is a weak consideration because in many places dominated by anti-Semitism, the Jews were among the oldest portions of the population. A stronger reason is that they have lived for the most part as minorities among other peoples. Echoing a theme that is so prominent in Carl Schmitt's friend/enemy distinction, Freud claims that "the communal feeling of groups requires, in order to complete it, hostility towards some extraneous minority, and the numerical weakness of this excluded minority encourages its suppression" (23:90). There are two other characteristics of the Jews that are considered unforgivable. They are in some respects different from their "host" nations. Although they are not *fundamentally* different, "the intolerance of groups is often, strangely enough, exhibited more strongly against small differences than against fundamental ones" (23:91). A further ground is one that Freud himself emphasizes—and indeed was proud of: "They defy all oppression, . . . the most cruel persecutions have not succeeded in exterminating them, and, indeed, . . . on the contrary they show a capacity for holding their own in commer-

cial life and, where they are admitted, for making valuable contributions to every form of cultural activity" (23:91).

These grounds for the hatred of the Jews are what Freud would
call manifest reasons. But there are deeper motives for hatred
of the Jews that operate in the unconscious of peoples. There is
the jealousy of the people who claimed that they are the favorite
children of God—that they are God's "chosen people." Furthermore, among the customs that distinguish the Jews from other
people, circumcision has a special importance because it recalls
"the dreaded castration and along with it a portion of the primaeval past that is gladly forgotten" (23:91). But perhaps Freud's most
speculative hypothesis concerns what he calls the last motive in
this series. This is especially significant because this is the place in
his text where Freud explicitly mentions the Nazis.

> We must not forget that all those peoples who excel to-day in
> their hatred of Jews became Christians only in late historic
> times, often driven to it by bloody coercion. It might be said
> that they are all "mis-baptized." They have been left, under a
> thin veneer of Christianity, where their ancestors were, who
> worshipped a barbarous polytheism. They have not got over a
> grudge against the new religion which was imposed on them;
> but they have displaced the grudge on to the source from
> which Christianity reached them. The fact that the Gospels
> tell a story which is set among the Jews, and in fact deals only
> with Jews, has made this displacement easy for them. Their
> hatred of Jews is at bottom a hatred of Christians, and we
> need not be surprised that in the German Nationalist-Socialist
> revolution this intimate relation between the two monotheist
> religions finds such a clear expression in the hostile treatment
> of both of them. (23:91–92)[11]

We might consider this claim outlandish, but Freud is also suggesting that the Nazis' hatred of the Jews is a hatred of *Fortschritt
in der Geistigkeit*, epitomized by Moses's strict ethical iconoclastic monotheism. This hatred is a regression to a "barbarous poly-

theism." For Freud, there is a close association between religion (including Judaism) and violence. There is the paradigmatic violence of the murder of the primeval father; there is the violence by which Moses imposes a strict monotheism on the crude Semitic tribe; there is the violence of a monotheism that excludes all paganism and idolatry; there is the violence of the rebellious Jews who murder Moses; and there is the violence of the "return of the repressed." Finally, there is the violence of those who hate (and murder) the Jews because of their iconoclastic strict ethical monotheism epitomized by *Fortschritt in der Geistigkeit*. We might also add the violence of those who hate psychoanalysis because it is the secular successor of this pure monotheistic tradition.

Jan Assmann succinctly captures the way in which *Fortschritt in der Geistigkeit* is closely and intimately related to "reactionary violence."

> Progress in intellectuality [*Der Fortschritt in der Geistigkeit*], and the sense of superiority it brings with it, always precipitates reactionary violence. Moses was its first victim, and in this sense one could say that the Jews who killed him were the first anti-Semites. For anti-Semitism—a particularly pressing concern for Freud at the time he wrote the book—is a reaction against intellect, which this world is prepared to tolerate only grudgingly. Anti-Semitism is anti-monotheism, hence anti-intellectualism.[12]

THUS FAR, I have attempted to present a sympathetic sketch of Freud's views about "how the Jews have come to be what they are and why they have attracted this undying hatred." But I want to step back and examine how Freud's reflections might help to shed light on the recent outbreak of anti-Semitic incidents. To do this, we need to begin to reflect on Freud's ambivalent relation to the Enlightenment tradition. Freud clearly stands in this tradition in his own passionate commitment to reason and to furthering the progress in intellectuality. Throughout his career—in both theory and practice—Freud is thoroughly committed to this Enlightenment ideal. However, at the same time, Freud is also one of the sharpest critics of what he takes to be the Enlightenment's naïve and superficial understanding of and faith in reason. Ironically, Freud can be viewed as consistently pursuing the Enlightenment ideal of reason in order to show what is inadequate about the Enlightenment conception of human beings and the human psyche—the failure to appreciate the power of the unconscious in shaping who and what we are. The unconscious is *intractably ambivalent*. "Ambivalence" in the psychoanalytic lexicon is not a vague term but has a precise meaning. As Jean Laplanche and Jean-Bertrand Pontalis tell us,

> The novelty of the notion of ambivalence as compared to earlier evocations of the complexity of the emotions and the fluctuations of attitudes consists on the one hand in the maintenance of an opposition of the yes/no type, *wherein affirmation and negation are simultaneous and inseparable*; and, on the other hand, in the acknowledgment that this basic opposition is to be found in different sectors of mental life.[13]

To my mind, one of Freud's greatest insights is to realize the depth and pervasiveness of this type of ambivalence. We might say that Freud's affirmation and negation of the Enlightenment legacy is itself "simultaneous and inseparable." We can also say that the progress in intellectuality and reactionary violence are inseparable.

But if we grant this, we might still ask how it sheds any light on the recent outbreak of incidents of violent anti-Semitism. It is important to keep in mind Freud's claim that a phenomenon of such intensity as the hatred of the Jews must have more than one ground. When we seek to account for the outbreak of anti-Semitic incidents in any historical period, we need to take account of *specific* cultural, sociological, political, and economic factors. But we can also ask: what does a psychoanalytic orientation contribute to comprehending this hatred? More specifically, we can ask, how do Freud's reflections in *Moses and Monotheism* shed light on anti-Semitism and hatred of the Jews? To answer these questions, I want to take what may seem to be an indirect path, but I hope to show that it will take us to the core of the issue.

I want to consider Jan Assmann's work on cultural memory as it pertains to what he calls the "Mosaic distinction"—the distinction essential to revolutionary monotheism. In *Moses the Egyptian*, Assmann introduced this distinction in order to characterize what he takes to be *distinctive* about the revolutionary monotheism that can be traced back to Akhenaten but that has been primarily associated with Moses. This is the idea of an exclusive monotheism that affirms that there is one and only one true God and one true religion. No God but God! Revolutionary monotheism sets itself against all forms of paganism, polytheism, and cosmotheism. Although there was plenty of hatred and violence in these earlier, primary religions, revolutionary monotheistic religions "brought a new form of hatred into the world: hatred for pagans, heretics, idolaters and their temples, rites, and gods."[14] Assmann appropriates from Freud the cultural pattern of trauma, latency, and the return of the repressed. "The concepts of latency and the return of the repressed are indispensable for any adequate theory of cultural memory."[15] This means that in the course of history—or, more precisely, what Assmann calls "mnemohistory"—there are traumas, which after periods of latency and repression break forth as the return of the repressed. This pattern of trauma–latency–return of the repressed happens over and over again. Assmann closely follows Freud's own analysis of what has happened with Moses's monotheism in the course of history. In describing Freud's theory, Assmann writes, "The theory of repression contends that there is such a thing as a *preserving forgetfulness*. According to Freud, the idea of exclusive monotheism was cloaked by this *preserving forgetfulness*, which allowed it to be retained by the Jews from the fourteenth all the way through to the fifth century BCE."[16] The memory of the true spiritual God is preserved, but, at the same time, it is repressed and forgotten. In this sense, there is a "preserving forgetfulness."

When Assmann published *Moses the Egyptian*, in which he sets forth his idea of the Mosaic distinction, he was severely criticized by historians of religion, biblical scholars, theologians, and many others. He was even falsely accused of being anti-Semitic and presumably advocating a return to polytheism. In a subsequent book, *The Price of Monotheism*, he sought to answer his critics, refine his position, and advance the discussion of the basic issues. I want to highlight some of his key claims that are relevant to my primary concern—the outbreak of hatred against the Jews and anti-Semitic incidents.

Rather than speaking of "a single 'monotheistic shift' with an unambiguous 'before' and 'after,'" Assmann proposes that we refer to "'monotheistic moments' in which the Mosaic distinction is struck with all severity."[17] This can occur—and indeed has occurred—throughout history when some version of revolutionary monotheism is used to "justify" the hatred and even the murder of infidels and heretics.[18] And indeed something like this is now occurring in the most extreme forms of militant religious fanaticism. There is *always* a danger that the Mosaic distinction will return with renewed force and become a "murderous distinction." "The times are over when religion could be viewed as the 'opium of the people.' Nowadays, in the hands and minds of certain movements, religion appears as the 'dynamite of the people.'"[19]

There is a violent *potential* in exclusionary monotheism. This, of course, does not mean that this *potential* will be *actualized*. Although we also find in the sacred texts of the great monotheistic religions the resources for countering this potential violence, it would, nevertheless, be naïve to deny this potential. If one firmly believes that there really is one and only one true

God, and one and only one true religion, then in extreme *political* circumstances, one can use or (misuse) this credo to "justify"
and "legitimize" the elimination or extermination of nonbe-
lievers and infidels. Like Freud, Assmann defends this "price of
monotheism." "If the violent potential of its semantic implications remains the price of monotheism, it is also important to
remember for what this price has been paid. Monotheism means
exodus, that is, enlightenment."[20] Consider what Freud himself
declares:

> The Jewish people had abandoned the Aten religion brought
> to them by Moses and had turned to the worship of another
> god who differed little from the Baalim of the neighbouring
> peoples. All the tendentious efforts of later times failed to
> disguise this shameful act. But the Mosaic religion had not
> vanished without leaving a trace; some sort of memory of it
> had been kept alive—a possibly obscured and distorted tradi-
> tion. And it was this tradition of a great past which continued
> to operate (from the background, as it were), which gradually
> acquired more and more power over people's minds and which
> in the end succeeded in changing the god Yahweh into the
> Mosaic god and in re-awakening into life the religion of Moses
> that had been introduced and then abandoned long centuries
> before. (23:70)

This is the noble story that Freud tells about the fate of Moses's
ethical, iconoclastic monotheism and how it shaped the character
of the Jews. Freud clearly identifies himself with this noble tradition. And he thinks that secular psychoanalysis is the proper
successor of this religious tradition. But let us not forget the significance and depth of psychoanalytic ambivalence. There is also
a dark side of revolutionary monotheism and its historical fate.
Despite Freud's consistent atheism, despite the fact that he was a
"godless Jew," he does not subscribe to the Enlightenment belief
that, in the course of history, reason will ultimately triumph over
superstition and magic.

Whether we emphasize Assmann's understanding of the dynamics of cultural memory or Freud's controversial claims about how acquired characteristics are transmitted over long periods of history, there is a convergence on the central thesis that we can discern the pattern of trauma, latency, and return of the repressed in cultural history. If we accept Freud's linkage between the progress of intellectuality and reactionary violence, then Freud is presenting a deep challenge to any and all conceptions of historical progress that claim that there can be a "final" triumph over irrationality, superstition, and hatred. There is no escape from psychic ambivalence regardless of whether we focus on individuals or groups and peoples. Freud is warning us to be wary of optimistic secularization theories and modernization theories that underestimate the compulsive power of religious belief. It is utopian to think that rational arguments are sufficient to put an end to anti-Semitism and Jew hatred. This, of course, does not diminish the responsibility of intellectuals to seek to understand the psychological dynamics of religious hatred—and to oppose it. At times, we find Freud in a more positive mood in which he does hope that the soft voice of reason, after many rebuffs, will triumph over irrational prejudice. In *The Future of an Illusion*, he affirms, "This is one of the few points on which one may be optimistic about the future of mankind" (22:53). But Freud's dominant mood is one of a clear-sighted realism in which he emphasizes the depth and intractability of psychic ambivalence. I do not think that Freud would be surprised by the outbreak of anti-Semitic incidents today and the new forms of Jew hatred that we witness. This is also an outbreak of the return of the repressed. Some people are shocked that after the revelations of the full horrors of the Shoah, anti-Semitism and Jew hatred can manifest themselves again in Europe. The mantra "Never Again" may express a wishful fantasy, but it obscures the dynamics of potential reactionary violence that is *always latently* present and can be triggered into actuality by political events.

I have cited Lou Andreas-Salomé's comment about how Freud's idea of the return of the repressed, which had hitherto been understood in the context of neurotic processes, was employed to explain how "noble and precious elements return despite long intermixture with every conceivable kind of material." Andreas-Salomé is right and perceptive in detecting how this provided a key for grasping the "return" of the strict, ethical Mosaic monotheism in shaping the character of the Jewish people. Although she was right, we might say she was only half right because she neglects the dark side of development. She does not note how these "noble and precious elements" are inseparable from the reactionary violence that they provoke.

There are some scholars (including Yerushalmi) who think that Freud leaves us with a bleak, pessimistic, and "un-Jewish" understanding of the fate of religion, since Freud presumably leaves no place for messianic hope. Yerushalmi writes,

> In your psychoanalysis of history you have presented us with a haunting vision of Eternal Return more seductive, because so much more subtle, than that of Friedrich Nietzsche. Beneath the dizzying multiplicity of events and phenomena that history throws up to the surface you have discerned a pulsating repetition: patricide, repression, return of the repressed, followed by reenactment of the entire cycle, though disguised under different forms, in a seemingly endless spiral. . . . At one point of the cycle the Father must be slain by the son, at another, that of the return of the repressed, the Father returns, but his return is only partial, illusory, temporary, for the cycle will begin again.[21]

I think that this is a serious misreading of Freud and a serious misreading of *Moses and Monotheism*. Freud is not a pessimist, and his reading of history is not pessimistic. It only appears pessimistic against an understanding of history as the linear, progressive realization of human emancipation. On the contrary, Freud is a serious and critical realist. He defends the cultural contribution of ethical, iconoclastic monotheism and the crucial significance of *Fortschritt in der Geistigkeit*. He hopes that this will be the legacy of psychoanalysis, which he takes to be the successor of the tradition of Moses's ethical monotheism. However, Freud is also the great realist who knows that we never escape from psychic and cultural ambivalence, that the progress in intellectuality provokes reactionary violence. Freud would certainly agree with Walter Benjamin's famous dictum, "There is no document of civilization which is not at the same time a document of barbarism."[22]

What does this mean in relation to the issue of the contemporary outbreak of anti-Semitic incidents and Jew hatred? Freud warns us against simplistic reductive psychoanalytic accounts. The explanation of such outbreaks requires a grasp and sensitivity to multiple political, economic, sociological, and cultural factors. If we take seriously Freud's cultural psychoanalytic analysis, then we should not be surprised or shocked by what is happening, but we can also not be indifferent to what is happening or accept the cyclical pattern of violence and hatred. Throughout his life, Freud was passionately committed to furthering the development of *Geistigkeit* and to opposing and fighting against all sorts of irrational prejudices. It is a dangerous illusion to think that reason can *finally* triumph over the dark forces of violence and hatred. But without succumbing to false utopian fantasies, we must nevertheless also constantly engage in the task—the *Aufgabe*—of combating destructive violence and hatred. The lesson that we learn from Freud is that this is a task that can *never* be completed. When we fully unpack the meaning of Freud's formula "Moses created the Jews," we understand why he believed that he could account for "how the Jews have come to be what they are and why they have attracted this undying hatred." Freud has a deep understanding of the cultural contribution of *Fortschritt in der Geistigkeit*, which has one of its key sources in Moses's ethical monotheism. At the same time, Freud had a deep understanding of the dark side of this development, which also provokes violence. We never quite know when anti-Semitism, hatred, and violence will break out in unanticipated new forms, but we must remain vigilant and committed to opposing them whenever and wherever they become manifest. This is what I take to be Freud's critically realistic, but hopeful, legacy.

Notes

[1]   Sigmund Freud to Arnold Zweig, September 30, 1934, *Letters* (New York: Harcourt Brace Jovanovich, 1970), 91–92.

[2]   Ibid., 92.

[3]   All references to Freud's works are to Sigmund Freud, *The Standard Edition of the Complete Works of Sigmund Freud*, 24 vols., translated under the editorship of James Strachey (London: Hogarth Press, 1953–74). References to Freud in the texts are to volume and page number.

[4]   For a discussion of this draft, see Yosef Hayim Yerushalmi, "Freud on the 'Historical Novel': From the Manuscript Draft (1934) of *Moses and Monotheism*," *International Journal of Psychoanalysis* 70 (1989): 375–395. Yerushalmi reproduces the German and provides an English translation of the introduction to this early draft in *Freud's Moses: Judaism Terminable and Interminable* (New Haven, CT: Yale University Press, 1991).

[5]   Yerushalmi, *Freud's Moses*, 78.

[6]   Lou Andreas-Salomé to Sigmund Freud, mid-January 1935, *Letters* (New York: W.W. Norton, 1972), 206–207.

[7]   Richard J. Bernstein, *Freud and the Legacy of Moses* (Cambridge: Cambridge University Press, 1998), 1.

[8]   Bernstein, *Freud and the Legacy of Moses*, 82.

[9]   Jan Assmann, *The Price of Monotheism* (Stanford, CA: Stanford University Press, 2010), 86. Philip Rieff gives an interesting twist to Freud's admiration for Moses: "And religious leaders like Moses are for Freud sympathetic figures so far as they elevate the moral standards of the rabble. Far from admiring instinctual revolt, Freud's own identification is with the benevolent culture despots of the prescientific ages who raised the level of popular aspiration and occasionally succeeded in transforming their own superegos into law." Philip Rieff, *The Jew of Culture: Freud, Moses, and Modernity* (Charlottesville: University of Virginia Press, 2008), 66.

[10] Jan Assmann, who provides a sympathetic and perceptive account of the *Fortschritt in der Geistigkeit*, criticizes Freud for having too weak a concept of cultural memory. "Cultural memory is not just *mémoire voluntaire*, but a *mémoire involontaire* as well; much is contained in its lower strata that can

break out again and seize hold of people's imagination after a long phase of latency." In opposition to Freud, Assmann claims that "the trauma of monotheism, if there is such a thing, rests in my opinion not on a twofold patricide, whose victims were the first primal father and then Moses, but a twofold deicide, whose victims were first the 'pagan' gods and then the god of monotheism himself." Assmann, *Price of Monotheism*, 96–97.

[11] It is striking that Freud speaks of "the two monotheisms." There is no mention of Islam in this context. Freud (like many Europeans of his time) does not ever seriously discuss Islamic monotheism. On the contrary, he tends to be dismissive about Islam. Consider the following remark about the "Mahommedan religion": "From my limited information I may perhaps add that the case of the founding of the Mahommedan religion seems to me like an abbreviated repetition of the Jewish one, of which it emerged as an imitation. It appears, indeed, that the Prophet intended originally to accept Judaism completely for himself and his people. The recapture of the single great primal father brought the Arabs an extraordinary exaltation of their self-confidence, which led to great worldly successes but exhausted itself in them. Allah showed himself far more grateful to his chosen people than Yahweh did to his. But the internal development of the new religion soon came to a stop, perhaps because it lacked the depth which had been caused in the Jewish case by the murder of the founder of their religion" (23:92–93).

[12] Assmann, *Price of Monotheism*, 93.

[13] Jean Laplanche and Jean-Bertrand Pontalis, *The Language of Psychoanalysis* (New York: Norton, 1973), 138 (emphasis added).

[14] Assmann, *Price of Monotheism*, 16.

[15] Jan Assmann, *Moses the Egyptian: The Memory of Egypt in Western Monotheism* (Cambridge, MA: Harvard University Press, 1997), 215.

[16] Assmann, *Price of Monotheism*, 94 (emphasis added).

[17] Ibid., 20.

[18] Assmann distinguishes *revolutionary monotheism*, the exclusive monotheism ascribed to Moses that declares that there is only one true God and all other gods and religions are false, from *evolutionary monotheism*, an inclusive form of monotheism "that is nothing other than a mature stage of polytheism." Ibid., 36.

[19] Jan Assmann, *Of God and Gods: Egypt, Israel, and the Rise of Monotheism* (Madison: University of Wisconsin Press, 2008), 5. Assmann is emphatic in declaring,

"The atrocities of the twentieth century—including the horrors of September 11, 2001—have lent tremendous resonance to the sacred texts of our monotheistic tradition. It is impossible to speak of religion, especially with a focus on violence, without thinking of and referring to the

Holocaust and/or to the events of 9/11. It is therefore of prime importance to make clear at the outset, before broaching the subject of monotheism, that the atrocities of the twentieth century did not stem from but rather were directed against monotheism. They were part of a modernity that had not only lost contact with but was violently reacting against its religious traditions. However, they must also not be associated with any "essence" of monotheism that would of necessity provoke such murderous reactions. Yet it would be equally wrong to make the Enlightenment responsible for Auschwitz. . . . Instead of opposing monotheism to the Enlightenment, I would prefer to see the two movements in closer proximity to one another, subscribing . . . to Sigmund Freud's phrase "Fortschritt in der Geistigkeit" (progress in intellectuality/spirituality). It is precisely this intellectual/spiritual "Geistigkeit" against which German fascism mobilized the masses and used the most "unspeakable forms of violence."

In recent years, Assmann has significantly modified his views about the Mosaic distinction. Based on his new interpretation of Exodus and the "Exodus myth," he now thinks that he was mistaken in emphasizing the concepts of a true and false religion. Furthermore, he emphasizes the role of the Covenant and the demand for loyalty by a jealous God in the development of monotheism. But even with these modifications and revisions, he still highlights the significance of potential violence in monotheism— especially God's violence directed against those who are disloyal and are tempted by idolatry. This is the significance of the demand for the Jewish people (the chosen people) to remember (*Zahor*) their covenant with God. See Jan Assmann, *Exodus: Die Revolution der Alten Welt* (Munich: C. H. Beck Verlag, 2015). See also Assmann's lecture "Exodus and Memory: Remembering the Origin of Israel and Monotheism" (paper presented at the University of San Diego "Out of Egypt Exodus Conference," San Diego, California, May 31–June 1, 2013), https://www.youtube.com/watch?v=rSMO1Knz4JM (accessed December 19, 2016).

[20] Assmann, *Of God and Gods*, 125.

[21] Yerushalmi, *Freud's Moses*, 95.

[22] Walter Benjamin, "Theses on the Philosophy of History," in *Illuminations* (New York: Schocken Books, 1968), 256.

Joel Whitebook

2 *Geistigkeit*: A Problematic Concept

I

THE DATE WAS the second of August 1938.[1] The lights were about to go out over Europe for the second time in less than thirty years, and the International Psychoanalytic Association was holding its fifteenth congress in Paris. It was the last meeting that the organization would convene before continental Europe was almost completely emptied of its analysts and before the creator of their field died the following year. It was therefore the last opportunity that Freud had to address his assembled troops before taking leave of them. But he was dying of cancer in London and too weak to attend, so he dispatched his daughter, Anna, to represent him. The text that he chose to have her read on that occasion was a section from his final major work, *Moses and Monotheism*, titled "Der Fortschritt in der Geistigkeit," which James Strachey translates as "An Advance in Intellectuality" in *The Standard Edition* of Freud's psychological works.[2]

Just as Moses sought to put his affairs in order and provide the Israelites with his last testament before ascending Mount Nebo to die at the age of 120, so, it has often been suggested, Freud, another "important Jew who died in exile," drafted his final testament in *Moses and Monotheism* before he returned "to the earth in London" at eighty-three.[3] Whatever the more esoteric and obscure truths contained in *Moses and Monotheism*, the passage that Anna delivered in Paris would appear to contain the exoteric message that Freud wanted his followers to carry with them after his death. In that section, Freud proudly identifies with the idea of *Geistigkeit* as a fundamental value of the Jewish people. (As we will see, he also believes that their articulation of it was a source of much of the hatred that has been directed at the Jews throughout history.) And it has also often been argued that, for Freud, *Geistigkeit* constituted the ur-norm not only for the Jews but for psychoanalysis as well.[4]

Because of the position that the concept occupies in Freud's last major work and because of the encomium that Anna delivered to it at that historic meeting, the concept of *Geistigkeit* has often been surrounded by an honorific aura that has shielded it from critical scrutiny. While there are very compelling reasons to praise the concept and the role that the Jewish people played in articulating it, the idea of *Geistigkeit* is not without serious difficulties that I examine in this chapter. It is a well-known fact that Freud has been criticized, from the earliest days of his career, for the masculinist and misogynist biases in his thinking. Indeed, at times he has been portrayed as one of the prime ideologues of patriarchy.

Research in feminism, pre-Oedipal theory, and psychoanalytic historiography in recent decades has not only sharpened and refined those criticisms but also traced the sources of those difficulties to previously unappreciated facts concerning Freud's biography.[5] We now know that, contrary to the idealized account promulgated by Freud and many of his followers, his early relationship with his mother, Amalie Nathanson Freud, was relatively traumatic and that his early traumas produced serious distortions in his views of femininity, masculinity, and culture. More specifically, there is now a consensus that, owing to his troubled relationship with Amalie, the figure of the mother—especially the early mother—is largely absent in his thinking and work. My thesis is that those distortions manifest themselves in his theory of *Geistigkeit* and account for the difficulties attached to it.

II

FREUD, LIKE ARNOLD Schoenberg, turned to Moses as a response to the rise of Hitler. The more obvious and less troubling question for him to have asked at the time would have been this: What was it about the German (and Austrian) character and culture that gave rise to Nazism? However, because of his consistent commitment to self-reflection, Freud raised a different question—one that he knew would not go down well with his persecuted coreligionists: What was it about "the particular character of the Jew[s]" that had "earned [them] the hearty dislike of every other people" throughout much of history?[6] This question presupposes a specific psychological theorem. Contrary to a popular conception, paranoia does not consist in pure projection "into the blue" but attaches itself onto some anchor, however minimal, that exists in extrapsychic reality. Likewise, prejudice is not a purely projective phenomenon either. As with paranoia, it also "leans on" some feature in the person who is persecuted.[7] Individuals who have been the object of hatred, if they are honest with themselves, often recognize that something in them provided a hook for their persecutor's projections. Having made this psychological point, however, we must immediately register a warning to forestall a pernicious and not uncommon interpretation of it. To say that there is something about the Jews that provokes anti-Semitism—or that there is something about any persecuted group that provokes its persecution—*in no way implies that they got what they deserved.*

Freud answers the question in the following way. What he considers the highest achievement of the Jewish people, namely, their comprehensive articulation of a monotheistic worldview that is fully "dematerialized" or transcendent, is also the source of the remarkable hatred that has regularly been directed at them. (We should note that, while the revolutionary Egyptian pharaoh Akhenaten first enunciated the monotheistic vision, according to Freud, it fell to Moses and the Israelites, whose "peculiar psychic aptitude" was well suited for the task, to complete his project.)[8] Freud takes one of "the precepts of the Moses religion" to be of central importance: "the prohibition against making an image of God" or, to put it differently, "the compulsion to worship a God whom one cannot see."[9] By analyzing the ban on idolatry, he believes he can elucidate the civilizational significance of Jewish monotheism. His thesis is that this prohibition introduced "an advance in *Geistigkeit*" into world history: "[It] meant that a sensory perception was given second place to what may be called an abstract idea—a triumph of *Geistigkeit* over sensuality or, strictly speaking, an instinctual renunciation, with all its necessary psychological consequences."[10]

The German philosopher Karl Jaspers introduced the idea of the Axial Age to connote a group of related phenomena that occurred in China, India, Palestine, and Greece at roughly the same time—phenomena associated with such names as Confucius, Socrates, Buddha, and Jeremiah—that constituted the emergence of a new level of spiritual awareness for humankind. And although Akhenaten's and Moses's creation of monotheism occurred before the Axial Age, according to the customary chronology, they can be seen, as the Egyptologist and cultural historian Jan Assmann suggests, as axial phenomena. The feature unifying the diverse achievements that are generally subsumed under the idea of the Axial Age is, Assmann argues, "a breakthrough to a kind of transcendence."[11] In one way or another, axial figures posited a sphere of second-order being and thinking—for example, a notion of a "dematerialized" God with the Jews and the idea of Reason with the Greeks—that made it possible not only to understand first-order thinking and the world as it is given but also to criticize them.

The point that needs to be stressed is that positing the existence of a transcendent sphere creates a standpoint from which "actually existing reality" can be criticized. Moses's introduction of monotheism made a new form of critique possible, and, for Freud, this is perhaps its most significant accomplishment and one that he appropriated. The Mosaic attack on idolatry, in other words, was the precursor of Freud's own destruction of the idols through the psychoanalytic critique of illusion.

The fact that asserting the demands of *Geistigkeit* over those of sensuality (*Sinnlichkeit*) required the "renunciation" of instinctual life and the devaluation of the body constitutes the linchpin for Freud's explanation of anti-Semitism. To accomplish "higher" *geistig* achievements, one must renounce and repress the distracting perceptions and seductive temptations offered by the material world as well as the immediate demands of the drives. Like most obsessional attempts to control the instincts, with the Jews, the *geistig* demands for renunciation steadily proliferated over "the course of the centuries" until, according to Freud, they assumed a central position in Judaism. "The religion" that began with the *Bilderverbot*, he observes, developed "more and more . . . into a religion of instinctual renunciations." As the Prophets never tire of telling us, "God requires nothing other from his people than a just and virtuous conduct of life—that is, abstention from every instinctual satisfaction."[12]

Freud's celebration of *Geistigkeit* is unabashedly androcentric and patriarchal and involves a repudiation of femininity and maternity. He offers a particularly concrete and somewhat strained explanation of why "this turning from the mother to the father points to a victory of *Geistigkeit* over sensuality—that is, an advance in civilization." Because birth, the physical emergence of the infant from the mother's body, is an observable fact, he argues, "maternity is proved by the evidence of the senses." By contrast, insofar as no comparable empirical evidence existed for establishing the identity of the father prior to the discovery of DNA, "paternity" is a "conceptual" matter, that is, "a hypothesis, based on an inference and a premise."[13] We might note that this is an argument that legions of deadbeat dads have deployed in less *geistig* situations. The triumph of patriarchy over the chthonic deities—of the Father of the primal horde over the Great Mother—represents an advance in *Geistigkeit* because to determine paternal lineage, one must rely on "conceptual" considerations, inferences, rather than "sensual" evidence.

There is another, more important point to be made about Freud's account of "the advance in *Geistigkeit*." Not only does it represent a "triumph" of patriarchy; it is an expression of Freud's "matraphobic" devaluation of the pre-Oedipal realm in that it also represents the debasement of the maternal dimension. The early breast-mother, with the warmth, comfort, smells, closeness, and pleasure that she offers her child, is, after all, the apotheosis of *Sinnlichkeit*. From the heights of the *geistig* Mosaic perspective, that sensuality is, as Ilse Grubrich-Simitis argues, demonized as "the fleshpots of Egypt," which can be understood as a "metaphor" for the temptation to return to a state of symbiotic merger with the archaic mother.[14]

Freud had identified with Moses in various ways throughout his life, and when it came time to draft his last testament, he saw specific parallels between his current situation and the prophet's. Moses had devised an elitist, severe, and uncompromising monotheistic doctrine, which he attempted to impose on the common people from above—Freud refers to them as the "mob"—and which they ultimately found intolerable. Indeed, according to Freud's version of the legend, Moses's demands were so unbearable that Israelites rose up and murdered him. Similarly, Freud believed he had subjected a ragtag "gang" of marginal Viennese

Luftmenschen to his equally "harsh" doctrine, and they also had difficulty maintaining its rigorist demands. There had already been the defections of Adler, Rank, and Jung—not to mention the heterodoxy of Melanie Klein and her group in London— and he suspected that his discontented followers, who remained "murmurers" as long as he was alive, would become overt "blasphemers" once he died. And his concerns about the resistances within his own ranks applied a fortiori to the public at large.

With these considerations in mind, Freud had a particular template for explaining anti-Semitism: it is the hatred of Akhenaten and Moses, resulting from the demand for renunciation they imposed on their people, writ large. After Akhenaten's death, in reaction to his antisensual and aniconic revolution-from-above— which sought to eradicate the abundant visuality of Egyptian culture and religion—the priests he had purged allied with the common people, angrily rose up in a counterrevolution, and eradicated every trace of the pharaoh's monotheistic worldview. By the same token, when the Israelites in the desert found they could no longer tolerate the renunciations that Moses's ascetic and dematerialized monotheism was imposing on them, they not only yearned to return to "the fleshpots of Egypt" and danced naked around the Golden Calf but also, if Freud is to be believed, revolted against their leader and murdered him.

The central conflict at the heart of the notion of "an advance in *Geistigkeit*" is this. On the one hand, the introduction into history of a thoroughly "dematerialized" monotheistic religion constituted an undeniable epochal advance and represents one of the Jews' greatest contributions to civilization. On the other hand, the demand for renunciation that is integral to it has provoked formidable resentment among the other peoples of the world. It is here that we arrive at Freud's central thesis concerning anti-Semitism: *the anger that the Gentile world harbors toward the Jews for having imposed that demand for renunciation on them is the central cause of the Jew hatred that has regularly flared up over thousands of years.*

Writing during the Nazi period, Horkheimer and Adorno make the point aphoristically: "Because [the Jews] invented the concept of the kosher," which exemplifies their renunciatory ethic, they "are persecuted like swine."[15] We might add that, owing to the fact that persecutory structures of thought typically obey primary processes, the Jews are often simultaneously condemned as hypersexual and lascivious.

III

OSKAR PFISTER WAS a Lutheran minister and practicing psychoanalyst, whom Freud held in high regard and with whom he conducted a decades-long debate concerning religion. In a 1918 letter that Freud wrote to his Gentile colleague, the founder of psychoanalysis asserted that only "a completely godless Jew" could have discovered psychoanalysis. (In response, Pfister had made the completely *meshuga* assertion that no "better Christian" than Freud ever existed.)[16] Then eighteen years later, in Freud's 1930 "Preface to the Hebrew Translation of *Totem and Taboo*," he upped the ante and made the assertion that it was he, a nonbelieving psychoanalyst, who in fact instantiated the "very essence" of Judaism—although "he could not [at that time] express that essence in words."[17] Now, Freud was in effect making the *chuzpadik* (cheeky) claim that no better Jew than he had ever walked the earth. Far from having abandoned the tribe, he was irreverently asserting that, precisely as an "apostate Jew"—as an iconoclastic Jew—he was the essential Jew. Though the Jewish historian Yosef Hayim Yerushalmi clearly bristles at the idea, he is forced to conclude that Freud's "secret" is not only that he is "a godless Jew" but also that psychoanalysis "is godless Judaism."[18]

How can Freud make the seemingly outrageous claim that he embodies the essence of Judaism? By identifying Judaism with one particular strand in it: the Mosaic. He then assimilates Moses the prophet to Moses Mendelssohn and construes the Mosaic critique of idolatry as the ancient prefiguration of the *Aufklärung*'s critique of illusion. This in turn allows him to maintain that the psychoanalytic critique of religion has carried the Mosaic critique of idolatry to its ultimate conclusion by demonstrating that not this or that particular religion *but religion as such* is idolatrous. One might say that *The Standard Edition* becomes the new Torah.

Richard J. Bernstein maintains that Freud, although he does not explicitly flag it as such in *Moses and Monotheism*, in fact articulates the essence of Judaism he had gestured at in the preface to *Totem and Taboo*. And, according to Bernstein, it is epitomized in the phrase *"Der Fortschritt in der Geistigkeit."* There is no doubt that Bernstein is in some sense correct when he argues that "this is a legacy with which Freud proudly [identified]" and that he wanted to honor at the end of his life.[19] The thesis, however, is also problematic, in no small part because the concept of *Geistigkeit*, as I am arguing, is itself problematic, and Bernstein does not sufficiently pursue its problematic aspects. Whatever its positive content, there is one thing that the essence of Judaism, as Freud saw it, was not: flabby. As we have seen, the feature of the Judaic tradition—more precisely of the Mosaic tradition—that he cherished and identified with was its critical rigor, manifested in its hostility to icons and idols. It was the internalization of that iconoclasm that, Freud believed, allowed him to stand outside the "compact majority"—including the compact Jewish majority— and adhere to a transcultural standard of scientific objectivity. The flattering self-images that a group creates to boost its collective narcissism—"the idols of the tribe"—should not, he believed, be exempted from that skeptical rigor. Indeed, he may have been bending over backward to demonstrate his commitment to cosmopolitan and universalist values when he maintained that Moses was an Egyptian and told his critics that he refused to "put the truth aside in favour of what are supposed to be [the] national interests" of his own people, regardless of the profound historical crisis that was threatening them.[20]

Freud's somewhat hortatory celebration of *Geistigkeit* in *Moses* is flabby in that it does not adequately capture the critical iconoclasm that he saw as an essential feature of the monotheistic revolution. To be sure, given the multiple traumas that confronted him at the time—his cancer, the uprooting of the professional infrastructure he had created, Hitler's massive attack on the Jews, and his immigration to London—we can understand why Freud may have relaxed his critical standards and painted an idealized and inspirational portrait of his people.[21] Nevertheless, in so doing, he retreated from the skeptical, iconoclastic rigor that was central to his Jewish ego ideal. The concept of *Geistigkeit* is too uncritical and affirmative—indeed, too unanalytic—and contains more than a whiff of sanctimony and self-satisfaction. One can imagine a Reform rabbi in prewar Berlin presenting a variation of Freud's encomium to *Geistigkeit* as a sermon to the respectable members of the Jewish *Bildungsbürgertum*—the people whom Franz Kafka, Gershom Scholem, and Walter Benjamin revolted against.

There is also a more insidious side to Freud's affirmation of paternal *Geistigkeit* and denigration of maternal *Sinnlichkeit*: it can be seen as identification with the aggressor—namely, with Pauline Christianity. The adoration of the Madonna may be one aspect of Christianity, but Paul's teachings, which criticize *Israel carnalis* and Jewish legalism in the name of Christian spirituality, are more central to its history.[22] As Robert Paul observes, the opposition between "spirituality" and "carnality" is at the heart of Paul's denunciation of the Jews.[23] And Assmann notes that "it could be said that Christianity is primarily and fundamentally distinguished by a principle that could no better be characterized than with Freud's phrase, 'progress in [spirituality].'" Assmann is content to conclude that Freud's "use of a Christian topos" to articulate what he believed to be the greatest accomplishment of the Jewish people, although "it is not without a certain irony," "was quite unintentional."[24] Yet the whole thing is too peculiar to be left there and invites analytic scrutiny. It would seem that

Freud's eagerness to valorize the Jews led him to a certain identification with the aggressor.

IV

THE "THIRD EAR" of every self-respecting analyst should have perked up at the mention of *Fortschritt*, for, as Freud taught us, there is no unambiguous progress in psychic life or cultural history. Every advance exacts its price. In this respect, enlightened psychoanalytic thinking is similar to mythical thought, which holds, as Horkheimer and Adorno put it, that "everything that happens must atone for the fact of having happened."[25] The cost of creating monotheism was not only the repression and debasement of sensuality and the body but the maternal dimension in general. One of the most problematic features of Freud's celebration of *Geistigkeit* is his uncritical affirmation of its thoroughly androcentric and patriarchal orientation, which is particularly obvious after the rise of feminism and its critique of psychoanalysis. Indeed, the reader is taken aback when Freud criticizes Christianity's reintroduction of the figure of the mother as "a cultural regression" from transcendent heights of Jewish monotheism to a more primitive stage of religious development based on "the great mother goddess."[26] It could in fact be argued that the rehabilitation of the maternal dimension was a crucial factor in Christianity's triumph over Judaism in popularity.

The monolithic androcentrism of *Moses and Monotheism* has a psychological as well as a political source. Psychologically, Grubrich-Simitis argues that because Freud himself had never successfully confronted "the catastrophic events of [his] own early childhood," largely connected with his relation to his mother, when memories of those early traumatic experience were reactivated by the traumas of the 1930s, he could only deal with them through a displacement, namely, from the maternal world onto world history.[27] Instead of excavating his own prehistory and his relation to the archaic mother, Freud turned to an excavation of the "primeval" history of civilization through what the eminent historian Carl Shorske calls his second "Egyptian dig."[28]

In addition to the psychological factors that were undoubtedly at work, the masculinist bias of *Moses*, Shorske argues, also results from Freud's attempt to present an idealized picture of Akhenaten's Enlightenment and Moses's continuation of it in order to enhance the Jews' conception of themselves and stiffen their mettle in their struggle against Nazi barbarism. Shorske points out that Egypt had replaced Greece as the ancient culture that Freud idealized. Though the Jews had never achieved "an honored place in the gentile history" of Athens, Rome, or Vienna, "in Egypt," he argues, according to Freud's narrative, they "became the *Kulturvolk* that rescued the highest gentile civilization from the unholy alliance of priests and ignorant people." The implicit message in *Moses and Monotheism*, Shorske suggests, is this: "in modern times, the Jews and cultured gentiles were, through exodus and exile, [likewise] saving Europe's enlightened civilization from Hitler."[29]

For Freud to accomplish his goal, he—writing at the time of the Berlin Olympics—apparently believed it was necessary to portray the Jews not simply as a *Kulturvolk* but specifically as a "masculine *Kulturvolk*," and therefore he emphasized "Moses's imperial manliness."[30] By demanding instinctual renunciation, the prophet, Shorske maintains, "liberated the Jews not so much from Egyptian bondage as from their instinctual drives." Moses was "a father to the childish people who transformed them into a father-people," that is, a mature, manly, and tenacious *Kulturvolk*, whose commitment to *Geistigkeit* allowed them to survive, although eliciting the intense hatred of the Gentile world.[31] The demands of this "monumental" history of the ancient Near East, in short, gave rise to the androcentric and patriarchal biases of *Moses and Monotheism* and caused Freud to extol the "masculine" virtues of *Geistigkeit*, while debasing the "feminine" and "maternal" values of *Sinnlichkeit*.

Shorske argues, however, that an alternative route was available to Freud, which, had he taken it, might have resulted in a more accurate picture of the ancient Near East and avoided the one-sidedness of his patricentric theory of religion and civilization. What is more, it might have prevented mainstream psychoanalysis from cleaving to a narrowly androcentric and downright misogynist orientation that was detrimental to the field's development and required four decades to overcome. Shorske calls our attention to the fact that Freud had exhibited a distinctly different mind-set at the time of his earlier forays into the uncanny land of Sphinx and was thoroughly familiar with two texts that presented a radically different picture of Egyptian culture but chose to ignore them.

In addition to Freud's identification with Moses, it is likely that his curiosity about Egypt was also first aroused when, sitting by his father's side, he had read *The Philippson Bible*, which contained numerous woodcuts depicting various aspects of the Ancient Near East. Shorske tell us that after 1900—that is, after Freud's "conquest of Rome"—his curiosity about Egypt asserted itself and "nurtured interests [in him] that were in drastic contradiction to the faith of his fathers and even to the male orientation of psychoanalysis." Indeed, according to Shorske, Freud's "first Egyptian digs" raised "ultimate and even dangerous questions of the psyche" to which Freud had previously "devoted scant attention."[32] Jewish law, as Janine Chasseguet-Smirgel observes, is suspicious of "mixture" and many "Biblical prohibitions are based on a principle of division and separation"—of what can touch and not touch, what should be kept distinct and apart.[33] Exactly the opposite is the case with the Egyptian world that Freud was exploring in the first years of the twentieth century. It was characterized by mixture, ambiguity, and bipolarity, especially with regard to bisexuality, a topic in which Freud was keenly interested in the aftermath of his relation with Wilhelm Fliess.

In *Leonardo*, for example, Freud turns to Egyptian mythology to interpret the artist's early memory, in which what Freud believed was a vulture struck the boy on the mouth with its tail while he was resting in his cradle. The memory, Freud argues, comprises a homosexual fantasy, in which the vulture represents the phallic mother inserting her penis into the boy's mouth. With this interpretation, Shorske points out, "a new [bisexual] figure" appears "on the psychoanalytic scene: the phallic mother."[34] Because we are not primarily interested in Leonardo's psychic life but Freud's, the fact that the interpretation was infamously based on a mistranslation (the Italian word that Freud took for "vulture" actually meant "kite") is beside the point. For us, what is important is that Freud arrives at his interpretation of the memory through associations to the Egyptian goddess Mut, an early hermaphroditic Egyptian mother deity, who has the head of a vulture and is generally depicted possessing a phallus.

Contrary to the heterosexual bias that tends to characterize Freud's "official position," in this text, he praises the bisexuality of the Egyptian gods. In a remarkable statement, he notes "expressions of the idea that only a combination of male and female elements can give a worthy representation of divine perfection."[35] Shorske argues that just as the Egyptian world, with its indeterminate sexuality, can be viewed as the archaic history of humanity, so the pre-Oedipal world, with its unintegrated drives, can be seen as the archaic history of the individual. Unfortunately, Freud's excursion into bisexuality and pre-Oedipal development in *Leonardo*, which occurred on his "first Egyptian dig," remained a relatively isolated event that he did not systematically pursue in his later work. To do so might have resulted in destabilizing and fruitful insights that would have been productive for his creativity and avoided many serious errors in the development of psychoanalysis.

At the same time as Freud in writing *Moses and Monotheism* drew on extensively James Henry Breasted's *The History of Egypt*

(1905), he also chose to ignore important parts of it.[36] According to Shorske, Breasted had roots "in the progressivist spirit of America's New History" and sought to chart "Egyptian culture as it struggled out of chthonic darkness to the achievements of rational enlightenment in the reign of his hero, Akhenaten." Indeed, Freud's "portrait of Akhenaten" as a rational enlightener, expounding a demanding, rational, androcentric, and puritanical doctrine, "is firmly grounded in Breasted's account."[37] But Breasted also presents another deeply sensual side to Akhenaten's personality and his dynasty that Freud completely ignores. For example, the works of Akhenaten's reign, in contrast to the rigid and geometric Egyptian art that had preceded them, display "a sensuous, naturalistic plasticity worthy of art nouveau." Indeed, "frescoes depicting Akhenaten and his beautiful queen Nefertiti in tender communion," according to Shorske, "radiate the joy of Sinnlichkeit." None of this sensuality, however, can be found in Freud. He "selected from Breasted" only what served his purposes in connecting "the Egyptian Enlightenment" with the *geistig* portrait he wished to create of the Jews. "In his copy of Breasted's history," Shorske tells us, "Freud marked only those passages" that helped him further those aims.[38]

There is something particularly striking about a second text that Freud chose to ignore, namely, Karl Abraham's "Amenhotep IV."[39] Not only had Freud proposed the topic of Akhenaten to his colleague from Berlin, but he had also praised the article, which emphasized the feminine side of the pharaoh's personality and cultural innovations, when it was published in 1912. It has often been observed that there is a double Abrahamic repression in *Moses and Monotheism*: of Abraham the patriarch as the founder of the Jews and of Abraham the analyst as the author of this important article. According to Abraham's paper, Akhenaten's character is distinctly androgynous. Moreover, the young pharaoh was not only deeply attached to two powerful women— his mother, Queen Tiy, and his beautiful wife, Nefertiti—but was also deeply influenced by them. Indeed, it may be the case that Queen Tiy was the source and inspiration for his monotheistic revolution, which would mean that the origins of monotheism were matriarchal. While there was undoubtedly a *geistig* side to Akhenaten, according to Abraham, he was no ascetic: there were deeply sensual aspects to his personality and the culture that surrounded him. The exclusion of Abraham's article from *Moses and Monotheism* is, as the feminist Estelle Roith argues, another symptom of Freud's need to suppress the maternal dimension from his thinking in general and his account of religion in particular.[40]

As we mentioned, the idea that everything has its price is not foreign to psychoanalysis. And the price that Freud paid for creating an image of the Jews that he believed would strengthen them during perhaps the most profound crisis they had faced was the exclusion of the feminine and maternal dimension from his thinking. As Shorske puts it, "For the sake of the Jews in Hitler's Götterdammerung, Freud banished from his mind the promising insights into sexuality and culture he had found in Egypt, and abandoned them in *Moses and Monotheism*."[41] It is not our place to judge Freud's decision but only to understand the price that was paid for his repudiation of femininity and maternity, namely, the exclusion of an entire dimension of psychic life and cultural life from his thinking. Those of us who arrived on the scene after the feminist critique of psychoanalysis, which, in many important respects, dovetailed with the field's pre-Oedipal turn, are left with a particular task: to recoup that dimension and to use the resources that Freud, the ambivalent patriarch, provided us to criticize patriarchy.

Notes

[1] For a longer version of this chapter, see Joel Whitebook, *Freud: An Intellectual Biography* (New York: Cambridge University Press, 2017), 430–451.

2   Sigmund Freud, *Moses and Monotheism*, in *The Standard Edition of the Complete Psychological Works of Sigmund Freud,* trans. James Strachey, vol. 23 (London: Hogarth Press, 1964), 111–115.

3   W. H. Auden, "In Memory of Sigmund Freud," in *Freud as We Knew Him,* ed. Hendrik M. Ruitenbeek (Detroit: Wayne State University Press, 1973), 116–119.

4   See for example Richard J. Bernstein, *Freud and the Legacy of Moses,* Cambridge Studies in Religion and Critical Thought (New York: Cambridge University Press, 1998), 24.

5   See Whitebook, *Freud,* chapter 1.

6   Sigmund Freud to Lou Andreas-Salomé, Jan. 6, 1935, *Sigmund Freud and Lou Andreas-Salomé: Letters,* ed. Ernst Pfeiffer, trans. William Robson-Scott and Elaine Robson-Scott (New York: Harcourt Brace Jovanovich, 1966), 204; Freud, *Moses and Monotheism,* 105.

7   Sigmund Freud, "Some Neurotic Mechanisms in Jealousy, Paranoia and Homosexuality," in *The Standard Edition of the Complete Psychological Works of Sigmund Freud,* trans. James Strachey, vol. 18 (London: Hogarth Press, 1962), 226.

8   Freud, *Moses and Monotheism,* 111.

9   Ibid., 112–113.

10 Ibid., 113.

11 Jan Assmann, *Of God and Gods: Egypt, Israel, and the Rise of Monotheism,* George L. Mosse Series in Modern European Cultural and Intellectual History (Madison: University of Wisconsin Press, 2008), 79.

12 Freud, *Moses and Monotheism,* 118–119.

13 Ibid., 114. Perhaps for this reason, the discovery of DNA should be considered a *Fortschritt in der Geistigkeit.*

14 Ilse Grubrich-Simitis, *Early Freud and Late Freud: Reading Anew Studies in Hysteria and Moses and Monotheism* (New York: Routledge, 1997), 72.

15 Max Horkheimer and Theodor W. Adorno, *Dialectic of Enlightenment: Philosophical Fragments,* trans. Edmund Jebcott (Stanford, CA: Stanford University Press, 2002), 153.

16 Pfister to Freud, Oct. 29, 1918, *Psychoanalysis and Faith: The Letters of Sigmund Freud and Oskar Pfister,* ed. Ernst L. Freud and Heinrich Meng (New York: Basic Books, 1963), 63.

17 Sigmund Freud, *Totem and Taboo,* in *The Standard Edition of the Complete Psychological Works of Sigmund Freud,* trans. James Strachey, vol. 13 (London: Hogarth Press, 1955), p. xv.

18 Yosef Hayim Yerushalmi, *Freud's Moses: Judaism Terminable or Interminable* (New Haven, CT: Yale University Press, 1991), 99.

19 Bernstein, *Freud and the Legacy of Moses*, 84.

20 Freud, *Moses and Monotheism*, 7.

21 See Grubrich-Simitis, *Early Freud and Late Freud*, 61.

22 See Daniel Boyarin, *Carnal Israel: Reading Sex in Talmudic Culture* (Berkeley: University of California Press, 1993).

23 Robert Paul, *Moses and Civilization: The Meaning of Freud's Myth* (New Haven, CT: Yale University Press, 1996), 111.

24 Jan Assmann, *The Price of Monotheism*, trans. Robert Savage (Stanford, CA: Stanford University Press, 2010), 101.

25 Horkheimer and Adorno, *Dialectic of Enlightenment*, 8.

26 Freud, *Moses and Monotheism*, 88.

27 Grubrich-Simitis, *Early Freud and Late Freud*, 68.

28 Carl Shorske, "To the Egyptian Dig: Freud's Psycho-Archeology of Cultures," in *Thinking with History* (Princeton, NJ: Princeton University Press, 1998), 191–215.

29 Ibid., 209.

30 I would like to thank the psychoanalytically oriented classicist Richard Armstrong for drawing my attention to the fact that the Olympics constituted, with their celebration of physicality, part of the backdrop for *Moses*.

31 Shorske, "To the Egyptian Dig," 209.

32 Ibid., 205.

33 Janine Chasseguet-Smirgel, "Perversion and the Universal Law," in *Creativity and Perversion* (New York: Norton, 1984), 8.

34 Shorske, "To the Egyptian Dig," 206.

35 Sigmund Freud, *Leonardo da Vinci and a Memory of His Childhood*, in *The Standard Edition of the Complete Psychological Works of Sigmund Freud*, trans. James Strachey, vol. 11 (London: Hogarth Press, 1961), 94. In this context, Freud raises the boggling question of why humans endow "a figure which is intended to embody the essence of the mother with a mark of male potency which is the opposite of everything male." Had he been able to face the frightening power of his own mother, he might have been able to provide a better answer to this question than the dubious one he formulated with the castration complex.

36 James Henry Breasted, *A History of Egypt* (New York: Scribner, 1905).

37 Shorske, "To the Egyptian Dig," 109–110.

38 Ibid., 110.

39 Karl Abraham, "Amenhotep IV: A Psycho-Analytical Contribution towards the Understanding of His Personality and of the Monotheistic

Cult of Aton," in *Clinical Papers and Essays on Psycho-analysis*, ed. Hilda C. Abraham, trans. Hilda C. Abraham and D. R. Ellison (New York: Bruner/Mazel, 1955), 262–290.

40 Estelle Roith, *The Riddle of Freud: Jewish Influences on His Theory of Female Sexuality*, New Library of Psychoanalysis 4 (New York: Tavistock, 1987), 172–173.

41 Shorske, "To the Egyptian Dig," 213.

Willi Goetschel

3 Heine and Freud: Deferred Action and the Concept of History

SIGMUND FREUD'S *Moses and Monotheism* is a rather strange book, if we can, in fact, call this mix of three uneven essayistic texts a book at all. The textual quality of this series of essays poses a hermeneutic challenge whose severity cannot be ignored. But bracketing this hermeneutic challenge of how to read this book or nonbook, this trilogy of texts has the curious effect of encouraging the attitude of screening out its self-critical dimension, distracting attention from a compositional mode that twists its way through the text. Thus, we can easily forget our sense that this idiosyncratic and oddly conflicted piece of writing contains many doublings, reiterations, and duplications, as if built around a double bottom or even a false floor.

Freud's *Moses and Monotheism* is, in other words, a performative text, self-consciously stating a literary mode that is part and parcel of the critical function of the writing. This aspect presents a defining moment of Freud's argument as it demonstrates his argument through a literary performance that reflects its point by performing it at the same time. Freud's writing thus warns us against focusing solely on the text's rationalizations and asks us to attend at the same time to the tremendous struggle that underlies their articulation. This dual-level focus reveals Freud's strategic positioning of his *Moses and Monotheism* as a critical intervention into the discourse of religion and modernity, secularization and revolution, and one in which Freud inserts himself self-consciously as an active player. Part of Freud's argument, the book's particular form of writing and literary arrangement calls for the reader's attention down to the overt and covert intertextual references that *Moses and Monotheism* offers that will prove critical for understanding the full thrust of Freud's intervention. One of the literary references that stands out in this text is the way Freud deals with acknowledging Heinrich Heine, an author close to his heart who plays a central role in his work. Exploring the function of Heine's presence in Freud's work as a replay of "fort/da" highlights the way in which Freud's *Moses and Monotheism* reflects the book's theme by working through Freud's own relationship with Heine.

At the end of a rather long footnote early on in the second essay, Freud asks the question,

> And, incidentally, who suggested to the Jewish poet Heine in the nineteenth century A.D. that he should complain of his religion as "the plague dragged along from the Nile valley, the unhealthy beliefs of Ancient Egypt"?[1]

> Wer hat übrigens dem jüdischen Dichter H. Heine im 19. Jahrhundert n.Chr. eingegeben, seine Religion zu beklagen als "die aus dem Niltal mitgeschleppte Plage, den altägyptischen ungesunden Glauben"?[2]

It is very tempting to turn the question around and ask the following instead: who gave Freud the idea to argue for the Egyptian origins of Judaism? If this seems a cheap shot of the kind Freud tries to get away with in his suggestion that the Egyptian godhead Aten might be addressed in Judaism's signal lines of the "Sh'ma Israel," suggesting that the Hebrew "Adonai" might reference Aten (German: Aton), a closer reading of Freud shows us that this footnote is hardly incidental and signals Freud's covert acknowledgment of Heine. Of course, it is not just this one occasional poem by Heine that had suggestive force for Freud's conception of his Moses book.[3] Heine plays a crucial role for Freud, and it is no coincidence that Freud was so fond of Heine's striking description of Spinoza as an "Unglaubensgenosse" (fellow *un*believer) that he calls Heine at the end of the penultimate section of *The Future of an Illusion* "one of our Unglaubensgenossen": "one of our fellow unbelievers."[4] Freud had introduced Heine's word joke of the *Unglaubensgenosse* in his joke book, *Jokes and Their Relation to the Unconscious*.[5] There Heine prominently figures as a rich source— Louis Untermeyer calls him Freud's "chief exhibit"—as provider of priceless comic material.[6] But the Heine who figures in Freud's writings ever since the publication of the *Interpretation of Dreams* seems to get a mixed reception in Freud's work. Celebrated as a crucial informant for our understanding of the preconscious, the region where Freud situates much of the dynamics of the function of jokes, or as "chief exhibit," Heine's significance for the exploration of the unconscious remains curiously contained in Freud's work.[7] The Freud who explored the origins of Moses, it seems, was wary of giving Heine too much credit for a discovery he after all claimed primarily to have been his own. A central passage in *Jokes and Their Relation to the Unconscious* suggests that much. There, Freud shares a striking family anecdote that captures a conflicted attitude toward the poor relation that Heine also represents:

> I recall a story told by an old aunt of my own, who had married into the Heine family, how one day, when she was an attractive young woman, she found sitting next her at the family dinner-table a person who struck her as uninviting and whom the rest

of the company treated contemptuously. She herself felt no reason to be any more affable towards him. It was only many years later that she realized that this negligent and neglected cousin had been the poet Heinrich Heine.[8]

Ich erinnere mich der Erzählung einer eigenen alten Tante, die durch Heirat in die Familie Heine gekommen war, daß sie eines Tages als schöne junge Frau einen Sitznachbar an der Familientafel fand, der ihr unappetitlich schien und gegen den die anderen sich geringschätzig benahmen. Sie fühlte sich nicht veranlaßt, herablassender gegen ihn zu sein; erst viele Jahre später erkannte sie, daß der nachlässige und vernachlässigte Vetter der Dichter Heinrich Heine gewesen war.[9]

Just like his aunt, whose anecdote he finds himself compelled to share, Freud himself could not resist helping himself to Heine's literary wit and insights, while seating his predecessor at the lower end of the table of the psychoanalytic discourse over which he presided. For the purpose of my argument, it is sufficient to note this passage as an instance when Freud's family dynamics, in the case of Heine, comes to light as the experience of a conflict. Such drama, of course, does not prohibit Freud from taking utmost advantage of Heine's writing, while remaining careful and overly conscientious in giving his source full and due credit. And it is this attention to his intertextual resonance with Heine—whose traces Freud refuses to mute—that helps to bring out the performative mode of Freud's *Moses and Monotheism*.

Freud's Moses book is in this way—and above all—a study concerned with the function of tradition, the role of doubling and repetition, and the phenomenon of *Nachträglichkeit*, that is, deferred action or belatedness. If Freud is after the meaning and function of history, the study itself reflects its own embeddedness in the historical process. Freud suggests as much at the opening of the first essay, "Moses, an Egyptian," in which he emphasizes science's own increasing caution with regard to the transmission of traditions than it used to display "in the early days of historical criticism."[10] This theme of belated discovery of a different origin continues to resurface throughout the speculative narrative that Freud presents.

While science or *Wissenschaft* as such is only a relatively reliable instrument, as Freud keeps cautioning us, his depth-psychological approach, he claims, will yield a better grasp of the way tradition, history, and religion function. Freud thus offers an alternative approach to history, one that of course bona fide historians can only view as anathema to their disciplinary convictions. Freud, to be sure, is primarily interested in a history of the psyche rather than in brute facts, although the facts he posits are no doubt rather brute in and of themselves.

Far less brutal is the way Freud's Moses book resonates with Heine; a survey of Heine's writing on the themes that Freud introduces therefore provides us with a crucial background that helps us situate Freud's effort differently: as an intervention in a critical discourse that has a history of its own. Freud's *Moses* is therefore more than the brainchild of an aging psychoanalyst: we can read it as a pointed intervention in a larger discourse on the multiple origins of tradition, a discourse whose own historicity it critically reflects. In other words, Freud challenges the problematic forms of rationalization that the attempts at constructions of history driven by the desire to identify a particular moment as origin or foundational moment represent. Instead, his *Moses* suggests that the desire for historical origins displaces what it seeks to fasten.

A brief review of some of the relevant passages in Heine's prose and poetry shall demonstrate the importance of Heine for Freud that underlies the study of *Moses*. A text that plays a central role in this respect is Heine's story of the Messiah in Golden Chains that can serve as the key passage around which we can review Heine's other texts, for it is this text that poses, in explicit and challenging terms, the question of the relation between the Messianic and history—revised in Freud's *Moses and Monotheism* as a theory of the differential origins of tradition, a position Freud uses Moses to explore.

The Messiah in Golden Chains

IN *LUDWIG BÖRNE: A MEMORIAL*, Heine inserts at the end of book 4 the story of the Messiah in Golden Chains. On a visit in Poland many years ago, Heine the narrator tells us he heard the following story from a rabbi in Cracow:

> "The Messiah," he told me, "was born on the day when Jerusalem was destroyed by the villain Titus Vespasian, and since then he dwells in the most beautiful palace of heaven, just like a king, but his hands are bound with golden chains!"
>
> "What," I asked in surprise, "what do these golden chains mean?"
>
> "They are necessary," replied the great rabbi, with a sly glance and a deep sigh; "without these fetters the Messiah, when he sometimes loses patience, would otherwise suddenly hurry down and undertake the work of salvation too soon, in the wrong hour. He is, after all, no calm sleepy-head. He is a handsome, very lean but immensely strong man: flourishing like youth. The life he leads, moreover, is very monotonous. The greatest part of the morning he passes with the customary prayers or laughs and jokes with his servants, who are distinguished angels, prettily singing and playing the flute. Then he has his long locks combed and he is rubbed with ointments and dressed in a regal purple robe. The whole afternoon he studies the Kabbalah. Towards evening he summons his old chancellor, who is a disguised angel, just as the four strong state councilors who accompany him are disguised angels. The chancellor must then read to his master out of a great book what has happened every day. All kinds of events occur about which the Messiah smiles with pleasure or shakes his head in annoyance. But when he hears how his people are treated down below, then he gets into the most terrible rage and howls so that the heavens tremble. The four strong state councilors must then hold the furious man back so that he will not hurry down to the earth, and they would surely not overcome him if his hands were not bound with the golden chains. They mollify him by saying gently that the time has not

yet come, the right hour of salvation, and in the end he sinks onto his couch and covers his face and weeps."[11]

As Heine the narrator has the rabbi conclude, "certifying his reliability by reference to the Talmud," Heine the narrator notes about the days since his visit in Poland, "I have often had to think of his stories, especially in recent times, after the July Revolution. Indeed, in bad days I thought I heard with my own ears a rattling, as though of golden chains, and then despairing sobs."[12] Turning now to the present, Heine concludes this passage with an appeal to the Messiah and his guards that spells the problem of *Nachträglichkeit* in harrowing terms: "Oh, despair not, handsome Messiah, who wants not only to save Israel, as the superstitious Jews think, but all of suffering mankind! Oh, do not break your golden chains! Oh, keep him bound for a time so that he does not come too soon, the saving king of the world!"[13] If Heine, who never visited Cracow, seems to have made up this wonderful story, we can consider it as his own creative attempt at producing a "Midrash."[14] In any case, with Galileo Galilei, we can say, "se non e vero e ben trovato." For this Midrash-style version of the Messianic legend brings home some remarkable critical reflections on the critical function of the Messianic, and not just in Jewish tradition. Although the notion of the Messiah in chains does not appear in Jewish tradition until the Middle Ages, there is a medieval mystical midrashic tradition that features the Messiah in chains.[15] Whether Heine knew about this midrashic tradition and whether he heard accounts reflecting it on his trip to Poland is impossible to ascertain. But what is striking is that Heine's version suggestively resonates with such traditions and that his narrative stages them in a temporality of deferred action.

Now let us first look at the way this story is framed in Heine's text. Heine's account is introduced as a citation hailing from an earlier encounter with a Polish rabbi going back to one of Heine's first publications, his series of articles *On Poland*, published in 1823. A voice from the past in many ways, the fictionalized Polish rabbi's story resonates in Heine's memory as Heine sets out to frame the difference concerning the relationship to history and the present that distinguishes him from Ludwig Börne, the Frankfurt onetime brother in arms and eventual opponent whose stress on progress and advancement, Heine suggests, might in the larger scheme of the dynamics of history appear backward and retrograde: precisely because he—Börne, that is—mistakes himself as the harbinger of the new world that he fails to bring about. But again, it is tellingly only much later, in 1840, that the rabbi of Cracow's story catches fire, we could say belatedly afterward, or so Heine's text stages the fictionalized storytelling. Yet this afterward, Heine suggests, is never late because it is precisely its lateness—its working through, in a different scheme—that makes it so timely.

We will return to this image that in Heine becomes a striking expression of his claim of being in step with history while apparently lagging behind, while Börne's brash pretense of being in sync with the time or ahead of it ultimately betrays an attitude that must inevitably miss the transformative historical moment, garbed or linked as it is to the past. With the story of the Messiah fettered with golden chains, Heine rehearses a literary form of *Nachträglichkeit*, that is, the afterward of belatedness, as his account surfaces over one and a half decades after his fictional or fictionally condensed encounter with the rabbi of Cracow. This deferral of the narrative action, if you will, frames the story of the Messiah in a context of continued belatedness just as much as the Messiah's own reaction—when he hears at the end of the day about life on earth—must always be deferred, as late if not too late. As "the chancellor must then read to his master out of a great book what has happened every day," the facts have already become the history, as it were, that the Messiah himself seeks to correct. And any metadiscourse on history is just another reiteration and repetition of the afterward, the belatedness, and so a deferral of action in the present. In other words, even in the heavens, there is no way to escape time and the temporality of textuality and history.

Deferred action can therefore never be translated into straight-forward logic. It remains a self-recursive operation whose referent is never stable in itself but works "itself" as a function of a delayed attempt at making sense in inevitable hindsight. This self-recursive mode, however, does not necessarily have to be simply limiting—permanent chains—since it also holds the promise of a transformative opening of, and into, history. The Messianic does not simply denote the moment of hope but also the moment of activity, of praxis and action. Activating the image of deferral, this re-action performs itself through, as it were, a deferred action—a moment to be seized, after all—and one that Heine projects onto the scene as an emancipatory and transformative power.

As a result, an action is an intervention that operates in a temporality of afterward, a lateness that defines the nature of time, that is, makes it possible in the first place. While the moment of deferral and displacement defines action as historical, it also is the reason that makes it historically effective because history is defined by the moment of afterward. The Messianic, Heine's story of the Messiah in Golden Chains suggests, is the resistance to submit to the past, the insistence that the past informs the present and future and the present conditions the way we reconstruct the past.

Framed as deferred narrative action pointing back "many years" to Heine's journey to Poland, the apocryphal mock or quasi-midrashic compilation assumes a critical force that is so pregnant with the hope of the future because it is so unabashedly grounded in the past.

Opening the present to the past, that is, a past reimagined by a present that reflects back from a future it anticipates, this move opens the afterward as the moment that sets free the relationship between past, present, and future, a relationship whose dynamics function as a critical—analytical and active—moment in the recovery of the past for the present.

Dream, Imagination, History: Going Forward Going Back

THE SWISS PHILOSOPHER Adrien Turel asked the grippingly suggestive question, "How far does one need to back up in order to jump further than where one stands?"[16] His answer was of course that we need to go as far back as speculation allows us. For Heine, the answer seemed to be similar to the one that Freud would give. A genuine understanding of history, Heine would argue, was less to be found with the fact-finding mission of the historian and the bare-naked facts they produced than with the poet, who sees the past differently, by seeing the hidden difference in the past. Heine formulates this view in his *Pictures of Travel* installment "From Munich to Genoa," a reflective journey back into history. It is worthwhile to listen to Heine's programmatic pronouncement concerning the poet's mission, which highlights also the often misunderstood political mission that for Heine, of course, was inseparable from the poetic aspect of his writing:

> Strange fancies these of the multitude! They seek their histories from the poet, and not from the historian. They ask not for bare facts, but those facts again dissolved in the original poetry from which they sprung. This the poets well know, and it is not without a certain mischievous pleasure that they mould at will popular memories, perhaps in mockery of pride-baked historians and parchment-minded keepers of State documents. [. . .] History is not distorted by the poets.[17] For they give the sense in all its truthfulness, though it be clothed in invented [Leland has "inverted"] form and circumstance. [. . .] From the same point of view I would assert that Walter Scott's romances give, occasionally, the spirit of English history far more truthfully than Hume has done.[18]

> Seltsame Grille des Volkes! Es verlangt seine Geschichte aus der Hand des Dichters und nicht aus der Hand des Historikers. Es verlangt nicht den treuen Bericht nackter Tatsachen, sondern jene Tatsachen wieder aufgelöst in die ursprüngliche Poesie, woraus sie hervorgegangen. Das wissen die Dichter,

und nicht ohne geheime Schadenlust modeln sie willkührlich die Völkererinnerungen, vielleicht zur Verhöhnung stolztrockner Historiographen und pergamentener Staatsarchivare. [. . .] Die Geschichte wird nicht von den Dichtern verfälscht. Sie geben den Sinn derselben ganz treu, und sei es auch durch selbsterfundene Gestalten und Umstände. [. . .] In gleicher Hinsicht möchte ich behaupten, Walter Scotts Romane gäben zuweilen den Geist der englischen Geschichte weit treuer als Hume. (B 2:330)

Heine goes on to point out that poets capture the essence of history just as dreamers capture through their inner feeling what their soul feels to be external causes,

> since they at once assign on the spot by dreaming, to the latter [i.e. the real external causes—], altogether different causes from the real, which, however, in one respect, amount to the same thing, in that they bring forth the same feelings. (*Pictures of Travel*, 28)

> indem sie an die Stelle dieser letzteren [i.e., the real external causes] ganz andere äußere Ursachen erträumen, die aber insofern ganz adäquat sind, als sie dasselbe Gefühl hervorbringen. (B 2:331)

If such a *Traumgestalt*, or dream form as Heine calls it (*Pictures of Travel*, 28), itself might appear like a dream, it, too, reflects the truth and, as Heine seems to suggest, potentially more accurately and more profoundly than a description by a sober chronicler might be able to render (B 2:331). Let us keep in mind that at this point Heine's bold and ambitious attempt not only to compose a historical novel à la Sir Walter Scott but to produce with it historical source material for future historians lies several years behind him (his project of the *Rabbi of Bacherach* dates back to the days at the Verein für Cultur und Wissenschaft der Juden). From that point onward to the conception of history in *On the History of Religion and Philosophy in Germany* of the 1830s to Heine's final literary legacy in his *Romanzero* and especially the *Romanzero's* "Hebrew Melodies," there is a continuous reflection on, and renegotiation of, history as reality that is most adequately grasped by its creative poetic (re)imagination in poetical narrative and fiction. There are a couple of stops in the *Pictures of Travel's* journey "from Munich to Genoa," however—one might say a progressive delay—worth our attention.

With the visit to the battlegrounds of Marengo, the *Pictures of Travel* enter a force field of historical memory causing the narrator to wonder whether "world history is no longer a history of robbery [*eine Räubergeschichte*], but a ghost story" (103; B 2:375). For a site breathing history such as the battlegrounds of Marengo, from which Napoleon emerged as the great reformer of France and in the wake of this victory as the harbinger of modernity in Europe as a whole, suggests the ghostly character that haunts history. Walking on the battlegrounds, Heine's narrator experiences the resurfacing of historical reflections that appear in ghostly disguise, as if stray dogs that have lost their masters (B 2:378). But the theme of the after-effect of history writ large—the forgotten past that will make history proper, so to speak—is given further elaboration as Heine's narrator now asks some of the hard questions that others so lightly discard:

> But alas! every inch which humanity advances costs streams of blood, and is not that paying rather dear? Is not the life of the individual worth as much as that of the entire race? For every single man is a world which is born and which dies with him; beneath every gravestone lies a world's history [—][19] "Be silent," Death would say "as to those who lie here"; but *we* still live, and will fight on in the holy battle for the freedom of humanity. (108)

> Aber ach! Jeder Zoll, den die Menschheit weiter rückt, kostet Ströme Blutes; und ist das nicht etwas zu teuer? Ist das Leben des Individuums nicht vielleicht eben so viel wert wie das des ganzen Geschlechtes? Denn jeder Mensch ist schon eine Welt,

die mit ihm geboren wird und mit ihm stirbt, unter jedem
Grabstein liegt eine Weltgeschichte—Still davon, so würden
die Toten sprechen, die hier gefallen sind, wir aber leben
und wollen weiter kämpfen im heiligen Befreiungskriege der
Menschheit. (B 2:378)

If there is any poetically adequate expression of the moment of
belatedness and the effect of the afterward that this passage so
eloquently addresses, we can see it captured in this momentous
but mute dash or break, which the German language so suggestively calls *Gedankenstrich*: the punctuation sign that indicates a
pause for thought. Let us just focus on the operative moment that
precedes this moment of silence and break:

beneath every gravestone lies a world history [Leland has
"world's history"]

unter jedem Grabstein liegt eine Weltgeschichte

Rather than merely the burial ground of the bodies of the dead
victims of history, the battlefield is also the site of their dreams
and aspirations: their hopes that live on and that represent a
historical force precisely because their champions died and the
chance to realize their dreams was missed. Just as the dash breaks
but also links the statement from what follows, it becomes unde-
cidable whether the dash cuts the statement to a fragment that
awaits completion, or supplementation, or whether it is all but
completely cut off and remains a stand-alone remark. Only the
afterward will tell—but even when exactly remains in question.

We must leave this powerfully suggestive aphorism for now
and move on, if moving on can ever mean to leave it behind.
There is only one other aspect of this text that needs attention at
this point: the leitmotif-like recurrence of the figure of the "dead
Maria."[20] Signaling the recurrence of the same, the "dead Maria"
motif explores the question of temporality in history and of the
relation between past, present, and future. For history is not just

what has passed but a past that informs our present. It is a bit like one of the final lines from Woody Allen's movie *Another Woman*, which in a Wittgensteinian key asks, "Is memory something we have or something we have lost?" Similarly, the same must be asked for history, and Heine's motif figures just that.

Among the many instances in Heine where the effect of belatedness returns are a number of poems in *Romanzero* and especially in its third and concluding part, the "Hebrew Melodies." History, as this late collection of Heine's poetry highlights, can no longer be writ large with a capital *H*. Rather, history is a series of histories that weave themselves through human experience in pointedly nonteleological and forgotten, if not belated, ways.[21] If this is a pointed departure from that other *H* writ large, Hegel, we should also remember that Freud as well cannot be simply subsumed under any sort of teleological or ego-driven scheme. But before we turn to Freud, let me just note that the "Hebrew Melodies" finale, the very end of the brash poem "Disputation," concludes on a note that articulates its critical caveat in the poetic form of an after-effect that so suggestively continues to linger on. When Heine has Queen Blanche turn up her nose at both priest and rabbi, reducing them to residues of stinking humans, this gesture returns the motif of an uncanny afterward of medieval persecution of the Jews to the heart of the discourse of emancipation.[22]

Eulogy of a Dying God and Moses, the Builder of a People

WHILE FREUD'S MOSES book referenced the aforementioned poem from the early 1840s that describes Judaism as a disease the Jews carried with them when they departed from Egypt, the grand eulogy of "old Jehovah" that marks the finale of the second book of Heine's *On the History of Religion and Philosophy in Germany* deserves our attention for its almost verbatim formulation that matches Freud's later theory of the genesis of monotheism. It is worthwhile to read Heine's account with Freud's *Moses and Monotheism* in mind:

> We have gotten to know him so well, from his cradle, in Egypt, where he was raised among the divine calves, crocodiles, holy onions, ibises, and cats—We saw him bid farewell to the playmates of his childhood, along with the obelisks and sphinxes of his homeland, the Nile valley, and become a small God-King in Palestine over a poor shepherd people, living in his own temple palace.—We saw later how he came into contact with Assyrian-Babylonian civilization and gave up his all-too-human passions, no longer spewed pure wrath and vengeance, or at least no longer went into rages about every little trifle.—We saw him emigrate to Rome, the capital city, where he gave up all national prejudice and proclaimed the heavenly equality of all peoples. With such splendid phrases, we saw him form a party in opposition to old Jupiter, intrigue long enough to come to power and rule from the Capitol over city and world, *urbem et orbem.*—We saw how he became even more ethereal, how he gently whined, how he became a loving father, a general friend of mankind, a benefactor of the world, a philanthropist—none of this could help him.
>
> Do you hear the bell ringing? Kneel down—Sacraments are being brought to a dying God.[23]

> Wir haben ihn so gut gekannt, von seiner Wiege an, in Ägypten, als er unter göttlichen Kälbern, Krokodilen, heiligen Zwiebeln, Ibissen und Katzen erzogen wurde—Wir haben ihn gesehen, wie er diesen Gespielen seiner Kindheit und den Obelisken und Sphynxen seines heimatlichen Niltals Ade sagte, und in Palästina, bei einem armen Hirtenvölkchen, ein kleiner Gott-König wurde, und in einem eigenen Tempelpalast wohnte—Wir sahen ihn späterhin, wie er mit der assyrisch babylonischen Zivilisation in Berührung kam, und seine allzumenschliche Leidenschaften ablegte, nicht mehr lauter Zorn und Rache spie, wenigstens nicht mehr wegen jeder Lumperei gleich donnerte—Wir sahen ihn auswandern nach Rom, der Hauptstadt, wo er

aller Nationalvorurteile entsagte, und die himmlische Gleich-
heit aller Völker proklamierte, und mit solchen schönen Phrasen
gegen den alten Jupiter Opposition bildete, und so lange intri-
gierte bis er zur Herrschaft gelangte, und vom Kapitole herab die
Stadt und die Welt, *urbem et orbem,* regierte—Wir sahen, wie er
sich noch mehr vergeistigte, wie er sanftselig wimmerte, wie er
ein liebevoller Vater wurde, ein allgemeiner Menschenfreund,
ein Weltbeglücker, ein Philanthrop—es konnte ihm alles nichts
helfen—

Hört Ihr das Glöckchen klingeln? Kniet nieder—Man bringt
die Sakramente einem sterbenden Gotte. (B 3:591)

I am not claiming that Heine drafted the précis for Freud's cultural theory, but the resonances are so striking that we may
wonder why Freud, who otherwise demonstrated such intimate
familiarity with Heine, restrains himself from simply referencing
a marginal poem that only covered one aspect of his theory while
letting all the rich resonances with Heine pass unmentioned.
This passage—in a now belated but anticipatory construction—
offers the principles of Freud's account of the God of the Hebrews,
as mouthed by an uncouth tribal chieftain, then received by
the emperor, pope ("Papa," as the Latin has it), and eventually
ascending to the position of Father of All Mankind in Rome.

Let us now consider another passage that presents an equally
powerful vision, composed in Heine's last years when he was
completely bedridden and arguing with God, tortured by the pain
of his illness. In his "Confessions," as Heine titled one of his very
last publications in 1854, we find the celebration of a striking portrayal of Moses, as Heine formulates, who despite his animosity
against art was "nevertheless himself a great artist, and possessed
true artist's spirit [*Genius*]."[24] And Heine continues,

Only, this artistic spirit with him, as with his Egyptian countrymen, was applied to the colossal and the imperishable. But not,
like the Egyptians, did he construct his works of art from bricks
and granite, but he built human pyramids and carved human

obelisks. He took a poor shepherd tribe and from it created a nation which should defy centuries; a great, an immortal, a consecrated race, a God-serving people, who to all other nations should be as a model and prototype: he created Israel. [With greater reason than the Roman poet is this artist, son of Amram and the midwife Yochevet, able to claim to have erected a monument that shall survive all creations made from ore.]²⁵

Nur war dieser Künstlergeist bei ihm, wie bei seinen ägyptischen Landsleuten, nur auf das Kolossale und Unverwüstliche gerichtet. Aber nicht wie die Ägypter formierte er seine Kunstwerke aus Backstein und Granit, sondern er baute Menschenpyramiden, er meißelte Menschen-Obelisken, er nahm einen armen Hirtenstamm und schuf daraus ein Volk, das ebenfalls den Jahrhunderten trotzen sollte, ein großes, ewiges, heiliges Volk, ein Volk Gottes, das allen andern Völkern als Muster, ja der ganzen Menschheit als Prototyp dienen konnte: er schuf Israel! Mit größerm Rechte als der römische Dichter darf jener Künstler, der Sohn Amrams und der Hebamme Jochebet, sich rühmen, ein Monument errichtet zu haben, das alle Bildungen aus Erz überdauern wird! (B 6.1, 481)

But this is not where Heine's legacy ends. There is one crucial additional paragraph that highlights the concern of a dying "ex-God," as Heine calls himself just a few pages preceding the section on Moses,²⁶ a point that Freud's Moses shares in a profound manner, as Miriam Leonard has recently demonstrated in such eloquent terms.²⁷ In addition, the Moses discourse serves as a means for renegotiating the distinction between Hellenism and Hebraism, one Heine had already earlier challenged as a false distinction. In this passage, he feels the need to reject this theory of mono-origin without reservation—not just with ironic ridicule but as a matter of principle:

I have never spoken with proper reverence either of the artist or of his work, the Jews; and for the same reason—namely, my

Hellenic temperament, which was opposed to Jewish asceticism. My prejudice in favour of Hellas has declined since. I see now that the Greeks were only beautiful youths, but that the Jews were always men, strong, unyielding men, not only in the past, but to this very day, in spite of eighteen centuries of persecution and suffering. Since that time I have learned to appreciate them better, and, were not all pride of ancestry a silly inconsistency in a champion of the revolution and its democratic principles, the writer of these pages would be proud that his ancestors belonged to the noble house of Israel, that he is a descendant of those martyrs who gave the world a God and a morality, and who have fought and suffered on all the battlefields of thought. [28]

Wie über den Werkmeister, hab ich auch über das Werk, die Juden, nie mit hinlänglicher Ehrfurcht gesprochen, und zwar gewiß wieder meines hellenischen Naturells wegen, dem der judäische Ascetismus zuwider war. Meine Vorliebe für Hellas hat seitdem abgenommen. Ich sehe jetzt, die Griechen waren nur schöne Jünglinge, die Juden aber waren immer Männer, gewaltige, unbeugsame Männer, nicht bloß ehemals, sondern bis auf den heutigen Tag, trotz achtzehn Jahrhunderten der Verfolgung und des Elends. Ich habe sie seitdem besser würdigen gelernt, und wenn nicht jeder Geburtsstolz bei dem Kämpen der Revolution und ihrer demokratischen Prinzipien ein närrischer Widerspruch wäre, so könnte der Schreiber dieser Blätter stolz darauf sein, daß seine Ahnen dem edlen Hause Israel angehörten, daß er ein Abkömmling jener Märtyrer, die der Welt einen Gott und eine Moral gegeben, und auf allen Schlachtfeldern des Gedankens gekämpft und gelitten haben. (B 6.1: 481)

In other words, the Moses that Freud "inherited," as it were, came not from the "Egyptians" but from a notion of tradition that already viewed origins in a multiple, differential, and open form—a belated, as it were, but deeply original truth. Freud's critical engagement with Moses reflects his wrestling with Heine, a wrestling that acts out the dynamics it explores or, maybe more precisely, an exploration of the dynamics of the forces of tradition that is illuminating because it commits to facing the conflicted double bind that culture and psychoanalysis share.

Coda

FOR FREUD, NOT surprisingly, Moses represents the first Messiah.[29] And this sends us back to Heine's Messiah in golden chains. If we can say that Freud works out his relation to Heine in the Jewish sons' relation to Moses—a little bit pace Harold Bloom—Freud needs to distort the predecessor figure to acquire his legacy in a different way. That is, Heine offers a construct of tradition that Bloom never gives and Freud only gestures toward, which is the following: that this process of encountering different origins is enjoyable and that the guilt hides a pleasure that breaks traditional chains.[30] In Freud, Heine's Messiah might not be released from his golden—that is, historical—fetters, but he is certainly reimagined as the Moses that Heine portrays. But it is hopefully not too late to say more. We might therefore accurately summarize Freud's final point as the following: the Jews are not, on the one hand, really to be seen as being responsible for the invention of Judaism but rather only for their undying loyalty. The belated but contemporary meaning of his point, however, on the other Freudian hand, is that the Jews or the Jewish tradition—Freud is never too subtle about any such distinction—are certainly held to be responsible for the invention of Christianity and its own differential tradition "itself." Or as Heine might retort with emancipatory openness, even Christianity as well has fallen into the hands of the Jews.[31]

To translate this wit into more acceptable and a bit more serious parlance, if that is really necessary, Freud's most personal legacy, his conflicted but also liberating theory of Jewish tradition and history as psychoanalytic case study or rather speculation or, more precisely, fantasy of how tradition and culture function shows that working through an issue means always working it through one's predecessors. If Moses might have been killed by the Jews, as Goethe imagined,[32] Freud's claim of making him an Egyptian might have saved him from death by the hands of his own sons. Freud's footnoting Heine might just have been another and more liberating way to acknowledge that a father—if only in spirit and with rather extended family relations—might not always just be a form of repression but might be a helpful guide to one's own freedom—or at least, as another heir of Heine's put it, a "way out."

Notes

I thank David Suchoff for thoughtful discussions and comments on an earlier draft of this chapter.

[1] Sigmund Freud, *Moses and Monotheism*, in *The Standard Edition of the Complete Psychological Works of Sigmund Freud*, vol. 23 (1937–1939) (London: Hogarth Press and the Institute of Psychoanalysis, 1964), 29.

[2] Sigmund Freud, *Der Mann Moses und die monotheistische Religion*, in *Gesammelte Werke*, vol. 16 (London: Imago, 1950), 129. For the Heine lines, see Heinrich Heine, *Sämtliche Schriften*, 2nd ed., ed. Klaus Briegleb, vol. 4 (Munich: Deutscher Taschenbuchverlag, 1997), 420: Heine has the second line in the nominative, Freud sets it in the accusative. I hereafter refer to this edition as "B" and cite it parenthetically in the text, followed by the volume and page number. For an English translation of the two lines, see Hal Draper, *The Complete Poems of Heinrich Heine* (Boston: Suhrkamp/Insel, 1982), 399: "The plague they carried from the grim Nile valley, / The old Egyptian faith so long unhealthful."

[3] Heine composed the poem "The New Israelite Hospital in Hamburg," from which Freud quotes, to celebrate the generous donation by his uncle Solomon Heine, who had the hospital built.

[4] Sigmund, Freud, *The Future of an Illusion*, in *The Standard Edition*, vol. 21 (1927–1931) (London: Hogarth Press and the Institute of Psychoanalysis, 1961), 49; and Freud, *Die Zukunft einer Illusion*, in *Gesammelte Werke*, vol. 14 (London: Imago, 1948), 374.

[5] Sigmund Freud, *Der Witz und seine Beziehung zum Unbewussten*, in *Gesammelte Werke*, vol. 4 (London: Imago, 1940), 83; Sigmund Freud, *Jokes*

and Their Relation to the Unconscious, in *The Standard Edition*, vol. 8 (1905) (London: Hogarth Press and the Institute of Psychoanalysis, 1960), 76.

6   Louis Untermeyer, *Heinrich Heine: Paradox and Poet* (New York: Harcourt, Brace, 1937), 303.

7   For an illuminating reading of Heine in Freud's *Interpretation of Dreams*, see Stéphane Mosès, "'Selten habt Ihr mich verstanden': Zur Funktion eine Heine-Zitats in Freuds *Traumdeutung*," in *Heine und Freud: Die Enden der Literatur und die Anfänge der Kulturwissenschaft*, ed. Sigrid Weigel (Berlin: Kadmos, 2010), 91–98.

8   Freud, *Jokes and Their Relation to the Unconscious*, 140.

9   Freud, *Der Witz und seine Beziehung zum Unbewussten*, 158.

10   Freud, *Moses and Monotheism*, 6; Freud, *Der Mann Moses*, 104.

11   Heinrich Heine, *Ludwig Börne: A Memorial*, trans. Jeffrey L. Sammons (Rochester, NY: Camden, 2006), 103–104.

12   Ibid., 104.

13   Ibid.

14   Cf. Jeffrey Sammons's note to the passage: "No such rabbi has been identified, nor does Heine seem to have gone to Cracow during his visit to Poland. The scene is probably fictional." Ibid., 103n179.

15   The apparatus of the Düsseldorf Heine edition—Heinrich Heine, *Historisch-kritische Gesamtausgabe der Werke*, ed. Manfred Windfuhr et al. (Hamburg: Hoffmann and Campe, 1973–1997) (DHA)—lists the medieval mystical "Midrash Konen" dating from around 1000 as reference and gives as reference for the relevant passage the collection *Bet ha-Midrash*, ed. Adolph Jellinek (Jerusalem, 1938), part 1, number 2, 29, that Ernst Simon provided and translated for the edition in DHA 11, 610. Ernst Simon, a close friend of Martin Buber and Gershom Scholem, not only was the author of numerous studies on Jewish tradition but has also published a fine essay on Heine and Romanticism in the Festschrift collection *Essays Presented to Leo Baeck on the Occasion of His Eightieth Birthday* (London: East and West Library, 1954), 127–157.

16   Cf. Adrien Turel, *Generalangriff auf die Persönlichkeit und dessen Abwehr* (Zurich: Adrien Turel, 1955). Turel uses the question as the title of part 2 of the book.

17   This sentence is left out in Leland's translation.

18   Heinrich Heine, *Pictures of Travel*, vol. 2, in *The Works of Heinrich Heine*, trans. Charles Godfrey Leland, vol. 3 (London: Heinemann, 1906), 27. Subsequent cites to this source appear parenthetically in the text.

19   The dash is missing in the English translation.

20   See for the motif of the dead Maria, B 2:344, 346, 366, etc.

21 For a discussion of Heine's critical approach to history, see also the two concluding chapters, "Heine's Dis/Enchantment of Hegel's History of Philosophy" and "Tradition as Innovation in Heine's 'Jehuda ben Halevy': Counterhistory in a Spinozist Key," in Willi Goetschel, *Spinoza's Modernity: Mendelssohn, Lessing, and Heine* (Madison: University of Wisconsin Press, 2003), 253–276.

22 I have discussed this in Willi Goetschel, "Nightingales Instead of Owls: Heine's Joyous Philosophy," in *A Companion to the Works of Heinrich Heine*, ed. Roger F. Cook (Rochester, NY: Camden, 2002), 162.

23 Heinrich Heine, *On the History of Religion and Philosophy in Germany and Other Writings*, trans. Howard Pollack-Milgate, ed. Terry Pinkard (Cambridge: Cambridge University Press, 2007), 76.

24 Heinrich Heine, "Confessions," in *Heine's Prose Writings* (London: Walter Scott, 1887), 307; Heine, *Geständnisse*, B 6.1: 481.

25 Heine, "Confessions," 307; Heine, *Geständnisse*, B 6.1:481. Ellis skipped the sentence in brackets. The translation of this sentence is mine.

26 Heine calls himself "ich armer Exgott" of this revocation of any divine claims (*Geständnisse*, B 6.1:476).

27 Miriam Leonard, *Socrates and the Jews: Hellenism and Hebraism from Moses Mendelssohn to Sigmund Freud* (Chicago: University of Chicago Press, 2012). See also my review essay "Tangled Genealogies: Hellenism, Hebraism, and Discourse of Modernity," review of *Socrates and the Jews: Hellenism and Hebraism from Moses Mendelssohn to Sigmund Freud*, by Miriam Leonard, *Arion* 21, no. 3 (2014): 111–124.

28 Heine, "Confessions," 308.

29 Freud, *Moses and Monotheism*, 196; Freud, *Der Mann Moses*, 196.

30 See Harold Bloom, *The Anxiety of Influence: A Theory of Poetry* (New York: Oxford University Press, 1997).

31 Heine, "Die Stadt Lucca," B 2:513.

32 Johann Wolfgang Goethe, *West-östlicher Divan*, in *Sämtliche Werke*, ed. Ernst Beutler, vol. 3 (Zurich: Artemis, 1948), 514.

Gabriele Schwab

4 Freud's Moses: Murder, Exile, and the Question of Belonging

> *Li'l Moses was found in a stream*
> *Li'l Moses was found in a stream*
> *He floated on water*
> *Till Ol' Pharaoh's daughter*
> *She fished him, she said, from dat stream.*
> —Gershwin, *Porgy and Bess*

The Story

WHEN WE WERE children growing up in a small German town at the edge of the Black Forest, the Moses story was handed down to us in somber Catholic sermons and Bible classes. From those times, I remember Moses mainly as an incorporation of two figures: he was an "abandoned child" put into the river Nile in a little wicker basket and saved by an Egyptian princess; and he became a leader and prophet who freed his people from slavery and led them to the Promised Land. God endowed Moses with magic powers, we were told, powers that enabled him to divide the waters of the Red Sea to create a pathway for the Israelites on the way to exile. Like many Bible stories, the story of Moses was colorful and exciting, full of mysterious events such as God speaking through a burning bush or giving Moses supernatural powers. We were also fascinated by the story of the Golden Calf and Moses's murderous rage against the idol worshipers that led him to smash the plates with the Ten Commandments. Above all else, we were drawn to the story of Moses the abandoned child, perhaps because it resonated with the stories of abandoned children from Grimm's fairy tales and the routine threats of child abandonment during the so-called black pedagogy of Germany's postwar years.[1]

Looking back at the figure of Moses the abandoned child through the perspective of Freud's *Moses and Monotheism* opens up questions of belonging and exile. In the book of Exodus, Moses's abandonment is explained through the history of slavery. He was allegedly born in Egypt as the child of Jochebed, a Hebrew mother and member of the enslaved minority of Israelites. Fearing an uprising by this slave population, the Pharaoh ordered all newborn Hebrew boys to be killed. To protect Moses, Jochebed left him in a wicker basket in the Nile, whereupon the Pharaoh's daughter, Princess Bithiah, rescued him and raised him in the royal family. With this story of a male infant who, threatened by the genocidal policy of a despotic Pharaoh, is saved by two women, one his Hebrew mother, the other the Egyptian Pharaoh's daughter, the book of Exodus counterbalances the murderous patriarchal politics with the nurturing and life-saving role of two women from enemy camps.

In the Hebrew tradition, both in the Bible and the Rabbinic Midrash, Bithiah is exiled by the Pharaoh for bringing Moses the Levite into the Pharaoh's house and claiming him as her own child. After leaving Egypt with Moses during the Exodus, Bithiah marries Mered, a Judahite and is said to be the only female not to be affected by the ten plagues. Moses thus occupies a position of contested belonging, torn by heritage and culture between the Egyptians and the Israelites. Raised Egyptian, he is exiled from Egypt and claimed by the Israelites as their liberator from slavery and founder of their religion. Strictly speaking, he belongs to both people while not exclusively belonging to any of them.

Different nations, cultures, and religions have generated an abundance of diverse versions of the story of Moses the abandoned child. Elie Wiesel adds a version in which he places the emphasis on Moses as the carrier of the tragic transgenerational legacy of the Jewish people. Wiesel tells how Moses's life began with tears. When Bithiah,[2] the Pharaoh's daughter, finds a basket with an infant floating down the Nile, she identifies him as a Jewish infant "because it cried not like an infant but like an adult, like a community of adults—his entire people was crying in him."[3] For Wiesel then, Moses already incorporates the tragic history of the Jewish people ranging from the enslavement of the Israelites in Egypt to the Holocaust.

Freud places the story of Moses's abandonment and rescue within a genealogy of archetypal myths of the births of the hero. In these myths, the hero is usually the son of noble or royal parents whom the father perceives as a threat and intends to kill. In order for the mother to save her son, she abandons him, whereupon he is found and raised by parents of lower status. In his adult life, he returns as a hero who takes vengeance, triumphs over his father, and assumes a position of power. Freud emphasizes that the Moses story occupies a special position within this genre because it inverts the usual pattern: while his original, allegedly Israelite family is of modest origin, the family who rescues and raises him is the royal family of Egypt. In the case of historical figures such as Moses, Freud argues, one of the families has most likely been invented for the sake of the myth, and he concludes that the historical Moses must have been a noble Egyptian whom the myth turned into a Jew.[4] Against the grain of familiar myths of the abandoned male infant, Freud asserts, Moses became a hero not because he returned to defeat the father who had given the order to kill all male Hebrew infants but because he descended from his royal height to liberate the enslaved children of Israel.[5]

Freud pays scant attention to the gender politics in the Moses story even though it bears on the prominent role that murder plays in his analysis. In both the Hebrew and the Muslim version, the Pharaoh retaliates against the women for saving Moses's life. In the Hebrew version, both of Moses's mothers, Jochebed and Bithiah, become victims of exile and persecution. In the Islamic tradition, Bithiah is known as Asiya and said to have been not the Pharaoh's daughter but his wife.[6] She rescues Moses twice, once when she finds him in the river and the second time when the Pharaoh orders him to be killed. Defiantly, Asiya exclaims, "Why do you kill this innocent child, the whereabouts of whose parents are not known?" According to the Qur'an (ch. 66), Asiya then appoints Moses's biological mother as his wet nurse. When Moses preaches his new religion, Asiya follows him, is persecuted by the Pharaoh, and is tortured to death on the Pharaoh's orders. Both the Hebrew and the Muslim versions of the story thus stress the opposition between a murderous male politics and a female assertion of life.

More generally, the Moses story was able to generate a rich and diverse reception across centuries, cultures, nations, religions, and literatures because its enormous adaptability (*Anschliessbarkeit*) to different cultural and religious contexts provides a highly fertile ground for transference.[7] I want to mention only one example here, mainly because it has been, as far as I know, completely ignored in critical discussions. It is a Roma story, which can be found in Diane Tong's *Gypsy Folktales*, which claims that the Pharaoh is of Roma origin.[8] Titled "Why the Jews and the Gypsies Are Enemies," this Bulgarian tale refers to the tradition that locates the origin of the Roma in Egypt. The story identifies the Egyptian Pharaoh as a "Gypsy king" who was allegedly approached by "the Jewish leader Moses" and asked to worship the Jewish god as the only true god. The Pharaoh replied that, as proof of the Jewish religion's superior truth, he needed Moses to perform a miracle and asked him to make the waters of the Nile flow backward.

Moses was unable to do so, but the Pharaoh's engineers had the technology to build an installation that reversed the river's flow. Triumphantly, the Pharaoh said to Moses, "You see, our brains can do more than your god." Furious, Moses, in one of his legendary acts of wrath, called on God to curse the Pharaoh and his people. In response, God condemned the Gypsies to wander forever over the face of the earth, and, the story concludes, since that day, the Gypsies and the Jews have been enemies.

Demonstrating how easily the Moses story can travel across cultures, nations, and religions and serve as a ground for transference,[9] this Roma story operates with a series of what Jan Assmann calls "normative inversions."[10] Instead of Moses performing the miracle of dividing the waters, the Roma Pharaoh's superior technological knowledge makes the Nile flow backward. And yet the Mosaic God, asserting his ultimate power, condemns the Roma, not the Jews, to the fate of becoming eternal wanderers. While there is no mention of the Exodus of the Israelites, it is the Roma who are exiled from their Egyptian homeland.

Archaic Traces: The Brother Horde, Akhenaton, and the Murder of Moses

THE PREVIOUS SKETCH of the diverse Moses stories from different religions, cultures, and nations provides the basic archive with which Freud works to write *Moses and Monotheism*. Like most archival researchers, Freud of course selects from this archive according to the specific interests he brings to it: first, to envision a psychohistory of monotheism and its archaic traces in the myth of the brother horde; second, to outline a geopolitical genealogy that provides evidence for Moses's Egyptian origin and for the existence and eventual merger of two historical figures of Moses; and third, to develop a plausible argument for the murder of the Egyptian Moses by the Jewish people. By tracing these lines of interest, we will hopefully be able better to understand both Freud's motives in returning repeatedly to this material and his specific interventions in debates not only about the psychohistory of monotheism but also about the use of psychoanalysis in working with archives. Moreover, his specific use of the Moses archive also sheds light on the role his own personal transference plays in his analysis.

First of all, Freud introduces an entirely new turn in rewriting the Moses story, choosing to focus on patricide as its most central element. Assuming that the Israelites murdered Moses, the father of their religion, Freud identifies patricide as a foundational event in the establishment of Judaism. According to Freud, this patricide arcs back to the "archaic heritage" of the original patricide he analyzed in the myth of the brother horde in *Totem and Taboo*.[11]

With his assertion that the myth of the brother horde is inscribed in the Moses story as an archaic trace, Freud establishes a historical genealogy of monotheism that begins with an original father-god (*Vatergott*) who is murdered by the brother horde. As is well known, Freud sees this patricide and the cannibalistic devouring of the father as the foundation of both the law and totemism, the first form of religion in human history. At the level of what we could call with Derrida a "psychic archive,"[12] this original patricide also becomes, for Freud, the instance of a transgenerational trauma transmitted over thousands of years. Finally, as a response to the traumatic patricide and as an effect of the brothers' belated mourning and guilt, the mechanism of psychological incorporation develops that is crucial for the dynamic of memory, forgetting, mourning, and the crypt.

After the unlimited rule of the original father-god, Freud envisions a period of matriarchal law and polytheistic rule by mother-goddesses. Eventually the sons assume the status of male gods who initially rule next to the mother deities before they establish a period of polytheistic patriarchal rule that precedes the first monotheistic religions. Within Freud's genealogy, Moses's foundation of monotheism thus appears as a rupture with Egypt's polytheistic or cosmotheistic religions and a return to the legacy of despotic patriarchal rule.

There is, however, also another, more recent Egyptian trace inscribed in the Moses story. Freud draws on the biblical scholar Ernst Sellin's reading of the prophets and a variety of other historical documents to suggest that the Mosaic God was modeled after Amenhotep's/Akhenaten's god Aton. Despite Amenhotep's sun worship, he was allegedly the first to introduce monotheism, which brought Egypt religious intolerance as well as a pervasive disenchantment of the world.[13] Facing the hostile and vengeful revolt of the priests of Amon against this imposed monotheistic religion, Amenhotep had to change his name to Ikhnaton or Akhenaten, erase the name of the old god from all inscriptions, and go into exile.

Freud sees in the Mosaic religion a return of Akhenaten's monotheism after a long period of latency, arguing that even the Hebrew word *Adonai* might be traced back to the Egyptian *Aton* (or *Atum*).[14] He portrays Moses as following the model of Akhenaten as an "enlightened despot," murdered by his people, who rebelled against the imposition of a monotheistic religion.[15] Driven by belated guilt, they later repressed this murder and erased it from their historical narratives. However, Aton—just like Akhenaten, his earthly representative—had been a pacifist god. By contrast, Freud alleges, Jahve is a violent warrior god who induces the Israelites to invade a foreign land and commit genocide of the native people.

Freud seems clearly troubled by this constitutive tension in portrayals of the God of the Mosaic religion. In a scrupulous yet highly speculative analysis of archival material, Freud comes to the stunning conclusion that there must have been two different historical figures: an Egyptian Moses who never heard of the name Jahve and a Midianite Moses who never heard the name Aton and who had never been in Egypt.[16] Unlike the Egyptian Moses, Freud's Midianite Moses leads his people to the new god Jahve, who promised them the land of "milk and honey."[17] Handed down by different religious traditions, Freud concludes, the stories of Moses eventually became blended in a dreamlike condensation, with the two historical figures who both had the name Moses merging into one. If Freud's assumption is right that the stories of the two Moseses and their different religions were eventually blended into one, Judaism would have emerged out of a compromise formation, built on a hidden double history that involves two religious founders, both named Moses, who created two different religions, the first of which was repressed by the second but reappeared later as the victorious one.[18] Freud surmises that the god of the Egyptian Moses casts a silent shadow over the god Jahve who replaced him, until the shadow becomes stronger than Jahve, asserting its ultimate victory.

Imperialism and Monotheism

TURNING TO THE question of Freud's own transference, we may ask, what is at stake for him in his highly provocative rewriting of the Moses story? A closer look at Freud's mobilization of the Moses archive reveals the importance he places on the impact of Egypt's political situation on its religious formations, naming imperialism as the most profound and sustained influence.[19] As a result of the warfare of the conqueror Thotmes III, Egypt had become a world power, usurping Nubia in the South, Palestine, Syria, and parts of Mesopotamia in the North. "This imperialism," Freud states, "was now mirrored in religion as universalism and monotheism."[20] Since the Pharaoh had become the sole and uncontested imperial ruler of the world known to the Egyptians at the time, they also had to abandon the national delimitation of their god.[21]

The link Freud establishes between monotheism and imperialism warrants further exploration in light of the new imperialisms of our time. Freud's main concern at the time was that the historical link between imperialism and monotheism entails a possible return of monotheism's repressed violent underpinnings. A related concern leads Edward Said to argue that *Moses and Monotheism* provides the basis for a sustained critique of Zionism and Jewish fundamentalism.[22] Freud's forcefully antinationalist stance is, Said reminds us, deeply colored by both National Socialism's treatment of the Jews as expendable foreigners and by the Zionist settlement in Palestine:[23] "By 1948 the relevant non-Europeans were embodied by indigenous Arabs of Palestine and, supporting them, Egyptians, Syrians, Lebanese and Jordanians who were the descendants of the various Semitic tribes, including the Arab Midianites, whom the Israelites had first encountered south of Palestine and with whom they had a rich exchange. In the years after 1948, when Israel was established as a Jewish state in Palestine, what had once been a diverse, multiracial population of many different peoples . . . seemed like a parodistic reenactment of the divisions that had been so murderous before."[24]

Said, in other words, posits the establishment of the Jewish state as yet another return of the repressed history of the Exodus of Moses and the subsequent settlement of the Israelites in the "Promised Land" after the conquest of its indigenous peoples. Moreover, Said points to the symbolic murder at the heart of official narratives of the Jewish state, namely, its erasure of the non-Jewish heritage that Freud took such pains to expose: "This other non-Jewish, non-European history has now been erased, no longer to be found in so far as an official Jewish identity is concerned."[25] The strength of Freud's thought, Said concludes, is that its insistence on heterogeneity refuses to resolve identity into a nationalist or religious fundamentalism. This is what, according to Said, enables *Moses and Monotheism* to "speak to other besieged identities" and perhaps even to "aspire to the condition of a politics of diaspora life."[26] Reading and expanding Freud in this vein remains a profound political task today.

Forensic Turn and Textual Murder

MOSES AND MONOTHEISM presents yet another challenge that concerns less its ability to speak to diasporic identities in a global world than its ability to interfere in a certain politics of *reading history through archives, otherwise.*[27] "What confirms or demonstrates a certain truth of Freud's *Moses* is not Freud's book, or the arguments deployed there with more or less pertinence. It is not the contents of this 'historical novel'; it is rather the scene of reading it provokes and in which the reader is inscribed in advance," writes Derrida in *Archive Fever.*[28]

This other scene of reading is opened up first and foremost by Freud's engagement with the archive of the Moses stories, which he puts under pressure from a psychoanalytic perspective, paying attention to gaps, inconsistencies, and contradictions. Rather than tracing the layered histories of the reception and rewriting of the Moses story in various cultural and religious origins, Freud assembles a truly astounding arsenal of material textual evidence and logical arguments to prove the two main tenets highlighted earlier, namely, Moses's Egyptian heritage and his murder by the Jews. In a psychoanalytic vein, he takes subsequent versions of a Jewish Moses who died on the mountain as belonging to a revisionist history of forgetting and distortion.

Historical narratives work, Freud asserts, according to a logic similar to that of dreamwork. Deciphering the textual unconscious allows one, he argues, to envision an alternative historicity, that is, a collective and internally conflicted psychohistory in which competing narratives such as the different Moses stories are, over long periods of time and in different geopolitical contexts, formed to serve competing national and religious interests. A psychoanalytic anamnesis of historical narratives that pursues the traces and inscriptions of erasures and distortions in the textual/religious unconscious will reveal, he trusts, the concealed historical truth.

In Freud's taking apart the Moses archive in order to write his own version, his psychoanalytic perspective guides him in relating repetitions, distortions, gaps, contradictions, and willful forgetting to the collective cultural and religious unconscious. A rhetorical analysis that focuses on these textual operations, he asserts, will reveal things that were not intended for communication. Reading the textual unconscious of the Moses story, Freud opens up a perspective on an alternative history of religion, if not on historicity more generally.

Exposing Moses's Egyptian heritage and his murder by his own people as the disavowed core of Jewish religion, Freud, as we have seen, retells the Moses story as one of exile, conflicted belonging, and patricide. Murder looms so large in Freud's version that it becomes a cornerstone of his transference. A murder, allegedly committed by Moses himself, when he slayed an Egyptian man who mistreated a Jewish slave, is named variously as the initial reason for Moses's need to flee Egypt. The story of the Exodus is full of murderous incidences that for Freud culminate in the murder of Moses. Undoubtedly, Freud's intense personal transference in his engagement with this material is, among other things, the result of his ambivalent fascination with the monumental figure of Moses, whose identification with the enslaved Israelite population in Egypt leads to his political assassination of a slaveholder, his leadership role in the Exodus, and his foundation of the Jewish religion, as well as his violent occupation of a new territory and his assassination by his own people.

But Freud makes a major and consequential move beyond this archival deconstruction that insists on Moses's actual murder. He contends that the very erasure of this patricide in the Hebrew versions of the story amounts to a second symbolic murder with tremendous consequences. "The distortion of a text resembles a murder. The difficulty lies not in committing the deed but in erasing its traces," Freud writes.[29] He thus portrays Moses as the victim of a double murder: an actual one and a symbolic textual murder that is designed to erase or displace the traces of the first one. It is the textual murder, that is, the erasure of the actual murder's traces in the symbolic order, that leads first to periods of historical latency and then to the return of the repressed. For Freud, the compulsion to repeat the murderous act manifests itself, for example, in the later juridical murder of Jesus by the Jewish people.[30]

How are we then to understand Freud's retelling of the story in light of the tremendous weight he places on this second symbolic murder of Moses? As Freud insists, the Hebrew version of the story is already based on a double erasure/murder, namely, that of Moses's Egyptian origin and that of his actual murder. But if we accept these premises, then Freud's own reading in which he tries to unearth the hidden traces of the Moses story must be seen as performing an inversion of this double textual murder. His reading of the historical and textual unconscious would accordingly appear as a concomitant act of reparation. If the Jews, as Freud seems to suggest, "murdered" the story of their origins, his own revelation of the traces of this symbolic murder is an attempt to repair the resulting damage.

But things are more complicated. We need to ask, what kind of reparation this could be and what Freud wanted to repair? The closer we read the composition of Freud's Moses pieces, the clearer it becomes that he is trying to repair the murder of historical truth in a general sense. The slippery concept of "truth" becomes in Freud's archival work an almost obsessive preoccupation. I would argue that Freud's retelling of the Moses story with his almost forensic pursuit of historical truth that preoccupied him for years, and indeed tortured him during the last months of his life, is designed to facilitate a work of historical, political, and psychological reparation.[31] Perhaps we could even push this further and argue that Freud's method of tracing historical erasures in historical, national, and religious archives might also speak to the concerns of truth and reconciliation commissions with uncovering censored evidence and stories. What Freud says about murders, for example—namely, that the difficulty lies not in making them happen but in erasing their traces—is also true for willful "disappearances" more generally. Freud's belief in the permanence of traces would then carry a hopeful message for those who, like the mothers of the disappeared, for example, are searching for bones of their disappeared loved ones in order to provide forensic evidence.[32]

The forensic, in fact, assumes increasing prominence as a new paradigm in the search for truth and justice, including, for example, attempts to preserve the traces of the Israeli occupation of Palestine. Eyal Weizman, who works in the occupied territories on a "forensic architecture" project, even speaks of a "forensic turn."[33] In the course of the three versions of the Moses story that Freud writes in the period before and after his own exile from Austria, he increasingly turns into a detective obsessed with uncovering the traces of the actual murder that were meant to be erased. As Jan Assmann argues, Freud "began writing a historical novel and ended up by using almost juridical forms of authentification to present his historical evidence."[34] In light of Weizman's "forensic turn," we could compare Freud's psychoanalytic treatment of the archive to a forensic ecology of mind that searches for the political unconscious in material evidence.

To return to Freud's own personal transference, his obsession to prove Moses's Egyptian origin as a historical truth could actually be compared to a forensic turn in his treatment of the Moses story. However, we also notice that in his transference, this turn seems to remain unresolved and internally conflicted. We can understand it only if we see it as a powerful defense related to something that haunts Freud not only about the question of Moses's belonging but also about his own belonging to the Jewish people at a time of their persecution during the genocidal Nazi politics. Freud's assertion that he will never be able to publish his second Moses piece is not only based on the prohibition of psychoanalysis as a Jewish science under the Nazi regime; it is, one would assume, also based on the fact that Freud might have felt reluctant to publish a piece that questions the very core of the Jewish religion at a time when the Jews were suffering from a new period of relentless persecution and exile. Freud's search for "forensic" evidence might then be designed to protect him from the criticism and rejection that he can easily anticipate. At the same time, the belief that the piece will not appear in print during his lifetime might also be designed to ease the censorship that Freud might otherwise have imposed on himself. Freud's decision to consign the publication of his story to a period of latency or to exile it, so to speak, is thus multiply motivated.

The relationship between writing, violence, forgetting, the trace, and transference that Freud highlights in the passage on textual murder thus becomes much more than a mere topic he pursues in his deconstruction of the Moses story. It evolves into a relationship that increasingly begins to haunt Freud's own text. Unlike any of his other texts, *Moses and Monotheism* is a singularly tortured sequence of pieces or, as Freud himself called it, a "haunted work." Haunted by the "dark times" in which it was written, it was, as several critics including Said have pointed out, also haunted by Freud's unresolved belonging to Judaism as a secular, indeed professedly atheist Jew.[35]

The persecution of Freud's people under the Nazis and the prohibition of psychoanalysis as a Jewish science provide him with a fertile ground of identification with Moses as a transitional figure who, neither entirely Egyptian nor Jew, inhabits two cultures without unequivocally belonging to any of them. Freud identifies with Moses as the stranger who is always insider and outsider at once or, as Akira Lippit calls it, with Moses's "radical exteriority."[36] While Freud might feel that his being Jewish is conflicted by his professed atheism, he is also culturally conflicted, endowed with a German/Austrian formation and a classical European *Bildung* that shapes his scholarly perspective in a profound and, as

Said says, decidedly Eurocentric way, and this at a time when his belonging to the German/Austrian people is radically questioned because of his Jewish heritage.

What adds to the complexity of Freud's rewriting of the Moses story is that his personal transference is deeply embedded both in the political upheavals of the time and in his desire to establish the validity of psychoanalysis as a social theory at the time when it is under attack as a Jewish science. Far beyond his initially declared goal of writing a historical novel, Freud ends up composing a hybrid text that straddles the boundaries between a historical treatise, a psychoanalytic study of the foundations of Judaism, and a theoretical reflection on trauma, erasure, and latency in collective memory and the writing of history. Freud was also aware that the new (Jewish) science of psychoanalysis that he offers his people and the world has been compared by his adversaries to a new secular religion. And regarding this "religion," did he not also feel threatened with a symbolic murder by some of his followers or disciples, including Jung, whom he suspected of anti-Semitism? Moreover, at the time when he was writing the third version of the Moses story in England, he bears with Moses the burden of exile. Finally, knowing that he is going to die, Freud also shares with Moses the sorrow of knowing that he will never see the Promised Land.

This rich ground for transferential identification may explain why Freud became haunted by the story of Moses during the last years of his life. Regarding Freud's "forensic turn," we may wonder whether his obsession with historical truth is unconsciously designed to offset what ultimately amounts to a textual murder that he himself performs when he "murders" Moses the Jew in order to resurrect him as Moses the Egyptian. When he talks about the repressed guilt of the Jewish people for murdering the founding father of their religion and then for repeating this murder in the juridical murder of Jesus,[37] could it be that Freud feels some guilt of his own for having symbolically murdered the

God of his people when he became an atheist and then when he repeated this murder by attempting to take Moses away from the Jews at the time of their worst persecution and enslavement? Is this not what Freud indirectly acknowledges in his opening statement? "To deny a people the man whom it praises as the greatest of his sons is nothing that one will like to do light-heartedly, especially when one belongs to this very people."[38] At issue is once again the question of belonging—a belonging that is for Freud inseparable from historical truth: Moses does not "belong" to you, Freud seems to say to his own people; even though you claim him as your liberator, lawgiver, and religious founder, he is not one of you by birth.

As we have seen, Freud performs this expropriation of Moses from an exclusively Jewish heritage through a scrupulous deconstruction of the archive of Moses stories. In *Archive Fever*, Derrida claims that the importance of *Moses and Monotheism* lies in the fact that these pieces exemplify the signature that Freud left on the archive, archivization, and historiography.[39] If, as Derrida insists, "Freudian psychoanalysis proposes a new theory of the archive," then this theory must be linked to Freud's notion of historical forgetting and repression or erasure from the archive.[40] In other words, a psychoanalytic theory of the archive is concerned with what I have called "textual murder." We may further ask how textual murder is connected to the operation of the death drive in the writing of history, which Freud implicitly invokes and which Derrida emphasizes in *Archive Fever*.[41] Through the transgenerational heritage of momentous historical erasures and symbolic murders such as the ones that Freud exposes at the heart of the Hebrew version of the Moses story, the death drive would become prominent in shaping national and religious histories.[42]

We may then wonder if part of Freud's attempt at repairing the symbolic murder of Moses, the Egyptian, might also be read as a work against the death drive. Releasing the story of the Egyptian Moses from a national crypt, Freud performs a work of mourning the loss of diversity and religious tolerance that was brought about by the story's erasure. Encrypted histories contain a historical truth that is both political and psychological. In this sense, they belong to the order of a "psychic archive."[43] Unearthing encrypted histories and offering them to the public is a gift of reparation to the collective memory. With Freud's opening of the national crypt that had buried the Egyptian Moses, he disrupts the transgenerational legacy of the symbolic murder by releasing the ghosts of the past that had haunted his contorted composition of *Moses and Monotheism*. This is how we must understand Freud's forensic turn and his obsession with the historical truth of Moses, the Egyptian who emerges as the spectral return of the repressed. This is also the "scene of reading" that *Moses and Monotheism* provokes and in which, as Derrida claims, "the reader is inscribed in advance."[44] Freud's inscribed reader is invited to help his cause by offering a hospitable reception to the ghosts released from national and religious crypts that continue to shape future global histories.

Finally, the spectral return of the repressed ghosts of history is also a return of the abandoned. Moses, the abandoned child, returns as a religious leader. After a period of latency, the abandoned God returns with a vengeance and displaces the one who had been installed in his stead. The abandoned pieces of *Moses and Monotheism* return in new versions. From his exile, Freud himself, abandoned by his home country, returns his Moses texts as the gift of a restored history of Judaism. The abandoned child who copes creatively with his fear had earlier played a crucial role in Freud's theory when he analyzed his nephew's *fort/da* game that was designed to restore in fantasy the mother who had temporarily abandoned him. *Moses and Monotheism* is Freud's own *fort/da* play. Individual or collective, memory traces never disappear, he affirms. He can bring back Moses, the Egyptian who had been abandoned by his people. In exile, he can bring back the text that he had to abandon in his homeland. Freud knows that, like Moses, he is going to die, but he also knows that death both destroys and preserves the archive, albeit spectrally. As readers inscribed in *Moses and Monotheism*, we are invited to play *fort/da* with Freud's archival ghosts.

Notes

[1] See Katarina Rutschky, *Schwarze Pädagogik: Quellen zur Naturgeschichte der bürgerlichen Erziehung* (Stuttgart: Ullstein Taschenbuch, 1997).

[2] Spelled "Batya" in Wiesel's tale.

[3] See Elie Wiesel, "Moses: Portrait of a Leader," in *Messengers of God: Biblical Portraits and Legends* (New York: Simon and Schuster, 2005), 183; see also *Moses, the Most Human Prophet*, Abigail Sarah Bagraim's website, www.abigailsarah.co.za/myart/TheHebrewBible/mosesmosthumanprofit.html.

[4] Trying to prove that Moses is in fact of royal Egyptian origin, Freud curiously pays scant attention to the role of the two maternal figures, Moses's biological mother, a Jewish Levite, and the Egyptian princess who raised him. He accepts the version told in the second chapter of Exodus that the Egyptian princess who saved him gave him his name "Mose," but he explicitly refutes critics such as Ed Meyer who assume that there must have been a different original story. In this story, the Pharaoh is warned by a prophetic dream that a son of his daughter will bring danger to him and his empire. He therefore orders that his daughter's son be abandoned in the Nile after his birth. The infant is then saved by Jewish people and raised as their child. Interestingly, however, Freud refutes this version, arguing that the Jewish people could not possibly have created a story that turns their great man into a foreigner.

[5] Sigmund Freud, *Gesammelte Werke: Chronologisch Geordnet*, vol. 23 (London: Imago, 1991), 112.

[6] While Freud reads the Muslim version as an imitation of the Jewish one, he remarks that Allah is a much more benign God than the original Jahve is. Highlighting that Moses's role in the Hebrew religion is so much more prominent than in Islam, Freud speculates that the murder of Moses by the Israelites becomes the very reason for the further differentiation and depth (*Vertiefung*) of Jewish monotheism. Reminiscent of *Totem and Taboo*, in which patricide becomes foundational for a deepening of religious law, Freud also emphasizes the role of unconscious guilt in the elaboration of Judaism.

[7] It can be read as an allegory of imperialism or of liberation from slavery; it can be read as an allegory of exile, vexed belonging, and living under diasporic conditions; and it can be read as an allegory of the tensions between patriarchal warfare and women's nurturing and life-sustaining politics.

8   Diane Tong, *Gypsy Folktales* (Orlando, FL: Harcourt Brace, 1989), 137–138.

9   Not surprisingly, the Moses story has also been appropriated in African American culture as an allegory of liberation from slavery. The most prominent examples are Zora Neale Hurston, *Moses, Man of the Mountain* (New York: Harper Perennial, 2009); and Martin Luther King Jr., "I've Been to the Mountain Top" (speech, Memphis, TN, April 3, 1968), *King Encyclopedia*, http://kingencyclopedia.stanford.edu/encyclopedia/ documentsentry/ive_been_to_the_mountaintop/. In this speech, King said, "I have gone to the mountaintop. I have seen the Promised Land." Tragically, the story of Martin Luther King is yet another repetition of the murder of a great prophet/father/leader-figure. Like Moses, King comes to the mountain and sees the Promised Land but is murdered before he can reach it.

10 See Jan Assmann, *Moses the Egyptian: The Memory of Egypt in Western Monotheism* (Cambridge, MA: Harvard University Press, 1997). The concept of "normative inversion" plays a crucial role in Assmann's analysis, beginning with the definition by Tacitus that the basic principle of the new religion founded by Moses is the "exact opposite of all other religions." In this "normative inversion," the Jews, according to Tacitus, "consider everything that we keep sacred as profane." See ibid., 37.

11 The story of an original brother horde was not new. Adopting it from Darwin, Freud elaborates it into a fully fledged myth in which the murder of the despotic father functions as a psychological allegory of patricide. Freud clearly states that this myth is a condensed figuration of a historical process that extends over thousands of years and is repeated innumerable times. A cornerstone of Freud's psychoanalytic theory, the ubiquity of patricide and patricidal fantasies equally informs his analysis of Moses's foundation of Jewish monotheism.

12 Jacques Derrida, *Archive Fever: A Freudian Impression*, trans. Eric Prenowitz (Chicago: University of Chicago Press, 1996), 19.

13 Freud, *Gesammelte Werke*, vol. 23, 121–125.

14 Along with the new religion, Freud adds, Moses also introduced circumcision into the Jewish religion. I refrain here from intervening in the controversial debates about circumcision that Derrida analyzed in detail in *Archive Fever*.

15 Freud, *Gesammelte Werke*, vol. 23, 148. For Freud, the story of the Golden Calf did not end with Moses's violent outburst against the idol worshipers but with his murder by them.

16 Ibid., 141.

17 In stark contrast to the pacifist Aton, who was the model of the Egyptian Moses, Freud describes Jahve as a "rough, narrow-minded local god, violent and bloodthirsty," who commands his followers to exterminate the native local population (ibid., 151).

18 Ibid., 154.

19 For Freud's discussion of the relationship between imperialism and religion, see ibid., 119. See also Herbert Marcuse, *Sigmund Freud* (Hamburg: Rowohlt, 1956), 101.

20 My translation of "Dieser Imperialismus spiegelte sich nun in der Religion als Universalismus und Monotheismus." Freud, *Gesammelte Werke*, vol. 23, 119.

21 Freud also speculates about foreign influences, especially that of Asian princesses who became royal wives and might have imported the idea of monotheism from Syria.

22 *Moses and Monotheism*, Said argues, has gained new relevance in light of the post–World War II period, the "fall of the classical empires," the forces of globalization and decolonization, and the emergence of postcolonies in Africa, Asia, and the Americas. Edward W. Said, *Freud and the Non-European* (London: Verso, 2003), 17.

23 "To say of Freud's relationship with Judaism that it was conflicted is to venture an understatement. At times he was proud of his belonging, even though he was irremediably anti-religious; at other times he expressed annoyance with and unmistakable disapproval of Zionism." Said mentions Freud's refusal to "join in an appeal to the British to increase Jewish immigration to Palestine" (ibid., 36). Similarly, Freud condemned the transformation "of a piece of Herodian wall into a national relic, thus offending the feelings of the natives" (quoted ibid.).

24 Ibid., 41.

25 Ibid., 44.

26 Ibid., 54, 55.

27 I refer here to Shoshana Felman's concept of psychoanalytic reading developed in her edited volume *Literature and Psychoanalysis: The Question of Reading: Otherwise* (Baltimore: Johns Hopkins University Press, 1982).

28 Derrida, *Archive Fever*, 67.

29 My translation of "Es ist bei der Entstellung eines Textes ähnlich wie bei einem Mord. Die Schwierigkeit liegt nicht in der Ausführung der Tat, sondern in der Beseitigung ihrer Spuren." Freud, *Gesammelte Werke*, vol. 23, 144.

30 The abandoned child/son is another parallel with Jesus: "Mein Gott, mein Gott warum hast Du mich verlassen?" Psalm 22:2.

31 Despite the fact that Freud acknowledges up front that there is no conclusive evidence that Moses was an actual historical figure, he relies on the fact that most historians believe in the historical truth of the story of Moses and the Exodus from Egypt. Freud also reminds his readers that without such an assumption, the history of Israel would become incom-

prehensible (*Gesammelte Werke*, vol. 23, 104). This assumption, however, does not yet provide any uncontestable evidence for one true version of the story.

32 See *Nostalgia de la luz*, directed by Patricio Guzmán (2010; Brooklyn, NY: Icarus Films Home Video, 2011), DVD.

33 Eyal Weizman, *Forensic Architecture: Violence at the Threshold of Detectability* (Cambridge, MA: MIT Press, 2017).

34 Assmann, *Moses the Egyptian*, 148.

35 See Said, *Freud and the Non-European*, 31.

36 Akira Mizuta Lippit, *Atomic Light (Shadow Optics)* (Minneapolis: University of Minnesota Press, 2005), 15.

37 Freud, *Gesammelte Werke*, vol. 23, 208.

38 My translation of "Einem Volkstum den Mann abzusprechen, den es als den grössten unter seinen Söhnen rühmt, ist nichts, was man gern oder leichthin unternehmen wird, zumal wenn man selbst diesem Volke angehört." Ibid., 101.

39 See Derrida, *Archive Fever*, 5.

40 Ibid., 29.

41 There would be no desire or possibility for the archive, Derrida asserts, without a death drive, that is, a place of violent forgetting and erasure that leads to a compulsion to repeat (ibid.).

42 See also ibid., 34.

43 See ibid., 19.

44 Ibid., 67.

Yael Segalovitz

5 A Leap of Faith into *Moses*: Freud's Invitation to Evenly Suspended Attention

> *There is no Freud, there are Freuds.*
> —Christopher Bollas, "Unconscious Perception" (lecture)

PAINFUL, REPETITIVE, PECULIAR, serpentine, contradictory, frustrating, odd. If asked to name which of Freud's texts these words describe, any reader of psychoanalysis would quickly pick *Moses and Monotheism* from the Austrian thinker's expansive oeuvre. Indeed, this is only a small sample of the variety of adjectives used to characterize this seminal work's form. To account for Freud's divergence in *Moses* from his otherwise famously lucid writing style, scholarship has focused primarily on the historical circumstances, whether personal or collective, that conditioned the production of this book. Early reviews emphasize the "tragic vicissitudes of the author's last years"[1] and "the persecution of Freud on ideological as well as racial grounds,"[2] Cathy Caruth identifies the text's repetitive quality as "the site of a trauma,"[3] Peter Gay suggests that Freud's language is "an intellectual game,"[4] and Ilse Grubrich-Simitis reads *Moses* as "a kind of *daydream* generated under . . . extreme distress."[5] But what would happen if, instead of asking what led Freud to produce stylistic "irregularities . . . unknown elsewhere in [his] writings,"[6] we asked what theory of reading *Moses*'s style prescribes? Could new aspects of this exceptional work surface if we engage it not through the frequently examined publication history but with a view toward its poetics as a whole?

As these questions make clear, my investigation does not approach *Moses* as a historical text by examining the factuality of its observations or as a psychoanalytical one by unpacking its descriptions of the psychic mechanism, but rather as a literary work, as per its original title, "The Man Moses: A Historical Novel" (*Der Mann Moses, ein historischer Roman*). For the analysis of *Moses* as literature, I employ Freudian theoretical tools and follow Chana Kronfeld's suggestion to theorize from, rather than into, "the works we deem important."[7] That is, in lieu of importing literary tools foreign to this work, I attempt to read Freud on his own terms. In doing so, I wish to heed Benjamin and Thomas Ogden's warning against conducting a psychoanalytic reading that applies "a set of analytic formulations to a literary work in order to 'solve' or 'decode' it."[8] Instead, I try to open up to *Moses* with a psychoanalytic "ear" and listen to the kind of reading it invites. It is my impression that *Moses* lends itself to being read in the perceptual state of "evenly suspended attention," which Freud advises his colleagues to practice in the therapeutic scene as early as in 1909.[9] This mind-set entails a temporary abandonment of sense-making procedures, as I explain later in more detail. Reading *Moses* in such a manner, along with Freud's earlier texts about attention, not only sheds new light on this specific Freudian work but also calls for a wider reevaluation of what a Freudian reading is typically understood to mean in the humanities.

Freud, of course, engages with literature throughout his writings: Jensen's *Gradiva*, Sophocles's *Oedipus Rex*, Shakespeare's

Hamlet, Dostoyevsky's *The Brothers Karamazov*, and Hoffmann's "The Sand Man" are just a few of his literary objects of study. His interpretations of these texts, nevertheless, depict a very specific Freud-as-reader, who, I postulate, is not necessarily the reader *Moses* calls for. After all, as Christopher Bollas reminds us in this chapter's epigraph, there is more than one Freud to be found in the Jewish psychoanalyst's body of work. The literary interpretations mentioned here, along with several of his "readings" of the psyche, earned Freud his reputation as a hyperobservant (or, as Eve Kosofsky Sedgwick would claim, paranoid) *archeologist* or *detective*: a reader whom no detail escapes, who ties all elements of the text together with perfection, and who is able to demonstrate how the most trivial of features is in fact crucial.[10] In literary terms, this Freud can be thought of as the ideal "close reader," and his own readers might wish to model their interpretative practices on his. With such an intention, however, it is no wonder that *Moses* seems frustrating and clumsy. Who needs a detective when the details of the mystery are so candidly presented, repeating themselves over and over again? Or when a "constant hammering of a few *leitmotifs*" takes place, in the words of the legendary Jewish historian Salo Baron?[11] As Freud himself writes in an apologetic tone, "I might, however, console myself with the reflection that the things I am treating are in any case so new and so important . . . that it can be no misfortune if the public is obliged to read the same thing about them twice. There are things that should be said more than once and which cannot be said often enough" (a quote we will return to later on).[12] Close reading such a text, that is, following its features with acute concentration, does prove to be an extremely vexing experience.

I have so far used the term "close reading" quite incautiously, but in order to continue this journey, let me suspend the discussion of Freud for a moment and turn to explore the term's meaning and origin. Close reading emerges as a technique during the 1930s, around the same time that Freud writes and publishes

Moses and Monotheism. Nonetheless, it is not the aim of this chapter to investigate whether Freud was acquainted with this literary method; what I propose is that Freud's text engages the assumptions undergirding this technique, which were part and parcel of the contemporary Western intellectual climate.

CLOSE READING IS developed as a practice by Anglo-American New Criticism.[13] The intellectuals associated with this movement, established in the United States in the 1930s and 1940s and influenced by British theory of the 1920s, succeeded in ushering literature through the university's gates and constructed what is now considered one of the first modern, Western, systematic accounts of literary analysis. Though these scholars, both British and American, held diverse and complex views about the literary text, they practiced, defined, and championed quite a unified reading technique. This method is by far the most prominent in the discipline, as evidenced by the numerous undergraduate introductory courses to critical reading and writing that even today tout it as the central method, both within and outside the United States. This reading practice, its assumptions, and its transnational history are themselves the subject of much contemporary research that deserves a nuanced review, which is unfortunately beyond my scope here.[14] I would like to focus specifically on the affinity between textual analysis and the mental state of "attention," which is of interest to both the New Critics and Freud, as I will go on to demonstrate. For the New Critics, close reading is fundamentally an attentive practice, as expressed, for example, in Jonathan Culler's account of this pioneering literary movement:

> It [New Criticism] focused attention on the unity and integration of literary works . . . and examined the interactions of their [poems'] verbal features and the ensuing complications of meaning rather than the historical intentions and circumstances of their authors. . . . Focusing on ambiguity, paradox, irony and the effects of connotation and poetic imagery, the

new criticism sought to show the contribution of each element of poetic form to a unified structure.[15]

It is not accidental, I claim, that Culler employs the terms "focus" and "attention" to describe the New Critics' method of interpretation. Though this is rarely acknowledged, the concept of "attention," which for the most part appears undefined, haunts definitions of close reading from its very inception. In this manner, Terry Eagleton depicts the New Critics as thinkers who "stressed the centrality of . . . a disciplined attention to the 'words on the page,'"[16] Paul de Man describes close reading as involving "patient and delicate attention . . . to the reading of form,"[17] *Close Reading: The Reader* states, "As a term, *close reading* hardly seems to leave the realm of so-called common sense, where it would mean something understandable and vague like 'reading with special attention,'"[18] and a recent article by Nicholas Gaskil argues that "the protest of the New Critics has to do, in part, with the insistence that there is a unique way of attending to things as together, that there are objects designed for such attention, and that there's something to be gained in so attending."[19] What these definitions stealthily unearth is that the New Critics are invested in an attempt to construct an attentive subject through their practice of reading. They intensely preoccupy themselves with controlling and disciplining their readers' minds, as indicated by their continuous use of the verbs "ordering," "controlling," "limiting," and "training" in delineating their method.

But the New Critics are in no way alone in their endeavor to fortify attention. Both they and Freud are developing their theories in the context of what Jonathan Crary terms "a disciplinary regime of attentiveness."[20] In his seminal work on attention and modernity, Crary claims that at the turn of the twentieth century, attention is understood as an invaluable mental procedure that allows the subject to transcend sensory uncertainty and inaccuracy by disengaging "from a broader field of attraction, whether visual or auditory, for the sake of isolating or focusing on a reduced number of stimuli."[21] Crary does not investigate, or even mention, the work of the New Critics, but his work provides a background against which one can understand why these thinkers give priority to the mental processes of selection (i.e., directing their readers' perception toward the minute details of texts) and exclusion (i.e., urging their readers to disregard, in Culler's aforementioned words, "the historical intentions and circumstances of their authors"). These are, after all, the mental processes considered most efficient in the cultural context in which they are producing their intellectual work.

What does not seem to jive with this "disciplinary regime" is Freud's depiction of attention as it should be practiced in the therapeutic scene, in his 1912 "Recommendations to Physicians Practicing Psycho-Analysis."[22] Freud opens this article, which offers advice to other practitioners of (the then still very young) psychoanalysis, with a question about the limitations of cognition. He asks, how can an analyst seeing six, seven, or even eight patients a day remember all the names, dates, and narratives he is exposed to?[23] What kind of attention could and should he pay to these myriad details? One would expect Freud, writing in a zeitgeist of what Paul North has termed "greedy" attention, to provide his colleagues with a method for "catching" the various details thrown their way and storing them in cognition.[24] Instead, he entirely dismisses the effort to focus and remember, making the bold claim that the analyst should "listen, and not bother about whether he is keeping anything in mind."[25] The technique Freud proposes is, in his words, a very simple one: "it consists simply in not directing one's notice to anything in particular and in maintaining the same 'evenly-suspended attention' . . . in the face of all that one hears."[26] Freud's complex original term for "evenly suspended attention," *gleichschwebende Aufmerksamkeit*, posed a challenge to various translators. To name just a few examples, what is rendered as "suspended" in English is termed "hovering and even" in Hebrew (*t'sumet lev merachefet va-achida*) and "floating" in Spanish and Portuguese (*atención flotante/atencão flutuante*). These different translations imply that Freud understands the unique form of attention he has in mind primarily in terms of mobility. For a physician practicing evenly suspended attention, perception swings from side to side like a ball suspended by a thread or hovers about unanchored. In contrast, Freud understands "deliberate attention"—the name he gives to the more conventional form of attention that he hopes to mute in the analytic scene—as being static. If the analyst applies such concentration, "one point will be *fixed* in his mind with particular clearness, and some other will be correspondingly disregarded";[27] in such a way, a "part of one's mental activity is *tied up*."[28] While evenly suspended attention involves a "swinging over . . . from one mental attitude to the other," deliberate attention entails a stagnant "brooding over."[29] Freud believes that this mental movement prevents exactly the analytic processes that the New Critics advocate: selection and exclusion. "As soon as anyone deliberately concentrates his attention to a certain degree, he begins to select from the material before him," Freud writes; and since selection, he claims, is always guided by previous inclinations and expectations, it is bound to lead to "never finding anything but what he [the analyst] already knows."[30]

Freud, to differentiate from the New Critics, urges the analyst to abandon all those cognitive processes with selection at their core. The analyst must relinquish all sense of purpose, ward off all speculation, erase all presuppositions, and steer clear of any form of synthesis. That is, the analyst is asked to shut down his conscious judging mechanism; the material entering his field of perception should be neither filtered nor categorized. And this stringent demand is a mirror image of the one placed on the analysand. Freud explains, "It will be seen that the rule of giving equal notice to everything is the necessary counterpart to the demand made on the patient that he should communicate everything that occurs to him without criticism or selection."[31]

This description is, of course, a reiteration of the "free associa-tion" technique, which, as Freud explains in *The Interpretation of Dreams*, involves a perceptual state called "mobile attention." The title of this mental state suggests it is quite similar to evenly sus-pended attention, as is indeed the case:

> I have noticed in my psycho-analytical work that the whole frame of mind of a man who is reflecting is totally different from that of a man who is observing his own psychical pro-cesses. . . . In both cases attention must be concentrated, but the man who is reflecting is also exercising his *critical* faculty; this leads him to reject some of the ideas that occur to him after perceiving them. . . . The self-observer on the other hand need only take the trouble to suppress his critical faculty. . . . What is in question, evidently, is the establishment of a psychical state which, in its distribution of psychical energy (that is, of mobile attention), bears some analogy to the state before falling asleep—and no doubt also to hypnosis. As we fall asleep, "involuntary ideas" emerge, owing to the relaxation of a certain deliberate (and no doubt also critical) activity. . . . As the involuntary ideas emerge they change into visual and acoustic images. . . . *In this way the "involuntary" ideas are trans-formed into "voluntary" ones.*[32]

The patient, like the therapist, is asked to invest all of his con-scious energy in suppressing his "critical faculty" and its inclina-tion to "reject" certain materials. He, too, is urged to practice an attention of movement rather than of stasis, a "mobile attention," which Freud likens to the state of mind of drowsiness and hyp-nosis. The ideal therapeutic scene for Freud, then, involves an "evenly suspended attention" on the side of the therapist and a "mobile attention" on the side of the patient, two terms that point to a similar state of mind.

LET ME NOW return to *Moses* and the question of reading. This book, through its form, works against the assumption that deliberate attention—and specifically "attentive reading"—is the only perceptual state in which we can fruitfully encounter a text. Relying on Freud's discussion of nondeliberate attentive states, I suggest that *Moses* invites us to think of the dyad mobile attention and evenly suspended attention in terms of reader-text relations. What I have in mind is not a simplistic equivalence in which the text is a producer of "free association" and the reader is an analyst. Texts are not human agents, and reading is not psychotherapy. What does seem productive, however, is to think of the relation between text and reader, in this context, as that between *potentiality* and *fulfillment*. While the text cannot practice any "attentive state," it can facilitate or invoke different forms of perception in the reader, such as a "mobile" or an "evenly suspended" attention.[33] These attentive states, on the reader's end, might enable an engagement with language and meaning that differs from those evoked by "close reading." This interchange, I believe, proposes itself in *Moses*.

Moses is an infamously unedited text. Sentences that could easily have been erased to create a more continuous argument are left undisturbed; contradictory arguments and radical swings in thought are everywhere; and seemingly unnecessary repetitions fill its pages. For example, Freud concludes the book's first chapter with the claim that "it will therefore be better to leave unmentioned any further implications of the discovery that Moses was an Egyptian"[34] and explains in the opening of the second section why he nevertheless maintains that assumption. He ends the fourth section of the first chapter with, "We shall have to admit that the thread which we have tried to spin from our hypothesis that Moses was an Egyptian has broken for the second time. And this time, it seems, with no hope of mending," and he opens the fifth section with, "Unexpectedly, here once more a way of escape presents itself."[35] Freud also includes the third chapter even though it is "nothing other than a faithful (and often word-for-word) repetition of the first part,"[36] and he prefaces this chapter twice, while admitting that the two introductions "contradict each other and indeed cancel each other out."[37] In that sense, the experience of reading *Moses* resembles an encounter with an unrevised literary text, as if every remnant of the writing and thinking process is presented to the reader in its initial articulation. This is not to claim that *Moses* was or was not historically edited or that it is in any way an inscription of the biographical Freud's "free associations" but that its rhetoric is one of "unselectivity"; the book gives the reader the impression that nothing whatsoever was edited out. This poetic principle resembles the imperative undergirding both the process of "free association" and the mental state of "evenly suspended attention" in which the analysand and analyst, respectively, are urged to avoid any internal "editing" of the psychic materials encountered. In fact, when reading Freud's instructions for the patient in his 1922 "Two Encyclopedia Articles," one cannot help but ask whether *Moses*'s narrator (to differentiate from the biographical Freud) is not following them as well:

> The treatment is begun by the patient being required to put himself in the position of the attentive and dispassionate self-observer, merely to read off all the time the surface of his consciousness, and on the one hand to make duty of the most complete honesty while on the other not to hold back any idea from communication, even if (1) he feels that it is too disagreeable or if (2) he judges that it is nonsensical or (3) too unimportant or (4) irrelevant to what is being looked for.[38]

Like Freud's free-associating patient, *Moses*'s narrator appears to not "hold back any idea from communication," notwithstanding its potential distastefulness, nonsensicality, or unimportance. The reader of *Moses*, as well, seems to have an affinity with Freud's patient relating his thoughts in a state of mobile attention. After all, Freud's uses in this paragraph the verb "to read" in order to describe the process of "free association": the patient must merely "*read off* all the time the surface of his consciousness." I would like to suggest that *Moses*'s rhetoric of unediting invites the reader to let down his guard and succumb, like Freud's analysand, to unselective reading.[39] That is, going back to the metaphor of the ball suspended by thread or evenly floating, *Moses*'s reader is prompted to allow his attention to move or "swing over" from one segment of the text to the next or from content explicitly expressed by the words on the page to content associatively triggered by it. He is encouraged to shut down the self-regulating mechanisms that, as we have seen earlier, are closely associated with the method of close reading and instead "simply listen" (or, in our case, simply read) "and not bother about whether he is keeping anything in mind."[40]

Moses not only invites but also facilitates this state of mind through its unique "hammering" structure, to echo Salo Baron's statement quoted earlier. Freud makes sure that verbatim repetitions are preceded in his book by an announcement, notifying the reader that he is about to encounter information already presented. This stylistic self-consciousness is usually presented in the form of an aesthetic apology for the text's "inartistic" quality, but it simultaneously functions as a pretext for informing readers of an upcoming reiteration. This format allows the reader who approaches the text "without criticism or selection" and without noticing "anything in particular" to drift away from the particulars of the argument and return to it immediately reassured that he had not missed a thing. The text apprises him that "all this" is "in part a repetition of [Freud's] second essay in *Imago*,"[41] that "what follows, from here to the end, is a slightly altered repetition of the discussion in Part I" of the third essay[42] or that "in spite of a risk of repetition, it will perhaps be as well to bring together here the facts which comprise the analogy that is significant for us."[43] These disclosures pave the way for the reader to surrender himself, at least momentarily, to a different form of concentration, without being required to reread with "deliberate attention" the parts he has risked missing. Put in another way, the concern to remain mentally stagnant in approaching a text in order to avoid letting any nuance fall between the cracks is abated by *Moses*, a work that seems to be more preoccupied with readers excessively looking over, rather than distractedly overlooking, its details.

LET US ASSUME, then, that the reader in fact "accepts" *Moses*'s proposal and abandons his self-imposed obligation to govern the text via thought processes of "selection" and "exclusion." Who then is the agent of reading in this process? Or, to put it in terms of Freud's clinical procedure, if the analyst is required not to select, judge, presuppose, construct expectations, reflect, and memorize, then where does apprehension or reception as a positive action take place? Not surprisingly, the active participant in this process for Freud is the unconscious—the subject's internal alterity. Freud clarifies this when he summarizes his argument as a rule of thumb: "He [the analyst] should withhold all conscious influence from his capacity to attend, and give himself over completely to his 'unconscious memory,'"[44] or, as he rearticulates it in "Two Encyclopedia Articles," "Experience soon showed that the attitude which the analytic physician could most advantageously adopt was to surrender himself to his own unconscious mental activity, in a state of *evenly suspended attention* . . . and by these means catch the drift of the patient's unconscious with his own unconsciousness."[45] To describe the workings of this enigmatic unconscious dialogue, Freud turns to a key metaphor of modernity: the telephone. This is how he puts it:

> [The analyst] must adjust himself to the patient as a telephone receiver is adjusted to the transmitting microphone. Just as the receiver converts back into sound waves the electric oscillations in the telephone line which were set up by sound waves, so the doctor's unconscious is able, from the derivatives of the unconscious which are communicated to him, to reconstruct that unconscious, which is determined by the patient's free associations.[46]

Breaking down this metaphor into its various components, the patient is the equivalent of the transmitting microphone, sending sound waves into the air or recounting free associations. The medium ("capacity to attend") is the telephone line, catching the various sound waves and transmitting them in the form of electric oscillations. The analyst's unconscious is the receiver that taps into the telephone line and does the interpretative work of converting the electric oscillations into the original sound waves or the free associations into the original unconscious materials. Can we develop the model Freud suggests here into a literary one in order to help us better understand *Moses*? Since Freud's metaphor relies on the patient's unconscious, it seems that thinking through it in terms of the reading process would bring us back to the familiar and complex question of the literary unconscious. However, in this present context, the concept of a textual unconscious does not seem to pose much difficulty since in "Recommendations" Freud does not delineate the unconscious in terms of human memory or conflict but rather in terms of production, use, machinery. In fact, we find in Freud a definition of the unconscious uncannily similar to that described in (of all places) Gilles Deleuze and Félix Guattari's self-proclaimed anti-Freudian work:

> The unconscious poses no problem of meaning, solely problems of use. The question posed by desire is not "What does it mean?" but rather *"How does it work?"* How do these machines, these desiring-machines, work—yours and mine? . . . How do they pass from one body to the other? . . . [The unconscious] represents nothing, but it produces. It means nothing, but it works. Desire makes its entry with the general collapse of the question "What does it mean?" No one has been able to pose the problem of language except to the extent that linguists and logicians have first eliminated meaning; and the greatest force of language was only discovered once a work was viewed as a machine, producing certain effects, amenable to a certain use.[47]

In light of this definition and to continue Freud's telephone meta-phor, the dialogue between the reader and the text's unconscious in *Moses* can be understood as one between two functioning appa-ratuses. The text's unconscious does not "mean" anything but "works" to challenge the reader's "deliberate attention" in order to allow him to approach the materials of *Moses* in a different way. The reader's unconscious does not pursue the question of "what does the text mean?" but works to "adjust" itself as best as pos-sible to the text's mode of operation, to "catch its drift," in Freud's words. The result is an invitation to a readerly state of evenly suspended attention, which, for Freud, entails a suspension of the question of "meaning" or "representation." Instead of reading in a constant attempt to understand the text, the reader is invited by *Moses* to loosen such a preoccupation and rely on his uncon-scious to do the work for him. In such a state of mind, Freud tells us in "Recommendations," meaning will always appear after the fact, unexpectedly, when the action of reading (or listening) has already ceased. He writes, "It must not be forgotten that the things one hears are for the most part things whose meaning is only recognized later on."[48]

On a practical level, it seems difficult to imagine that the con-scious question of "what does *Moses* mean?" will never appear during the reading process, even in the case of readers who indeed approach the text in an alternative form of attention and surrender themselves to their "unconscious memory." What I do believe is that *Moses* works to mitigate the governing power of this question over the reading as a whole and offers a different kind of knowledge to its readers in evenly suspended attention. Freud himself does not provide a clear answer in his investigations of counterattention as to the nature of the knowledge that these states of mind can yield. But what he does insinuate in his afore-mentioned discussion of "mobile attention" is that these mind-sets are similar to "the state before falling asleep—and no doubt also to hypnosis," during which "involuntary ideas . . . change into visual and acoustic images." Might it be the case, then, that reading *Moses* in a state other than "deliberate attention" creates an opportunity for a sensory form of knowledge to appear? Can accepting the text's invitation to read it in a state of evenly suspended attention lead to an experience, rather than to objectified knowledge in the sense of abstract thought?

To follow this line of thought, we might think of *Moses* as not only following a historical occurrence that takes place in a desert, but as also setting the stage for readers to sense the wasteland on the very surface of the body. The reader drags his legs through the thick sand of argumentation, in a trajectory that seems to progress but in fact moves in dizzy spirals; the horizon, that promise of clarification, constantly offers its hope only to quickly dissipate, leaving the reader once again disoriented in unbounded space; and signals in the text that momentarily lead the reader toward a captivating mirage are revealed to be misguiding— rushing toward them, the reader, time and again, encounters a void and finds that they were simply a ruse. The following paragraph exemplifies this desert-like experience:

> But it may not, perhaps, be quite useless to enquire under what condition we confer this title of honour ["the great man"]. We shall be surprised to find that it is not quite easy to answer this question. A first formulation—"we do so if a man possesses to a specially high degree qualities that we value greatly"—clearly misses the mark in every respect. . . . It would seem, then, that the qualities have to be mental ones—psychical and intellectual distinctions. As regards these . . . we should not unhesitatingly describe someone as a great man simply because he was extraordinarily efficient in some particular sphere. We should certainly not do so in the case of a chess master or of a virtuoso on a musical instrument; but not very easily, either, in the case of a distinguished artist or scientist. . . . If we unhesitatingly declare that, for instance, Goethe and Leonardo da Vinci and Beethoven are great men, we must be led to it by something

other than admiration for their splendid creations. . . . For the moment, then, we are inclined to decide that it is not worth while to look for a connotation of the concept of a "great man." . . . We will, however, keep this enquiry as short as possible, since it threatens to lead us far away from our goal.[49]

The length of this paragraph, which takes up two pages in the English translation, is significant in terms of the disorienting experience it creates. I have presented only a segment of it here for reasons of concision, but its internal structure is still apparent. At the beginning of the paragraph, the reader is promised an engaging investigation, or at least a "not-useless" one, into the meaning of the term "a great man." This inquiry, however, quickly becomes "not quite easy to answer" and ends up being "not worth while." During this serpentine journey, various definitions of the term "the great man" are examined, but they either are presented only to be immediately negated ("a first formulation . . . clearly misses the mark in every respect") or are depicted from the outset as impossible ("We should certainly not do so in the case of . . ."). Simultaneously, the reader is introduced to Goethe, Leonardo da Vinci, masters of chess, and musical virtuosos, all conjured with vividness and specificity, only to discover that these have no clear function in the argument. In this paragraph, then, the reader is taken through a digression that leads nowhere, that under the guise of progression remains "stuck," and that manages to provisionally fill the reader's space with names and voices that immediately withdraw into the desert aridness. Finally, the reader finds himself "far away from our goal," exhausted and yet exactly where he was before.

AND YET, AS I have mentioned before, the epistemology of evenly suspended or mobile attention can only be speculative, as Freud never explicitly delineates it in his writings. The consequences of this gap are substantial. It follows that Freud expects the therapist to "give himself over completely" to the machinery of the unconscious without knowing when and in what form the belated meaning of the materials he has encountered might arrive. In fact, all that Freud is willing to guarantee to the analyst in "Recommendations" is that this enigmatic knowledge *will* arrive. He writes, "These elements of the material which already form a connected context will be at the doctor's conscious disposal; the rest, as yet unconnected and in chaotic disorder, seems at first to be submerged, but arise readily into recollection as soon as the patient brings up something new to which it can be related and by which it can be continued."[50] To translate this statement into the terms of a reading experience, it seems that meaning might arise from a text, if approached with evenly suspended attention, in the form of a local correlation between different elements of the work, or as a result of the reader's encounter with new materials or old materials anew (i.e., when the text "brings up something new"). In any case, what remains unequivocal is that the therapist, the patient, and—I add here—the reader of *Moses* are all asked by Freud to perform a dangerous leap into the unknown when engaging with the materials at hand (whether psychic or textual) in a state of an alternative attention. That is, they are required to loosen their critical faculties without being certain of how the "reading" or "interpretation" they were assigned to perform will in fact be conducted. In the context of the current investigation, the question arises, then, how does (if at all) Freud convince his readers of *Moses* to make this audacious move? Can he urge them to slacken their "deliberate attention" when facing this text without presenting them with a fully developed alternative? It seems that here as well Freud uses his narrator as a model for the behavior he is asking his readers to conduct; the narrator himself is coping with the anxiety of losing control yet overcoming it and boldly visiting unfamiliar territory.

While the narrator of *Moses* recounts his intellectual endeavor, he continually admits to the profound danger embedded in his journey. In the conclusion of the second preface of the book's third chapter, he admits, "to my critical sense this book, which takes its start from the man Moses, appears like a dancer balancing on the top of one toe; however," he continues, "let us now take the plunge."[51] Freud's narrator, then, dares to let go, at least in part, of his "critical sense" when unfolding his investigation to readers. He also frequently reverts back to another verb of the same semantic family, *wagen*, translated in English as "venture," which further emphasizes the immense risk embedded in his endeavor ("I should now like to venture on this conclusion," "I venture to assert," "evidential value seems to me strong enough for me to venture on a further step").[52] To shed light on this hovering anxiety, Freud (as a narrator) describes the process of writing *Moses* as having at its core an uncanny interaction with an internal otherness:

> There are things which should be said more than once and which cannot be said often enough. But the reader must decide of his own free will whether to linger over the subject or to come back to it. He must not be surreptitiously led into having the same thing put before him twice in one book. It is a piece of clumsiness for which the author must take the blame. Unluckily an author's creative power does not always obey his will: the work proceeds as it can, and often presents itself to the author as something independent or even alien.[53]

It is no wonder, then, that *Moses* is replete with daring "plunges" and precarious "ventures"; Freud depicts *Moses* as a work potentially "alien" to its own creator, brought forth by internal forces foreign to the conscious self. This passage could undoubtedly be also read as a Freudian account of artistic creations as representations of unconscious conflicts (à la "Creative Writers and Day-Dreaming"). However, in his 1900 discussion of "mobile attention," Freud draws a definite correlation between the patient's willingness to allow the "alien" free rein during therapy and the writer's willingness to surrender to interior "creative powers." That is, surrendering to alterity is linked, for Freud, not only with being able to produce artistic work but also with being able to linger in a state of nondeliberate attention and the kind of thinking it permits:

> The adoption of the required attitude of mind towards ideas that seem to emerge "of their own free will" and the abandonment of the critical function that is normally in operation against them seem to be hard of achievement for some people. . . . If we may trust that great poet and philosopher Friedrich Schiller, however, poetic creation must demand an exactly similar attitude. In a passage in his correspondence with Körner . . . Schiller . . . replies to his friend's complaint of insufficient productivity: "The ground for your complaint seems to me to lie in the constraint imposed by your reason upon your imagination. . . . It seems a bad thing and detrimental to the creative work of the mind if Reason makes too close an examination of the ideas as they come pouring in—at the very gateway, as it were. . . . Where there is a creative mind, Reason—so it seems to me—relaxes its watch upon the gates, and the ideas rush in pell-mell, and only then does it look them through and examine them in a mass."[54]

The reader of *Moses*—like Schiller, his unprosperous friend, and Freud's narrator—is pressed to engage with the materials he encounters with a "creative mind," one that "relaxes its watch upon the gates" and allows ideas to "rush in pell-mell." This mind-set is synonymous for Freud with either mobile or evenly suspended attention, as two sides of the same coin. To go back to the previous quote, Freud hopes to position the reader in a place where he can "decide of his own free will whether to linger over the subject or to come back to it," but this freedom of movement, as we have seen before, necessitates a nondeliberate engagement with the text. By modeling through his narrator this creative mind-set, this unselective movement, this willingness to boldly encounter knowledge in an unknown form, Freud seems to invite readers of *Moses* to follow his lead and do the same.

BEFORE MOVING ON to the last section, I cannot help but take a short detour and point out that the model of attention, and possibly of reading, that Freud proposes in "Recommendations," "Two Encyclopedia Articles," *The Interpretation of Dreams*, and, as I have suggested here, in *Moses*, undermines the numerous claims made by central figures such as Fredric Jameson and the aforementioned Deleuze and Guattari that Freud is not only exclusively a close reader but even a *detective* with a single murder mystery in mind.[55] As we have seen, this is a partial truth at best. In the model presented here, Freud insists that in listening to the patient, it is detrimental to search for a specific model, meaning, or conflict.[56] This should be avoided, he maintains, both during therapy and later on when engaging with the belated meaning of the materials, since previous expectations "will certainly falsify what he [the analyst] may perceive."[57] Analysts are required, instead, to give themselves over to the logic of the other rather than imposing an a priori sense on the materials presented before them. The Freudian reader, then, is not (or at least not solely) a "psychoanalyst-as-cop," to quote Deleuze and Guattari, who views "those who do not bow to the imperialism of Oedipus as dangerous deviants."[58] In *The Infinite Question*, Bollas makes a similar claim, admonishing his colleagues for understanding Freudian interpretation as a "reduction . . . into pre-limited terms," and, like Freud, warns against the mental process of "selection":

> This is not to be selective listening: the analyst is to be without such desire. Compare this position with the view that the analyst should always observe the transference, or track the subject's slips of the tongue, or follow the opera of projection or projective identification. Such selectivity could be understood as a defense against the complexity of a session, whereas Freud's innovative method of listening honors this complexity and encourages the analyst to meet the analysand in an intermediate area in which they share something of the same frame of mind.[59]

As mentioned before, the set of texts presented here behooves us to rethink what a "Freudian reading method" entails. Or, more accurately, it asks us to consider, in the spirit of Bollas, the plural "Freuds-as-readers" that populate his work.

TO RETURN TO *Moses*, one is left with an urgent question at hand. If such audacity is needed to plunge into a reading of *Moses* in an evenly suspended attentive state, why would the reader consent to do so? What upholds the willingness to let go of deliberate attention? The answer lies, in fact, at the heart of *Moses*, at the heart of the problem of *belief*. Indeed, if one is to surrender to the "unconscious memory," one must first believe in its very existence and functionality. And though Freud never forthrightly admits to the critical role belief must play in practicing evenly suspended attention, it unwittingly leaves its trace in "Recommendations." There, Freud admits that psychoanalysis is not yet capable, at that historical moment, of accounting for the "psychology of the unconscious and . . . the structure of the neurosis."[60] It follows that Freud asks his therapists in this article to delegate, during therapy, all response-ability to an internal "machine," which he claims is more capable than the self but whose mode of operation he simply cannot explain. This inkling of metaphysics grows when Freud insists on humility toward this unconscious and inexplicable mechanism. In the moment of interpretation, Freud writes, the patient is likely to pay the analyst a compliment for remembering and putting together various disparate details. The analyst must remember, then, that this is always an "undeserved compliment." The agent of interpretation is not in fact the conscious self but the unconscious. The analyst is therefore required to answer with a humble smile, knowing that a "conscious determination to recollect would probably have resulted in failure."[61] These echoes of "belief" turn into a clear voice in the paragraph where Freud sows the seeds for what later develops into Wilfred Bion's famous "no memory, no desire" argument.[62] The therapist must approach the session with no "ambition" to achieve any "convincing effect" on the patient. This goal-oriented approach, Freud warns, will hinder the unconscious dialogue that is taking place in the therapeutic scene:

> I cannot advise my colleagues too urgently to model them-selves during psycho-analytic treatment on the surgeon, who puts aside all his feelings, even his human sympathy, and concentrates his mental forces on the single aim of performing the operation as skillfully as possible. Under present-day condi-tions the feeling that is most dangerous to a psycho-analyst is the therapeutic ambition to achieve by this novel and much disputed method something that will produce a convincing effect upon other people. . . . A surgeon of earlier times took as his motto the words: "Je le pansai, Dieu le guérit" [I dressed his wounds, God cured him]. The analyst should be content with something similar.[63]

If we unpack the quotation of this sixteenth-century surgeon, Ambroise Paré, to understand Freud's allegorical statement, then we must deduce that the "I" here refers to the analyst's conscious-ness, who should concentrate "on the single aim of performing the operation as skillfully as possible." The consequence of such an understanding, of course, is that "God" in Paré's quote, the true healer in this metaphor, is no other than the interpretative "receiver"—the unconscious. In other words, the model of evenly suspended attention, whether in the context of therapy or in that of the reading experience, is fundamentally dependent on the subject's belief in the potency of his or her internal alterity. If *Moses* invites us to practice such attention, it invites us to perform an act of belief.[64] In the context of *Moses*, this conclusion is far-reaching. It is in this late work that Freud repeats with greater force his argument in *Totem and Taboo*, asserting that psychoanal-ysis "leads us to a conclusion which reduces religion to a neurosis of humanity and explains its enormous power in the same way as a neurotic compulsion in our individual patients."[65] If we associate religion with belief, then this statement takes both out of the picture for Freud. But in *Moses*, belief seems to leave the realm of institutionalized religion. This exceptional text, if we "venture" to catch its drift, stealthily rescues the act of belief and returns it through the back door. It might not be a belief in one supreme and only God (after all, Freud declares in this text that he does not believe "there is a single great god to-day"),[66] but it could very well be a belief in many "alien" gods residing within the self and yet independent of it. As Julia Kristeva so deftly puts it in her famous discussion of psychoanalysis and faith, "The ordeal of analysis requires, at a minimum, that I (analyst or analysand) accept the existence of an other. . . . A certain fideism, or even degraded forms of spiritualism, thereby find their way into psychoanalytic ideology. . . . The result is not to prepare that other for some sort of transcendental existence but rather to open up as yet undefined possibilities in this world."[67] Freud's *Moses*, a hunchback wandering through history in its clumsy and peculiar ways, provokes its readers to make their very act of reading an act of faith, to "take a plunge" into their internal otherness and follow its lead.

BEFORE CONCLUDING, I allow myself to make one last digression and add a word about the conceptualization of the reading process in the contexts of the humanities more generally. It is my sense that reading *Moses* as a work of literature that solicits a unique perceptual state has ramifications not only for nuancing the conventional understanding of what a "Freudian reading" is but also for suggesting a different reading model that might fit other texts outside the realm of psychoanalysis. In *To the Lighthouse*, Virginia Woolf's masterpiece published between Freud's "Recommendations" and *Moses*, the modernist writer depicts Mr. and Mrs. Ramsey reading together:

> And she opened the book and began reading here and there at random, and as she did so she felt that she was climbing back-

wards, upwards, shoving her way up under petals that curved over her, so that she only knew that this is white, or this is red. She did not know at first what the words meant at all. . . . Don't interrupt me, he seems to be saying, don't say anything; just sit there. And he went on reading. His lips twitched. It filled him. It fortified him. . . . He felt that he had been arguing with somebody, and had got the better of him. . . . And he wondered what she was reading, and exaggerated her ignorance, her simplicity, for he liked to think she was not clever, not book-learned at all.[68]

Against the backdrop of Freud's model of alternative attention, we can perhaps understand more clearly the gendered power struggle between Mr. and Mrs. Ramsey. While Mr. Ramsey's reading fits with Freud's "deliberate attention" or the New Critics' "close reading," that is, a concentrated and undisturbed engagement with a text for the purpose of unpacking it to the maximum feasible extent, as in solving a riddle ("He felt that he had been arguing with somebody, and had got the better of him"), Mrs. Ramsey, in the terms of this chapter, seems to be engaged in an evenly suspended attentive reading. Her interaction with the text is random, zooms in and out, and involves a sense of experience ("climbing backwards," "she only knew that this is white and this is red") rather than of symbolic understanding ("She did not know at first what the words meant at all"). Could Woolf, then, be hinting here at a different method of approaching her own oeuvre? Can we find in the structure of her work, as we do in Freud's, formal features that direct its readers to imitate Mrs. Ramsey? I would like to close this chapter with the suggestion that not only Woolf but a wide corpus of works, from Freud to the Brazilian Clarice Lispector and the Israeli Yehuda Amichai, awaits a reading practice of evenly suspended attention. These texts, through formal devices such as metaphor construction, excessive detail, repetition, and imitation of clearly "attentive" genres (e.g., the detective novel or crime fiction), invite the reader, very much as

Moses does, to perform an unselective, sensory-oriented reading. For scholars trained in close reading who carry this practice in our very bodies, that would require a bold disciplinary leap of faith. Will we take it?

Notes

1 Robert P. Casey, "Exodus: Freudian Version," *Kenyon Review* 2, no. 2 (1940): 239.

2 Salo W. Baron, review of *Moses and Monotheism*, by Sigmund Freud, trans. James Strachey, *American Journal of Sociology* 45, no. 3 (1939): 471.

3 Cathy Caruth, *Unclaimed Experience: Trauma, Narrative, and History* (Baltimore: Johns Hopkins University Press, 1996), 20.

4 Peter Gay, *Freud: A Life for Our Time* (New York: Norton, 1988), 647.

5 Ilse Grubrich-Simitis, "Freud's Study of Moses as a Daydream: A Biographical Essay," in *Early Freud and Late Freud: Reading Anew Studies on Hysteria and Moses and Monotheism* (London and New York: Routledge, 1997), 60 (emphasis in original).

6 James Strachey, editor's note to *Moses and Monotheism*, by Sigmund Freud, in *The Standard Edition of the Complete Psychological Works of Sigmund Freud*, trans. James Strachey, vol. 23 (London: Hogarth Press, 1953), 4.

7 Chana Kronfeld, *The Full Severity of Compassion: The Poetry of Yehuda Amichai* (Stanford, CA: Stanford University Press, 2015). Kronfeld writes, "In making explicit my own theorization from the poets I read and the cultures I study, whether in their majoritarian or minoritarian formulations, I try to follow Barbara Christian's injunction in 'The Race for Theory,' to theorize from—rather than into—the works we deem important" (ibid., 145).

8 Benjamin H. Ogden and Thomas H. Ogden, *The Analyst's Ear and the Critic's Eye: Rethinking Psychoanalysis and Literature* (London and New York: Routledge, 2013), 2.

9 Freud first depicts the state of evenly suspended attention (without referring to it by name) in his case study of the "Rat Man"; see Freud, "Notes upon a Case of Obsessional Neurosis," in *The Standard Edition of the Complete Psychological Works of Sigmund Freud*, trans. James Strachey, vol. 10 (London: Hogarth Press, 1953), 159.

10 Sedgwick writes, "in the context of recent U.S. critical theory, however, where Marx, Nietzsche, and Freud by themselves are taken as constituting a pretty sufficient genealogy for the mainstream of New Historicist, deconstructive, feminist, queer, and psychoanalytic criticism, to apply a hermeneutics

of suspicion is, I believe, widely understood as a mandatory injunction rather than a possibility among other possibilities." Sedgwick, *Touching Feeling: Affect, Pedagogy, Performativity* (Durham, NC: Duke University Press, 2003), 125.

[11] Baron, review of *Moses*, 471.

[12] Freud, *Moses*, 104.

[13] My definition of New Criticism follows Lawrence H. Schwartz, who writes, "by New Critics I mean those poets, critics, and writers who developed formalist literary aesthetics based on the work of T. S. Eliot, I. A. Richards, and William Empson, dating from the 1920s. This movement had its early development in Nashville with the Agrarian/Fugitive group: Ransom, Tate, Warren, Brooks, and Davidson. Once the Agrarian ideology was dropped in the mid-1930s, the movement expanded rapidly. As commonly defined, the New Critics were those who were interested in explication of poetic texts and who published in and were involved with *Southern Review, Sewanee Review, Kenyon Review,* and the Kenyon School. Principal among them were: R. P. Blackmur, Yvor Winters, W. K. Wimsatt, René Wellek, Austin Warren, Robert Heilman, Robert Stallman, Mark Schorer, Arthur Mizener, William Van O'Connor." Schwartz, *Creating Faulkner's Reputation: The Politics of Modern Literary Criticism* (Knoxville: University of Tennessee Press, 1988), 5–6.

[14] New Criticism and close reading are at the heart of a lively debate that has taken place in the discipline of literature over the past decade or so. For several recent reevaluations of close reading in the context of New Criticism, see Isobel Armstrong, "Textual Harassment: The Ideology of Close Reading, or How Close Is Close?," *Textual Practice* 9, no. 3 (1995): 401–420; Michael Warner, "Uncritical Reading," in *Polemic: Critical or Uncritical,* ed. Jane Gallop (New York: Routledge, 2004), 13–38; Joshua Gang, "Behaviorism and the Beginnings of Close Reading," *ELH* 78, no. 1 (2011): 1–25; Joseph North, "What's 'New Critical' about 'Close Reading'? I. A. Richards and His New Critical Reception," *New Literary History* 44, no. 1 (2013): 141–157; Joseph North, *Literary Criticism: A Concise Political History* (Cambridge, MA: Harvard University Press, 2017); Nicholas Gaskill, "The Close and the Concrete: Aesthetic Formalism in Context," *New Literary History* 47, no. 4 (2016): 505–524.

[15] Jonathan Culler, *Literary History: A Very Short Introduction* (Oxford and New York: Oxford University Press, 2011), 136.

[16] Terry Eagleton, *Literary Theory: An Introduction,* 2nd ed. (Minneapolis: University of Minnesota Press, 1996), 27.

[17] Paul de Man, *Blindness and Insight: Essays in the Rhetoric of Contemporary Criticism* (Minneapolis: University of Minnesota Press, 1986), 29.

[18] Andrew DuBois, introduction to *Close Reading: The Reader,* ed. Frank Lentricchia and Andrew DuBois (Durham, NC: Duke University Press, 2002), 2.

19 Gaskill, "Close and the Concrete," 512. Gaskill astutely suggests that "attention" for the New Critics has to do with the mental process of bringing details into a harmonious whole ("attending to things as *together*"). He thus paves the way for a clearer definition of what "attention" means for these thinkers, even though this conception is not central to his argument.

20 Jonathan Crary, *Suspensions of Perception: Attention, Spectacle, and Modern Culture* (Cambridge, MA: MIT Press, 2001), 13.

21 Ibid., 1.

22 Sigmund Freud, "Recommendations to Physicians Practicing Psycho-Analysis," in *The Standard Edition of the Complete Psychological Works of Sigmund Freud*, trans. James Strachey, vol. 12 (London: Hogarth Press, 1953), 111–120.

23 Since in 1912 psychoanalysis was almost an exclusively male practice, I use masculine pronouns when discussing Freud's recommendations to his colleagues.

24 Paul North, *The Problem of Distraction* (Stanford, CA: Stanford University Press, 2011). North writes, "The hand of attention stretches out, *adtenere*, toward the things it wishes to take and possess, and it compels itself to do so again and again" (ibid., 3).

25 Freud, "Recommendations," 112.

26 Ibid., 111–112.

27 Ibid., 112 (emphasis added).

28 Ibid., 113 (emphasis added).

29 Ibid., 114.

30 Ibid., 112. Interesting in this respect is Gaskill's discussion of the New Critics as bringing the poem to a halt in order to analyze it. As he reminds us, William Wimsatt writes in the preface to *The Verbal Icon*, "The poem is an act, . . . but if we are to lay hold of the poetic act to comprehend and evaluate it, and if it is to pass current as a critical object, it must be hypostatized." William K. Wimsatt, *The Verbal Icon: Studies in the Meaning of Poetry* (Lexington: University of Kentucky Press, 1954), xvii; quoted in Gaskill, "Close and the Concrete," 518. It seems that the New Critics imagine both their readers' minds and their objects of inquiry in terms of stasis.

31 Freud, "Recommendations," 112.

32 Sigmund Freud, *The Interpretation of Dreams*, in *The Standard Edition of the Complete Psychological Works of Sigmund Freud*, trans. James Strachey, vols. 4–5 (London: Hogarth Press, 1953), 4:101–102 (emphasis in original).

33 As Mattheu Mullins so aptly puts it, "Texts have the . . . capacity to elicit and control cognitive and emotional responses through their formal fea-

tures. . . . I simply want to offer an approach that specifically calls attention to the text's participation in the dialogue of reading. Put another way, whereas [Stanley] Fish outlines 'effective stylistics' in an early essay titled 'Literature in the Reader,' here I examine the affective effects literature has *on* the reader." Mullins, "Antagonized by the Text, or, It Takes Two to Read Alice Walker's 'Everyday Use,'" *Comparatist: Journal of the Southern Comparative Literature Association* 37 (2013): 38.

34 Freud, *Moses*, 16.

35 Ibid., 36.

36 Ibid., 103.

37 Ibid., 57.

38 Sigmund Freud, "Two Encyclopedia Articles," in *The Standard Edition of the Complete Psychological Works of Sigmund Freud*, trans. James Strachey, vol. 18 (London: Hogarth Press, 1953), 238.

39 In a way similar to my treatment of "the analyst" (see note 23), I adhere in this chapter to the masculine grammatical inflection of "the reader" in accordance with Freud's imaginary as reflected in his texts. However, the conclusion of this chapter demonstrates that evenly suspended attention in fact holds the potential to undo the gender power structures that are both manifested in and reinforced by traditional Western reading practices.

40 The affinity between reading and listening has been intensively investigated in the past few years in the interdisciplinary field of sound studies. Exemplary is the work of Marília Librandi-Rocha on the "aural novel"; see Librandi-Rocha, "'Writing by Ear': Clarice Lispector, Machado de Assis, and Guimarães Rosa and the Mimesis of Improvisation," *Critical Studies in Improvisation / Études critiques en improvisation* 7, no. 1 (2011), http://www.criticalimprov.com/article/view/1250/2037; Librandi-Rocha, *Writing by Ear: Clarice Lispector and the Aural Novel* (Toronto: University of Toronto Press, forthcoming 2017). In the specific intersection of psychoanalysis and literature, the work of Thomas and Benjamin Ogden, mentioned earlier, discusses this issue at length; see Ogden and Ogden, *Analyst's Ear and the Critic's Eye*.

41 Freud, *Moses*, 61.

42 Ibid., 130.

43 Ibid., 73–74.

44 Freud, "Recommendations," 112.

45 Freud, "Two Encyclopedia Articles," 239 (emphasis in original).

46 Freud, "Recommendations," 115–116.

47 Gilles Deleuze and Félix Guattari, *Anti-Oedipus: Capitalism and Schizophrenia*, trans. Robert Hurley, Mark Seem, and Helen R. Lane

(Minneapolis: University of Minnesota Press, 1992), 109 (emphasis in original).

48 Freud, "Recommendations," 112.

49 Freud, *Moses*, 108–109.

50 Freud, "Recommendations," 112.

51 Freud, *Moses*, 58 (emphasis added).

52 Ibid., 24, 91, 99.

53 Ibid., 104.

54 Freud, *Interpretation of Dreams*, 4:102–103.

55 In *The Political Unconscious*, Jameson writes, "Indeed, one of the most dramatic of such recent attacks on interpretation—*The Anti-Oedipus*, by Gilles Deleuze and Félix Guattari—quite properly takes as its object not Marxian, but rather Freudian, interpretation, which is characterized as a reduction and a rewriting of the whole rich and random multiple realities of concrete everyday experience into the contained, strategically prelimited terms of the family narrative—whether this be seen as myth, Greek tragedy, "family romance," or even the Lacanian structural version of the Oedipus complex." Jameson, *The Political Unconscious: Narrative as a Socially Symbolic Act* (Ithaca, NY: Cornell University Press, 1982), 21–22.

56 Freud's model of evenly suspended attention has been returned to and elaborated on in recent years by leading analysts such as Wilfred Bion, Christopher Bollas, and Thomas Ogden, mentioned earlier in this chapter. Evenly suspended attention informed Bion's seminal concept of "reverie" in, among other texts, his 1962 *Learning from Experience* (London: Karnac, 1984). This psychic state is at the center of the psychoanalytic work of Ogden. Bollas's work is undergirded as a whole by Freud's concept of evenly suspended attention. As he writes after quoting Freud's description of this mental state, "let me repeat the last phrase because I think every psychoanalyst should put this on the wall and read it every day. '. . . and by these means catch the drift of the patient's unconscious with his own unconscious.'" Bollas, *The Freudian Moment* (London: Karnac, 2007), 13.

57 Freud, "Recommendations," 112.

58 Deleuze and Guattari, *Anti-Oedipus*, 108.

59 Christopher Bollas, *The Infinite Question* (London and New York: Routledge, 2009), 20.

60 Freud, "Recommendations," 114.

61 Ibid., 113.

62 Wilfred Bion, "Notes on Memory and Desire," *Psychoanalytic Forum* 2, no. 3 (1967): 279–281.

63 Freud, "Recommendations," 115.

64 Freud's invocation of belief in "Recommendations" might seem to be at odds with his "scientific" approach, made evident by his reliance on images such as the "telephone" and the "surgeon." However, this is only an alleged discrepancy since, throughout his writings, Freud consistently acknowledges the limitations of the scientific approach and locates an inarticulable alterity at the heart of any psychic object of study. This can be observed as early as in his "Project for a Scientific Psychology" or in *The Interpretation of Dreams*, in which he states, "There is often a passage in even the most thoroughly interpreted dream which has to be left obscure. . . . This is the dream's navel, the spot where it reaches down into the unknown." Freud, *Interpretation of Dreams*, 5:525.

65 Freud, *Moses*, 55.

66 Ibid., 129.

67 Julia Kristeva, *In the Beginning Was Love: Psychoanalysis and Faith*, trans. Arthur Goldhammer (New York: Columbia University Press, 1988), 26.

68 Virginia Woolf, *To the Lighthouse* (New York: Harcourt Brace Jovanovich), 119–121.

Jan Assmann

6 Freud, Sellin, and the Murder of Moses

1. Freud

IN SIGMUND FREUD'S last book, *Moses and Monotheism*, published in the year of his death (1939), he laid down some rather bold theses:

- That Moses was an Egyptian, a follower of Akhenaten and his new solar monotheism, who organized the Exodus from Egypt in order to rescue the new religion from being extinguished in Egypt

- That he was subsequently murdered by the Jews, who did not bear the high moral demands of Moses's abstract religion

- That this murder meant for the Jews a kind of retraumatiza- tion, being a reenactment of the "primal parricide" in the "primal horde" that had left its traces in the human soul (the thesis Freud had expounded in 1913 in *Totem and Taboo*)

- That this retraumatization resulted in a repression of Moses's monotheism and a long period of latency after which the

monotheistic religion returned with the compulsory power of
the return of the repressed

It does not seem worthwhile to engage again in a discussion of
Freud's arguments concerning the historical Moses, because they
lack any evidence both in the biblical text and in extrabiblical
sources. They function as a heuristic construction in the psychoanalytical sense and are meant to shed light on a present situation, to clear up an actual problem. One aspect of the present
situation that Freud had already dealt with in *Totem and Taboo* is
the diagnosis of religion as a compulsory neurosis that is rooted
in the repressed experience of the primal parricide:

> Early trauma—defence—latency—outbreak of neurotic
> illness—partial return of the repressed. Such is the formula
> which we have laid down for the development of the neurosis.
> The reader is now invited to take the step of supposing that
> something occurred in the life of the human species similar
> to what occurs in the life of individuals: of supposing, that is,
> that here too events occurred of a sexually aggressive nature,
> which left behind them permanent consequences but were for
> the most part fended off and forgotten, and which after a long
> latency came into effect and created phenomena similar to
> symptoms in their structure and purpose.[1]

Along the pattern "Early trauma—defence—latency—outbreak
of neurotic disorder—partial return of the repressed," Freud felt
himself able to explain the general course of religious history
with the stages of totemism, polytheism, and monotheism. This
diagnosis is now applied to Moses and the Mosaic religion:

> It would be worth while to understand how it was that the
> monotheist idea made such a deep impression precisely on
> the Jewish people and that they were able to maintain it so
> tenaciously. It is possible, I think, to find an answer. Fate
> had brought the great deed and misdeed of primaeval days,
> the killing of the father, closer to the Jewish people by caus-

ing them to repeat it on the person of Moses, an outstanding
father-figure. It was a case of "acting-out" instead of remembering, as happens so often with neurotics during the work of
analysis. (SE 23:88)

What he really wanted to explain is the structure and genesis
of the Jewish character. At the end of his book, he summarizes:
"We wanted to explain the origin of the special character of the
Jewish people, a character which is probably what has made their
survival to the present day possible" (SE 23:123). Freud's book
belongs to the genre of Jewish self-thematization and is triggered
by the outbreak of violent anti-Semitism in Nazi Germany. In
letters to Lou Andreas-Salomé and Arnold Zweig, he wrote, "In
view of the new persecutions one wonders again how the Jew
came to be what he is and why he attracted this undying hatred,"
and the answer he found was "Moses hat den Juden geschaffen":
Moses created the Jew.[2]

Freud wants to explain with his theory of the "return of the
repressed" how the monotheistic religion was able to assert itself
with such overwhelming power. The Jewish people had not forgotten the message of monotheism that Moses had brought them
but had only repressed it. This means that they had always, albeit
unconsciously, known it. For this reason, the message, when it
returned with the later prophets whom God sent to remind them
of what had been revealed to them at Sinai, could meet in the
Jewish soul with such an overwhelming and compulsive resonance:

> A tradition that was based only on communication could not
> lead to the compulsive character that attaches to religious
> phenomena. It would be listened to, judged, and perhaps
> dismissed, like any other piece of information from outside;
> it would never attain the privilege of being liberated from the
> constraint of logical thought. It must have undergone the fate
> of being repressed, the condition of lingering in the uncon-

scious, before it is able to display such powerful effects on its return, to bring the masses under its spell. (SE 23:101)

In another passage, he expresses himself in even more unequivocal terms:

It is worth specially stressing the fact that each portion which returns from oblivion asserts itself with peculiar force, exercises an incomparably powerful influence on people in the mass, and raises an irresistible claim to truth against which logical objections remain powerless: a kind of "credo quia absurdum." This remarkable feature can only be understood on the pattern of the delusions of psychotics. We have long understood that a portion of the forgotten truth lies hidden in delusional ideas, that when this returns it has to put up with distortions and misunderstandings, and that the compulsive conviction which attaches to the delusion arises from this core of truth and spreads out onto the errors that wrap it round. We must grant an ingredient such as this of what may be called *historical* truth to the dogmas of religion as well, which, it is true, bear the character of psychotic symptoms but which, as group phenomena, escape the curse of isolation. (SE 23:85)

The "curse of isolation" would be the necessary consequence of any liberation from the constraints of logical thinking, because this constraint is nothing else but the principle of socialization. The religious illusion, however, does not have isolating effects because as a collective neurosis, it is shared by the entire society.

Moses, however, did not just create the Jews by having caused their retraumatization through his violent death. He also and above all created them by his religious instruction (his Torah). In the first place, Freud identifies a peculiar ethnical narcissism. The Jews, he writes, "have a particularly high opinion of themselves, that they regard themselves as more distinguished, of higher standing, as superior to other peoples—from whom they are also distinguished by many of their customs. . . . They really regard themselves as God's chosen people, they believe that they stand especially close to him; and this makes them proud and confident" (SE 105). For Freud, it is evident

> that it was the man Moses who imprinted this trait—significant for all time—upon the Jewish people. He raised their self-esteem by assuring them that they were God's chosen people, he enjoined them to holiness and pledged them to be apart from others. . . . It was this one man Moses who created the Jews. It is to him that this people owes its tenacity of life but also much of the hostility it has experienced and still experiences. (SE 23:106)

Of equal importance as chosenness is for Freud the drive renunciation imposed by the prohibition of images and its subsequent progress in intellectuality:

> Among the precepts of the Moses religion there is one that is of greater importance than appears to begin with. This is the prohibition against making an image of God—the compulsion to worship a God whom one cannot see. In this, I suspect, Moses was outdoing the strictness of the Aten religion. Perhaps he merely wanted to be consistent: his God would in that case have neither a name nor a countenance. Perhaps it was a fresh measure against magical abuses. But if this prohibition were accepted, it must have a profound effect. For it meant that a sensory perception was given second place to what may be called an abstract idea—a triumph of intellectuality over sensuality or, strictly speaking, an instinctual renunciation, with all its necessary psychological consequences. (SE 23:112–113)

According to Freud, the Jewish character is formed by two different motives: a progress in intellectuality and a specific susceptibility to the neurotic father-religion of monotheism. It is obvious what an important role the murder of Moses plays in this theory. However, Freud was not the first to come to such a conclusion concerning the death of Moses, which, by the way, is left in the dark by the biblical report in a rather striking way. This fact led others before Freud to a similar conclusion, among them the German poet Johann Wolfgang von Goethe and the Old Testament scholar Ernst Sellin. Freud mentions both briefly in footnotes but relied especially on Sellin much more heavily than is commonly assumed.

2. Goethe

IN AN ESSAY written in earlier years but published only in 1819 in "Noten und Abhandlungen zum besseren Verständnis des West-östlichen Divan," titled "Israel in der Wüste,"[3] Goethe held that after years of aimlessly wandering in the desert, Moses was slain by Joshua and Caleb, who could no longer bear his weak and hesitant style of leadership and wanted to enter and conquer the Promised Land as soon as possible. In this hypothetical murder, Goethe saw the culmination and logical consequence of the numerous scenes of rebellion, mutiny, and infidelity that interrupt the march from Egypt to Canaan. These scenes of "murmuring," as they are traditionally called, led him to the following conclusion: "The proper, sole and deepest motive of global and human history, to which all the others are subordinate, remains the conflict of disbelief and belief."[4] In the same way as Freud, Goethe arrived at a very general theory, not of human history in general, as he believed, but of monotheism in particular. In the horizon of "Abrahamic" monotheism, not so much perhaps in Judaism but very much so in Christianity and Islam, history is stamped by the conflict of belief and disbelief. The conflict that broke out during the wandering through the wilderness continued in the Promised Land and is virulent until today. Goethe's diagnosis of monotheism comes closer to the truth, I think, than Freud's, but Freud comes closer to the tragic aspects of the figure of Moses.[5] Freud has Moses die for his message, as a martyr of monotheism, as it were (though Freud does not use this term, as far as I can remember). This term, however, plays a dominant role in the book that Freud quotes as his authority for the murder of Moses, the book by Ernst Sellin *Mose und seine Bedeutung für die israelitisch-jüdische Religionsgeschichte* (Moses and his significance for the history of Israelite-Jewish religion; 1922).

3. Sellin

SELLIN (1867–1946)[6] CULLED from passages primarily in Hosea that Moses must have been slain at Shittîm, the last resting place of the Israelites after the forty years of wandering through the desert. There, they participated in a feast that the Moabites held to the local god Baal Peor and raised thereby the jealousy and anger of YHVH, who sent a plague killing twenty-four thousand people and ordered Moses, "Take all the leaders of these people, kill them and expose them in broad daylight before the Lord, so that the Lord's fierce anger may turn away from Israel" (Num. 25:4). In order to prevent Moses from executing this cruel order, the Israelites—according to Sellin—killed Moses and his Midianite wife, Zippora, and had this crime covered up under the story of Zimri and his Midianite lover Cozbi, whom Phineas had killed, by which deed he stilled God's anger and stopped the plague. Sellin's construction is as fantastic as Freud's construction of an Egyptian Moses. But the conception of a murder covered up in the tradition by a screen memory may have set Freud on the track of constructing his case history of monotheism.

"Hosea," Sellin writes, "is still acquainted with the continuation of Numbers 25:3–5 in its original form; he knows that Moses has been killed at Shittîm by his own people after their defection to Baal Peor when he called them to penitence and demanded atonement. The whole is a tragic, gripping story par excellence."[7] With Moses, Sellin assumes, his message was also forgotten. "At most," he writes, "we may expect that here and there a spark pops up of the spiritual fire that he once ignited, that his ideas did not wholly disappear . . . until they later broke through under the impression of special events or personalities that were moved by his spirit and won influence on the population at large.[8] The possibility that the memory of Moses, his message, and his violent death has been preserved in a small and marginalized group has also been considered by Freud, whose lines read as a paraphrase of Sellin:

> The religion of Moses, however, had not disappeared without leaving a trace. A kind of memory of it had survived, obscured and distorted, supported, perhaps, among individual members of the priestly caste by ancient records. And it was this tradition of a great past which continued to work in the background, as it were, which gradually gained more and more power over men's minds, and which finally succeeded in transforming the god Yahweh into the god of Moses and in calling back to life the religion of Moses which had been established and then abandoned long centuries earlier. (SE 23:124)[9]

Freud, however, eventually discards this interpretation in favor of his own theory of repression. However, Freud's theory about the pathogenic effects of the repressed memory of Moses also has its precursor in Sellin's book, which influenced Freud much more strongly than he himself admits. Sellin is convinced that not only the memory of Moses but also and above all the remembrance of the grievous sin of his murder and all the crimes that have been committed against the prophets would have lingered on in the memory of the people and would eventually have caused a kind of collective psychic disease. He takes it for certain "that in spite of all the cover-up from the side of the priests the tradition of Moses' martyrdom stayed alive, that this murder and defection was resented as the great sin of the people which made them deadly ill and which has to be atoned for first before salvation may come."[10] The impression to live under the curse of the break of the covenant and under the wrath of God produced a "sick theology" of sorts, informed by a guilt complex. These feelings of guilt also play a major role in Freud's analysis of biblical religion. He related them to the ambivalence of the father-son relationship:

> Ambivalence is a part of the essence of the relation to the father: in the course of time the hostility too could not fail to stir, which had once driven the sons into killing their admired and dreaded father. There was no place in the framework of the religion of Moses for a direct expression of the murderous hatred of the father. All that could come to light was a mighty reaction against it—a sense of guilt on account of that hostility, a bad conscience for having sinned against God and for not ceasing to sin. (SE 134)

"The bad conscience for having sinned against God and for not ceasing to sin": this is exactly what Sellin has in mind when he speaks of the "deadly illness" of the people and its guilt-stricken theology. Since the situation of the Jews did not change with the building of the Second Temple, since they did not regain their political sovereignty but remained under foreign dominion, first by the Persians, then by the Seleucids, and finally by the Romans, they could not but feel that the curse and the wrath of God did not yet end.

For Sellin, the murder of Moses was not only the culmination of the scenes of rebellion during the march through the wilderness but also the beginning of violent acts against the prophets who followed Moses in the Promised Land and shared his tragic lot. His boldest claim was not so much that Moses was murdered—the biblical record is suspiciously vague about Moses's death—but that this murder was remembered and that this memory stayed alive until the times of the New Testament. For the historical Moses remains a mystery, and one cannot even be sure whether he ever lived; but the cultural memory of Israel is codified in the Bible—both testaments—and open to investigation and critique. In this respect, Sellin goes so far as to draw a line of tradition that leads from the alleged passion of Moses via the tradition about the violent fate of the prophets to the passion of Jesus of Nazareth. He quotes, for example, Nehemiah, who gives a recapitulation of YHVH's *magnalia* for Israel, including the gift of the law through Moses, his servant: "But they were disobedient and rebelled against you; they turned their backs on your law. They killed your prophets, who had warned them in order to turn them back to you; they committed awful blasphemies" (Neh. 9:26). This passage does not refer to the murder of Moses but to the murder of the later prophets, his followers, and it therefore testifies to the tradition of sinful opposition against the law. The same reproach occurs in the New Testament, in which Luke and Matthew have Jesus saying, "Jerusalem, Jerusalem, you who kill the prophets and stone those sent to you" (Luke 13:34 = Matt. 23:37), and in which Stephen in his great speech before his execution by stoning says, "Was there ever a prophet your ancestors did not persecute? They even killed those who predicted the coming of the Righteous One. And now you have betrayed and murdered him—you who have received the law that was given through angels but have not obeyed it" (Acts 7:52–53). Sellin, thus, connects the scenes of murmuring in the wilderness and the topic of the violent fate of the prophets in Canaan, and he even includes the four songs about the suffering servant, the man of sorrows, in Deutero-Isaiah, chapters 52–53, in this tradition. Nobody seems to have followed him in this construction except Klaus Baltzer in his commentary on Deutero-Isaiah.[11] Moses is never mentioned by name in these songs. But if we think not of a repressed tradition about the death of Moses but of a cultural pattern about the suffering that those who plead YHVH's cause, live by the law, and stay loyal to the covenant may incur by the hands of an infidel people and government, the idea that the suffering servant tradition also belongs to this pattern seems anything but absurd. There is not a literary but an associative connection that allowed Jesus to be seen by his disciples and followers both as a new Moses and as the paradigmatic suffering servant.

In 1967, forty-five years after Sellin and twenty-eight years after Freud, the New Testament scholar Odil Hannes Steck, who turned in the course of this project into an Old Testament scholar, took up this theme in his dissertation on "the violent fate of the prophets."[12] In this book, he does not mention Freud, which is small wonder, but he also never mentions Sellin, which is a crime. Sellin's pioneering work seems to have fallen into complete oblivion. Steck is able to substantiate the line of tradition from Nehemiah to Luke—that Sellin only briefly adumbrated—by a plethora of passages referring to the idea that Israel not only neglected the message of the prophets but even killed them. For an explanation, he points to the tendency to interpret the disasters of Israelite history as God's punishment for Israel's continuous disobedience, which characterizes the "Deuteronomistic history" (Deuteronomy, Joshua, Judges, Samuel, Kings). This leads to the formation of a fixed pattern that Steck reconstructs like this:

A The stiff-necked, disobedient people,
B warned by the prophets to turning back,
C remained resistant/C^1 killed the prophets
D and incurred God's punishment.[13]

In the form ABCD, this schema penetrates the whole Deuteronomistic history and the book of Jeremiah; in the exacerbated form ABC^{1}D, it occurs first in Nehemiah and then not only in the New Testament but in striking abundance in intertestamentary and postbiblical sources such as Qumran, Midrash, Talmud, and Flavius Josephus. Sellin could not wish for a better confirmation of his general thesis, which is not so much about the murder of Moses, the only point for which Sellin is mentioned by Freud, but about the tragic side of the "Israelite-Jewish history of religion." Both Sellin and Steck connect the topic of the "sin of the fathers" that YHVH is visiting on the next generations with a general feeling of guilt that kept haunting the Jewish people, because their sufferings were in no way over with the return to Jerusalem and the building of the Second Temple. Foreign domination continued with the Persians and assumed much more repressive forms under the Seleucids and finally under the Romans. Thus, the feeling of living under the wrath and curse of God persisted. While Freud feels able to treat this feeling or mentality like a neurotic illness by tracing it back to repressed traumatic experiences in primal history, Steck connects it with contemporary experiences and the Deuteronomistic view of history that stayed alive in liturgical confessions and penitential prayers.

Steck and Sellin are certainly right. We do not need the primal trauma and the Mosaic retraumatization. The historical traumas of experiencing the collapse of, first, the Northern Kingdom in 722 at the hands of the Assyrians and then the Southern Kingdom 587 at the hands of the Babylonians; the total loss of state, kingdom, territory, city, and temple; fifty and more years of exile; and continuous foreign domination under changing empires are quite sufficient to stress the tragic side of the new religion. It is not the ambivalence of the father-son relationship that is at play here but the ambivalence of the concept of covenant with its polarity of belief and disbelief, as Goethe had it, as well as loyalty and betrayal, blessing and curse, love and wrath.[14]

Goethe, Sellin, and Freud depart from the scenes of "murmuring" as they occur in the books of Exodus and Numbers, but only Sellin and Steck are able to give an explanation of this perplexing tradition. In connecting these problematic scenes with the tradition about the violent fate of the prophets and the Deuteronomistic critique of history, they integrate them into a comprehensive view of biblical history. This complex that Freud in his psychoanalytical approach interpreted as repression they interpret as resistance, with which the concepts of law and revelation met in the formative periods of early Judaism.

If seen in this broader context, the scenes of "murmuring" during the Exodus from Egypt receive their full importance. There are no less than fourteen of them. In closing, I propose to inspect them in more detail. They start in Exodus 14, when the Israelites arrive at the shore of the Yam Suf and see the Egyptian army approaching from afar. They lose faith immediately and want to return, but Moses splits the sea by God's command, and they pass through on dry ground, whereas the Egyptian army is drowned in the returning water. On the Israelites' way to Sinai occur three similar scenes of rebellion prompted by thirst and hunger. At Mara, they find brackish water that Moses, however, is able to transform into drinkable water by throwing into it a piece of wood. Later they rebel because of hunger, and YHWH sends quails and manna, but the murmuring does not subside. At Meriba, they are thirsty again and are on the verge of lynching Moses when at the last moment he draws water from the rock on God's command by hitting it with his rod. Up to here, these rebellions proceed without consequence. YHWH gives in and puts things right. This, however, changes in the most radical way once the covenant at Sinai is sealed. From then on, similar events raise YHWH's anger and are severely punished.

This new system of causality hits first the Israelites, who lose faith in seeing Moses again after forty days of his absence on the mountain and have Aaron make them a Golden Calf to represent their lost leader. Only after killing three thousand people and with much persuasion is Moses able to dissuade God from annihilating the whole people and to win him over to continue the broken covenant. On the Israelites' way from Sinai, the rebellions continue and are punished by fire and plague. Even Aaron and Miriam protest against Moses, reproaching him for his "Cushite wife," and Miriam is punished by a fit of leprosy that lasts for a week. The severest of these crises occur when the scouts return whom Moses had sent on God's command to spy out the land of Canaan. Some of them spread a rumor that the land is inhabited by giants. The people are stricken by fear and decide to kill Moses and Aaron and to choose other leaders who would lead them back to Egypt. This time their revolt is not about hunger and thirst but the central covenantal values: belief and disbelief, trust and betrayal, shedding doubt on the sense of the whole project. Again YHWH is resolved to annihilate the whole people but is persuaded by Moses to turn the death penalty into a life sentence: God says about the whole generation of those who set forth from Egypt, "Not one of those who saw my glory and the signs I performed in Egypt and in the wilderness but who disobeyed me and tested me ten times—not one of them will ever see the land I promised on oath to their ancestors" (Num. 14:22–23). "In this wilderness your bodies will fall—every one of you twenty years old or more who . . . has grumbled against me. . . . Your children will be shepherds here for forty years, suffering for your unfaithfulness, until the last of your bodies lies in the wilderness" (Num. 14:30, 33). This punishment intones the generation theme that also underlies the returning formula of the "sin of the fathers" for which YHWH is resolved to punish the sons through the third and fourth generation. Forty years designate the time span in which the murmuring generation will have died out so that only their children will enter the Promised Land.

It is significant that God speaks of ten such scenes of murmuring. The number is symbolical and puts the scenes of murmuring in parallel to the ten plagues and the ten commandments. Here, as elsewhere, the number ten has a mnemonic function: ten mighty deeds has God performed to liberate his people, ten commandments has he given them for a constitution as partner in his covenant, and with ten acts of infidelity or "harlotry" they have offended him.

But the scenes of murmuring continue even after the crisis of the scouts. Soon afterward occurs the rebellion of the Korach clan against the monopoly that Moses and Aaron are claiming in conversing with God. God punishes the whole clan, which is swallowed by the earth, and 14,700 people die of the plague that is sent by God. When the people revolt because of the many who had to die, God is again resolved to annihilate the whole people, but Aaron manages a quick expiation. A revolt because of thirst follows, doubling the scene at Meriba. This time Moses and Aaron are ordered to speak to the rock instead of hitting it, which they were however doing. For this mistake, they are punished by being forbidden to enter the Promised Land. Aaron is to die in the desert, Moses on Mount Nebo, from which he is permitted at least to see into the land.[15] The next murmuring is about hunger. The people are fed up with the eternal manna and long for meat. God sends them poisonous serpents for punishment but advises Moses to make remedy in the form of the Nehushtan, the brazen serpent the sight of which will heal the bites. At the end of the wanderings, the scene at Shittîm occurs that equals the scene of the Golden Calf as to the gravity of the offense. God sends a plague, calls for execution of all the leaders, and is only reconciled by Phineas, who transfixed Zimri and Cozbi in the act of lovemaking.

Let us consider again these fourteen scenes of rebellion against the will of God, from the western shore of Yam Suf up to the eastern shore of river Jordan. Four occur before sealing the covenant, *ante legem*, as Augustine has it, and remain without consequence. Ten scenes occur after the covenant ceremony, *sub lege*, attracting God's anger and entailing terrible punishment. Three scenes stand out among them: the Golden Calf (5), the scouts (9), and Shittîm (14). The Golden Calf at the beginning and the feast of Baal Peor at the end infringe the first commandment of absolute loyalty—no other gods!—the first by the Israelites' making and worshiping an image, the last by their "whoring" with another god. The scene of the scouts offends the command of absolute faith and trust—the Hebrew word *'aemunah* means both.

THE EXODUS MYTH is the founding myth of the Jewish people—this point is uncontested among scholars. What, however, in this context could these continuously repeated scenes of rebellion mean? What could be the sense of such an unfavorable self-representation of the Chosen People? Michael Walzer, the political philosopher, reads the Exodus narrative as a political myth and as a blueprint of political revolutions.[16] He sees in the scenes of murmuring an expression of the typical difficulties and drawbacks with which every revolution, every attempt at a radical political innovation, has to struggle. After each revolution, there are deserts to traverse if the arduous way toward a new order meets with deprivation, constraints, and violence. These counterrevolutionary crises are expressed by the scenes of murmuring. This is without any doubt a most ingenious interpretation, but it falls short of accounting for the continuation of such scenes in the Promised Land, which has to be seen in the context of the whole Bible, Old and New Testaments included.

Psalm 106, for example, is a liturgy of penitence enumerating the salvatory deeds of God and opposing them with the sins of the ungracious people, starting with the sins of the fathers during the Exodus from Egypt and continuing in Canaan:

> They did not destroy the peoples
>> as the Lord had commanded them,
> but they mingled with the nations
>> and adopted their customs.
> They worshiped their idols,
>> which became a snare to them.
> They sacrificed their sons
>> and their daughters to false gods.
> They shed innocent blood,
>> the blood of their sons and daughters,
> whom they sacrificed to the idols of Canaan,
>> and the land was desecrated by their blood.
> They defiled themselves by what they did;
>> by their deeds they prostituted themselves.
> Therefore the Lord was angry with his people
>> and abhorred his inheritance.
> He gave them into the hands of the nations,
>> and their foes ruled over them. (34–41)

The whole Exodus narrative has a triumphant and a tragic side. It is both a story of liberation and a story of passion. Liberation and passion belong inextricably together. Goethe identified this tension as the conflict of belief and disbelief. Freud saw in it the ambivalence of the father-son relationship and diagnosed monotheism as a collective neurosis. Neither Goethe nor Freud, however, were careful readers of the Bible; neither of them was interested in an exegesis of the biblical text. This was the merit of Sellin, who as an Old Testament scholar was able to reconstruct from a plethora of biblical passages a thick and well-attested tradition about the suffering servants of God, from Moses to Jesus, both of whom, one might add, appear in Christian tradition as liberators and as sufferers, as "men of sorrows." That this line of tradition, however, is not a purely Christian construction has been shown by Steck, who was able to adduce an additional plethora of references from extrabiblical Jewish sources. Jesus and his followers were firmly rooted in Jewish tradition when they interpreted the figure and fate of Jesus in the light of the passion narrative, seeing in Jesus both a second Moses and the paradigmatic suffering servant.

It is revelatory to read Sellin's book—which met with very little approval in its time and was soon forgotten—in the light of Freud. Freud—without fairly acknowledging this most important source—brings to the fore its central theme, which is the pathogeny of monotheism that we find already in Sellin but without the unfortunate mythology of the primal horde. Sellin's book deserves a better fate than surviving in a footnote of Freud's book (where he appears as "Ed. Sellin") and in footnotes of books on Freud. It is much more important for the theory of religion, especially of monotheism, than one would have guessed before Freud exploited it in his way.

Notes

1 Sigmund Freud, *Moses and Monotheism*, in *The Standard Edition of the Complete Works of Sigmund Freud*, trans. James Strachey, London 1953–74, vol. 23, 80. Subsequent references to the *Standard Edition* are cited parenthetically in the text as SE.

2 Sigmund Freud to Arnold Zweig, Sept. 9, 1934, in *The Letters of Sigmund Freud*, trans. W. D. Robson-Scott, London 1970, 91. For Freud to Lou Andreas-Salomé, Jan. 1, 1935, see Ilse Grubrich-Simitis, *Freuds Moses-Studie als Tagtraum*, Verlag Psychoanalyse, Weinheim 1991, 21–24.

3 Johann Wolfgang von Goethe, "Israel in der Wüste," in *West-östlicher Divan*, ed. Hendrik Birus, Berlin 2010, 229–248.

4 Ibid., 230 (my translation).

5 The tragic aspect of Moses does not seem to have played any role in the tragedy *Exagoge* by Ezekiel the Tragedian, because this drama was based on Exodus 1–15, in which the scenes of rebellion have not yet set in.

6 Ernst Sellin, *Mose und seine Bedeutung für die israelitisch-jüdische Religionsgeschichte*, Erlangen 1922; cf. also id., "Hosea und das Martyrium des Mose," in *Zeitschrift für die alttestamentliche Wissenschaft* 46, 1928, 26–33.

7 "Hosea kennt die Fortsetzung von Num 25,3,5 noch in ihrer ursprünglichen Gestalt, er weiß, daß Mose in Schittim, im Heiligtum seines Gottes, von seinem eigenen Volke nach dessen Abfall zum Baal Peor, wegen dessen er es zur Buße gerufen und jedenfalls Sühne verlangt hat, hinterlistig getötet ist. Mit ihm haben vielleicht seine Söhne den Tod erleiden müssen. Das Ganze ist eine tragische, ergreifende Schilderung sondergleichen." Sellin, *Mose*, 49–50 (my translation).

8 "Wir können von vornherein nur damit rechnen, daß bald hie bald da einmal ein Funke wieder auftaucht von dem Geistesbrande, den er einst entzündet hat, daß seine Ideen nicht ganz ausgestorben, sondern hie und da auf Sitte und Glauben eingewirkt haben, bis sie etwa früher oder später unter der Einwirkung besonderer Erlebnisse oder von seinem Geiste besonders erfasster Persönlichkeiten einmal wieder stärker hervorbrachen und Einfluss gewannen auf breite Volksmassen." Ibid., 52–53 (my translation).

9 "Die Moses-Religion war aber nicht spurlos untergegangen, eine Art Erinnerung an sie hatte sich erhalten, verdunkelt und entstellt, vielleicht bei einzelnen Mitgliedern der Priesterkaste durch alte Aufzeichnungen gestützt. Und diese Tradition einer großen Vergangenheit war es, die aus dem Hintergrunde gleichsam zu wirken fortfuhr, allmählich immer mehr Macht über die Geister gewann und es endlich erreichte, den Gott Jahve in den Gott Moses' zu verwandeln und die vor langen Jahrhunderten eingesetzte und dann verlassene Religion Moses' wieder zum Leben zu

erwecken." Sigmund Freud, *Der Mann Moses und die monotheistische Religion. Drei Abhandlungen* (1939), ed. Jan Assmann, Stuttgart 2010, 152.

[10] Sellin, *Mose*, 124.

[11] Klaus Baltzer, *Deutero-Jesaja: Kommentar zum Alten Testament*, Gütersloh 1999.

[12] Odil Hannes Steck, *Israel und das gewaltsame Geschick der Propheten: Untersuchungen zur Überlieferung des deuteronomistischen Geschichtsbildes im Alten Testament, Spätjudentum und Urchristentum*, WMANT 23, Neukirchen-Vluyn 1967.

[13] Ibid., 63–64:

> A Das widerspenstige, ungehorsame Volk,
> B durch Propheten zur Umkehr ermahnt,
> C blieb halsstarrig/C1 tötete die Propheten
> D und zog sich die Strafe Gottes zu.

[14] For a more detailed exposition of this interpretation of biblical history, see my book *Exodus: Die Revolution der Alten Welt*, Munich 2015; translated into English by Robert Savage as *The Invention of Religion: Faith and Covenant in the Book of Exodus*, Princeton, NJ, 2018.

[15] This is presumably the first case of mountaineering for the view's sake in literary history, two thousand years before Petrarch climbed Mount Ventoux.

[16] Michael Walzer, *Exodus and Revolution*, New York 1985.

Ronald Hendel

7 Creating the Jews: Mosaic Discourse in Freud and Hosea

FOR A SCHOLAR of the Hebrew Bible, Freud's _Moses and Monotheism_ is an oddity. As Yosef Yerushalmi states, "it has been rejected almost unanimously by biblical scholars as an arbitrary manipulation of dubious historical data," a judgment that, he adds, is "quite correct."[1] Within the field of biblical scholarship, William F. Albright's comment in 1940 is characteristic: "[Freud's] new book is totally devoid of serious historical method and deals with historical data . . . cavalierly."[2] More recently, William Propp writes in his Exodus commentary, "[Freud] was confecting fantastic pseudo-history, midrash if you like, both to legitimate a theory of religion's bloody origins and to work out a life-long conflict over his own Jewish heritage."[3] Among specialists, the book is rightly regarded as an eccentric failure.

Yet we still read Freud's book. As Propp hints, it is not the "fantastic pseudo-history" that makes the book resonant but the way that Freud deals with his "conflict over his own Jewish heritage." As Jan Assmann observes, "One reason readers are still fascinated by Freud's book is the unmistakable fact that it is itself written out of fascination, even obsession."[4] With what is Freud obsessed? Nothing less than the sources of religion and intellectuality, the origins of Judaism, and the motives for anti-Semitism.

Freud described an early version of his book in a letter to Arnold Zweig on September 30, 1934, one month after Hitler was elected as Germany's president:

> The starting point of my work is known to you. . . . Faced with the new persecutions, one asks oneself again how the Jews have come to be what they are and why they have attracted this undying hatred. I soon discovered the formula: Moses created the Jews. So I gave my work the title: *The Man Moses, an Historical Novel* [*Der Mann Moses, ein historischer Roman*]. . . . The material fits into three sections. The first part is like an interesting novel; the second is laborious and boring; the third is full of content and makes exacting reading. The whole enterprise broke down on this third section, for it involved a theory of religion—certainly nothing new for me after *Totem and Taboo*, but something new and fundamental for the uninitiated.[5]

Here we have the main themes of *Moses and Monotheism*: "how the Jews have come to be what they are" (*wie der Jude geworden ist*), "why they have attracted this undying hatred" (*warum er sich diesen unsterblichen Hass zugezogen hat*), and "a theory of religion" (*eine Theorie der Religion*). These are large and complex concerns. For Freud, the weight of these themes became evident in the context of Nazi persecution, which threatened his life and legacy. These issues—or obsessions—are still with us today. This is why we still read Freud's *Moses*. It is not simply that Freud is a towering intellectual father-figure with whom we must contend. It is because the issues that he raises—often unsatisfactorily—will not go away. And so we read a deeply flawed but fascinating book.

In my engagement with Freud's book, I have two aims. One is to clarify the basis for his "fantastic pseudo-history" in the work of the Berlin biblical scholar Ernst Sellin, whose short book *Moses and His Meaning for the History of Israelite-Jewish Religion* (*Mose und seine Bedeutung für die israelitische-jüdische Religionsgeschichte*, 1922) is the source for Freud's theory of Moses's violent death. The second is to reanalyze some texts of the prophet Hosea that are the basis of Sellin's and Freud's theory of Moses-cide. I submit that Hosea's discourse about Moses and monotheism—what I call his Mosaic discourse—is, when read attentively, far more interesting than Sellin's and Freud's fantastic conjecture. Hosea is a puzzling and generative text, which in unexpected ways illuminates Freud's formula "Moses created the Jews" (*Moses hat den Juden geschaffen*).

My remarks will, I hope, clarify and confirm Assmann's recommendation about how best to explore the issues that Freud raises:

> What Freud unearths and dramatizes as a revelation is not the historical truth, but merely some theoretical constructs that turn out to be superfluous. The truth can be found in the [biblical] texts themselves. They speak of memory, remembrance, forgetting, and the repressed, of trauma and guilt. In order to uncover this network of meanings we have no need to practice the hermeneutics of suspicion; nor need we read these texts against the grain. We need only listen to them attentively.[6]

The plain sense of the biblical texts, when read patiently, is all we need to discern the web of trauma, guilt, and remembrance that Freud sought to reveal with his pseudohistory. It is not the murder of Moses but the effects of what I call Mosaic discourse that, in a Freudian sense, created the Jews.

Freud's (and Sellin's) Moses

IN THE SECOND essay of *Moses and Monotheism*—the part that Freud characterizes as "laborious and boring" (i.e., historical scholarship)[7]—he writes,

> In 1922, Ernst Sellin made a discovery which affected our problem decisively. He found in the Prophet Hosea (in the second half of the eighth century B.C.) unmistakable signs of a tradition to the effect that Moses, the founder of their religion, met with a violent end in a rising of his refractory and stiff-necked people, and that at the same time the religion he had introduced was thrown off. This tradition is not, however, restricted to Hosea; it reappears in most of the later Prophets, and indeed, according to Sellin, became the basis of all the later Messianic expectations.[8]

This report of Sellin's "discovery" (*Entdeckung*) based on "unmistakable signs" (*unverkennbaren Anzeichen*) is a turning point in Freud's book. It provides, in his view, a scientific basis for his theory. In a prefatory note to the third essay, he emphasizes the importance of Sellin's discovery for the whole project:

> To my critical sense this book, which takes its start from the man Moses, appears like a dancer balancing on the tip of one toe. If I could not find support in an analytical interpretation of the exposure myth and could not pass from there to Sellin's suspicion about the end of Moses, the whole thing would have had to remain unwritten.[9]

Without Sellin's theory, the treatise—"like a dancer balancing on the tip of one toe" (*wie eine Tänzerin, die auf einer Zehenspitze balanciert*)—would doubtless tumble.

However, as scholars have long pointed out, Sellin's proposal is untenable. As Assmann comments, "[Sellin's] construction is as fantastic as Freud's."[10] Sellin, a distinguished biblical scholar at the University of Berlin, had a tendency to make daring textual emendations. In a 1940 review of Freud's book, the biblical scholar Philip Hyatt states, "Sellin's theory rests on very doubtful textual emendations and has not commanded the respect of other scholars. It is highly speculative, not to say fantastic."[11] Just so. The historian Salo Baron indicated in his 1939 review that even Sellin was having second thoughts: "the violent death of Moses [is no] more than a farfetched hypothesis, largely given up by its author and shared by no other biblical scholar."[12]

If Sellin's theory was so dubious, why did Freud adopt his theory? Surely to do so was, as he seems to admit, like building "a bronze statue with feet of clay" (*ein ehernes Bild auf tönernen Füssen*).[13] The answer, as he hinted in his letter to Zweig, involves his theory of religion in *Totem and Taboo*, which posits a primeval murder of the father. The murder of Moses is, in Freud's new theory, a historical instantiation of the primeval parricide and provides the basis for the peculiar character of biblical monotheism and Judaism. The violent death of Moses—and its concomitant guilt, repression, and return—is the key to Freud's historical and psychoanalytical narrative. As Freud summarizes his theory in the third essay,

> It would be worthwhile to understand how it was that the monotheist idea made such a deep impression precisely on the Jewish people and that they were able to maintain it so tenaciously. It is possible, I think, to find an answer. Fate had brought the great deed and misdeed of primeval days, the killing of the father, closer to the Jewish people by causing them to repeat it on the person of Moses, an outstanding father-figure. It was a case of "acting out" instead of remembering.[14]

After his primeval parricide theory in *Totem and Taboo*, Freud had a natural affinity for Sellin's theory of Moses-cide.

In Freud's exposition in *Moses and Monotheism*, he makes a concerted effort to present Sellin's theory in the best light. He repeatedly makes what Richard Bernstein calls a "slide from conjecture to established conclusion."[15] In doing so, Freud admits his own amateur status as a biblical critic while positioning Sellin as an objective authority. He writes, "I am not, of course, in a position to judge whether Sellin has interpreted the passages from the Prophets correctly."[16] After this honest admission, he continues, "We will borrow from Sellin his hypothesis that the Egyptian Moses was murdered by the Jews and the religion he had introduced abandoned. This allows us to spin our threads further without contradicting the trustworthy findings of historical research."[17] By this rhetorical "slide," Freud turns Sellin's "hypothesis" (*Annahme*) into the "trustworthy findings of historical research" (*glaubwürdigen Ergebnissen der historischen Forschung*). This enables Freud to elaborate his theory on a firm foundation. Here we see Freud's skill as a persuasive "historical novelist" (as he describes his project in the letter to Zweig, quoted earlier), a trait that is not, of course, absent from the rhetoric of professional historians.

This brings us back to Sellin. Sellin's theory rests on a few verses in Hosea that announce Israel's punishment for its "great iniquity" (Hosea 9:7). Sellin's conclusion, that the great iniquity was the murder of Moses, relies on his textual reconstruction and interpretation of Hosea 12:15a + 13:1 + 12:15b.[18] (Sellin reordered this sequence, inserting verse 13:1 into the middle of 12:15.) These verses are notoriously difficult and probably have suffered textual damage. Sellin's daring—and dubious—restoration of the text is as follows. (I have marked his emendations with brackets and his interpretation of the referents of the pronouns "he," "his," and "him" with parentheses.)

> 12:15a Ephraim provoked [him] (Moses),
> [Israel embittered him] (Moses).
> 13:1 As long as Ephraim spoke [my law],
> he (Moses) was [a prince] in Israel,
> but he (Moses) atoned because of Baal and was killed.
> 12:15b His (Moses's) blood, [I] will leave on [you] (Ephraim),
> and will bring upon [you] (Ephraim) his (Moses's) disgrace.

There are at least four problems with Sellin's reconstruction of these verses.

1. This is not the actual sequence of the text (12:15a + 13:1 + 12:15b), and there is no plausible reason to change the order in this way. Hosea 13:1 begins a new poetic unit and is editorially (viz. secondarily) appended to 12:15,[19] which concludes the divine "indictment" in Hosea 12. (See my translation of these verses below.)

2. Moses is not named in these verses; the subject in both is explicitly Ephraim. Moses is only implied if one accepts a series of arbitrary emendations: from "lifted, exalted" (נשא) to "prince" (נשיא); from "he provoked" (הכעיס) to "he provoked him" (הכעיסו); and from "bitterness" (תמרורים) to "embittered him" (ומררו). However, Moses is nowhere called a "prince," and there is no reason to supply the additional pronominal suffixes. These are unwarranted emendations and conjectures. In sum, there is no reason, grammatical or semantic, to take the pronouns ("he," "his," "him") as referring to anyone other than Ephraim. Similarly, there is no reason to change two of the pronominal suffixes in 12:15b to "you" in order to make a distinction between "him" (Moses) and "you" (Ephraim).

3. To translate ויאשם as "he atoned" in 13:1 is also unwarranted, since the verb nowhere has this meaning. Elsewhere it means "he became guilty." Similarly, to translate וימת as "he was killed" is unwarranted, since it always means "he died."

4. By emending and translating the text in this fashion, Sellin ignores (and eliminates) the poetic parallelism in both verses.

The following is my translation of these verses, which is equivalent to most modern treatments. While I grant that the text is corrupt in parts, I see no compelling preferable readings, so the text is that of the Masoretic Text.[20]

> [12:15] Ephraim has caused bitter provocation,
>   and the bloodguilt that is on him he leaves alone;
>   and his Lord will bring upon him his reproach.

^{13:1} When Ephraim spoke, trembling (?),²¹

he was exalted in Israel,

then he became guilty through Baal, and he died.

These lines are fairly obscure, but it is obvious they address Ephraim's (= Israel's) transgressions and guilt. The mentions of "his bloodguilt" (דמיו) in 12:15 and "he died" (וימת) in 13:1 are obscure and intriguing. On Ephraim's parallel transgressions in 12:15—"provocation," "bloodguilt," and "reproach"—Graham Davies's comments are apt:

> The nature of the *provocation* remains obscure, but the terms *bloodguilt* and *reproaches* are perhaps more specific than is usually recognized. On the one hand, while Hosea repeatedly condemns murder (1:4; 4:2; 7:7), one passage specifically links this charge with Gilead (6:8–9), mentioned above for its *iniquity* (12:12). On the other hand, *reproaches* are most likely to have been directed against Yahweh and as such recall the treatment of his prophets in 9:7–8.²²

In Hosea, Ephraim's transgressions are abundant. Most intriguing is the last line of 13:1, "Then he became guilty through [or "at"] Baal and he died." The guilt associated with Baal has multiple resonances, including the worship of local Baals (see Hosea 2:10, 18) and, perhaps more precisely, the incident at Baal Peor, where Israel worshiped the "Baal of Peor" (see Hosea 9:10, Numbers 25:1–3). The past death of Ephraim ("he died") as a consequence of serving Baal is arguably an ascription of social or moral death, a meriting of death, rather than an actual death. In prophetic retrospect, "he died" suggests that he earned death through his apostasy.

The following verses in Hosea 13 expand on the themes of Ephraim's apostasy and death, including harrowing descriptions of Yahweh's impending judgment:

> I will attack them like a bear deprived of her young,

I will rip open the covering of their hearts.
I will devour them like a lion,
The beasts of the field shall tear them. (Hosea 13:8)

In these texts, the themes of transgression, judgment, guilt, trauma, and death are explicit. There is no need for drastic emendation to uncover hidden crimes and punishments. The psychological complexity of the manifest text is plain to see, as I will elucidate shortly.

In the allusive network of Hosea's poetry, there are no "unmistakable signs" of the violent death of Moses. Sellin has turned some obscure biblical poetry into a historicizing Bible code. We can easily see why Hyatt describes Sellin's theory as "highly speculative, not to say fantastic."[23] Within biblical scholarship, Sellin's theory has been forgotten, for good reason.

Sellin's theory ultimately reflects his predilection to historicize Christian typology in his biblical exegesis. As the biblical scholar André Caquot comments, "it is not possible to ignore the Christian roots of Sellin's ideas, which in this way found in Moses the prototype of the mysterious suffering characters of whom the prophetic literature speaks."[24] These suffering characters include the "suffering servant" in Second Isaiah and ultimately Jesus Christ. The idea of Moses as a martyr, killed by the Jews, directly anticipates the salvific martyrdom of Christ. As Sellin writes in his history of Israel, written shortly after his Moses book,

[Moses] was murdered by his own people as a martyr for his faith, and this remained unforgotten in the circle of his followers. While Hosea simply stated that this unexpiated crime was the pinnacle of all the sins of Israel, which would now inevitably bring judgment in its wake (9:7, 11f., 12:15), the idea gradually formed that Moses, the most humble of all men (Num. 12:3), offered himself willingly as an expiating sacrifice. . . . With him, a great one passed through history, who won not only significance for his own people, but for all mankind, one far greater than most people could dream.[25]

As we can see, Sellin's theory and textual analysis are grounded in his apologetic orientation. In sum, there is nothing remotely plausible about Sellin's (and Freud's) conjectural history of Moses.

Hosea's Moses

LET US TURN to Hosea's history of Moses. I submit that there is no need to infer a secret history of Moses in order to understand Hosea's text. The plain sense suffices. There is only one place where Hosea refers to Moses, in a remarkable poetic unit that juxtaposes Jacob and Moses:

> Jacob fled to the fields of Aram,
> Israel served for a wife,
> and for a wife he guarded.
> By a prophet Yahweh brought up Israel from Egypt,
> and by a prophet he was guarded. (Hosea 12:13–14)

The context of this sequence in Hosea 12 is Yahweh's "indictment" (ריב, 12:3) against Israel, based on Ephraim/Israel's misdeeds. The story of Jacob (= Israel) is invoked as an ancestral charter for Israel's shady deeds, since Jacob is often an equivocal character. The nuances of Hosea's use of the Jacob story are hard to follow, but it clearly uses Jacob's flight to Aram and his servitude for a wife (v. 13) as a negative foil to Israel's exodus from Egypt (v. 14). As Hans Walter Wolff writes, "Verse 14 is formulated in complete antithesis to v 13, and thus vv 13 and 14 form a rhetorical unit."[26] The unnamed prophet in verse 14 who brings the Israelites up from Egypt and who "guards" them afterward is clearly Moses, who in some way is compared to Jacob.

There are several intersecting layers of meaning in these verses, which combine in a poetic articulation of Hosea's view of Moses. The terseness of the narrative details indicates that Hosea is mobilizing well-known traditions, activating his audience's tacit knowledge, which the prophet interprets to make his points.

Formally, the text comprises two parallelistic verses—a triplet and a doublet—that have numerous stylistic and semantic parallels across the verses. These interverse parallels and contrasts elucidate the textual nuances by indirection and allusion, what we may call the poetics of juxtaposition. This is most evident in the last lines of the two verses, which echo each other formally, semantically, and rhythmically: "and for a wife he guarded" (ובאשה שמר); "and by a prophet he was guarded" (בנביא נשמר).

The first lines of each verse juxtapose Jacob's flight to Aram with Yahweh's and the prophet's deliverance of Israel from Egypt. These are two journeys with different connotations. "Jacob," which is internally parallel to "Israel" (v. 13b), is distantly parallel to "Israel" in verse 14, with the latter shifted semantically and grammatically to the collective people as direct object. As the agent of the action, Jacob is juxtaposed with the "prophet" in verse 14. The focus on these two agents is emphasized by the repeated internal parallelism (Jacob/Israel; prophet/prophet). The actions of these agents—"flight" versus "bringing up"—is morally weighted against Jacob, since flight has the connotation of fear and cowardice, whereas leading the Israelites out of Egypt has a wholly positive connotation. In the focalized contrast of Jacob and the prophet, the former is subtly denigrated while the latter is exalted.

The same contrastive coloring obtains in the other lines of the two verses. In verse 13b, "Israel served" (ויעבד ישראל) is parallel to "he guarded" (שמר), and both have the same object, "for a wife" (באשה). This obviously refers to the story of Jacob becoming an indentured servant in Aram to his uncle Laban, "guarding" sheep as a bride-price for Rachel. In this verse's juxtaposition with verse 14, each of these terms takes on a different nuance. "Israel served," in the context of the Exodus, evokes Israel's slavery to Pharaoh. In this juxtaposition, Israel "serving" for a wife takes on a derogatory connotation.

The verb in verse 13b, "he guarded" (שמר), is parallel across the verses to verse 14b, "he (viz. Israel) was guarded" (נשמר). Jacob/

Israel's act of shepherding is parallel to the metaphorical shepherding of Israel by Moses. Moses was a former shepherd, but he now has a people as his flock. Jacob's "guarding" is denigrated by comparison, since it is an act of servitude. Moses's "guarding," in contrast, is a salvific act.

The motive for Jacob's servitude is the twice-repeated phrase "for a wife" (באשה באשה). This is formally and grammatically parallel with the twice-repeated phrase in verse 14, "by a prophet" (בנביא . . . בנביא). The last line of each verse, as noted earlier, constitutes a striking interverse parallel: "and for a wife he guarded" // "and by a prophet he was guarded." It is not immediately clear what this juxtaposition entails, but obviously the latter image— Israel guarded by Moses—trumps Jacob/Israel guarding for a wife.

Outside the semantic frame of the narrative traditions, the contemporary theo-political resonances of these juxtapositions can, to some extent, be inferred. During the time of Hosea's prophecies (ca. 750–725 BCE), Israel's "flight" to Aram and his servitude there arguably have a political connotation. As Wolff suggests, "Jacob's flight to 'Aram' and his work in the capacity of servant . . . might allude to Israel's submission to foreign powers."[27] The foreign power that Israel "served" was Aram-Damascus, in an alliance of rebellion against Assyria. This is consonant with Hosea's critique of political alliances with Assyria and Egypt (see Hosea 5:13, 7:11, 12:2). These alliances concern events during and after the Syro-Ephraimite war (735–732 BCE), in which Israel was allied with Aram-Damascus. In this historical context, Edwin Good proposes that Jacob/Israel's "servitude in Aram" evokes the disastrous alliance with Aram-Damascus (see 2 Kings 16; Isaiah 7).[28] He aptly observes that "going into servitude for a woman is the same sort of ironic metaphor that Hosea uses elsewhere for Israel's politics."[29] Hence, in Hosea's allusion to these details in the Jacob story, Israel's recent misdeeds are mirrored by Jacob's servitude in the ancestral past.

Erhard Blum has recently advanced additional arguments for this interpretation, noting that the destruction of Gilead and Gilgal in verse 12 probably reflects the Assyrian campaign of 733/732 BCE.[30] The line "their altars are like heaps [גלים] on the furrows of the fields [שדי]" arguably evokes the treaty between Jacob and Laban in Gilead (see Gen. 31:47, where Jacob calls the place גלעד, "heap of witness"), and provides a linking-word to the "fields (שדה) of Aram" in v. 13. As Blum observes, "Since [verse 12] is followed immediately by the name of the place to which Jacob fled, 'fields of Aram' (not 'to Laban'), and the text speaks of Israel's dependency (עבד) there, the contemporary reader cannot but think of the recent history of catastrophic events, namely, Israel's role as a junior partner in a pact with Damascus against Assyria."[31] This resonance coheres with the negative sense of Jacob's servitude in Aram in Hosea's poetry.

The deliverance and protection of Israel by Yahweh and his prophet is the positive foil to Jacob/Israel's alliance in Aram. The latter is colored negatively, both in the ancestral past and in its reflection in recent historical memory. Within the semantic frame of the narrative details, the prophet is clearly Moses. But in the theo-political semantics outside the stories, the prophet is clearly Hosea, who "guards" and criticizes his people. He is the prophet whom Yahweh appointed in the present age to instruct and judge the people. By drawing out these nuances, we can see the prophet's rhetorical strategy in *not* naming Moses. The title "a prophet" refers to Moses and Hosea. By this fruitful doubling, Hosea's discourse presents himself as the contemporary correlate of Moses, as a Mosaic prophet. The juxtaposition of narrative traditions serves to elucidate Israel's misdeeds *and* the abiding authority of the prophet, then and now.[32] The elevation of the Mosaic prophet includes his present successor, Hosea.

Both within and beyond the narrative frame, Hosea's poetry is a Mosaic discourse. The verse invokes Moses and the Exodus narrative, and it places Hosea—and his words—in the role of Mosaic prophet. It is also a Mosaic discourse in a broader sense, in that prophecy here presents itself as Mosaic; it is, as Hindy Najman states, "discourse tied to a founder."[33] Hosea speaks in his own name, not in Moses's name (as occurs in other biblical and post-biblical books of "Mosaic discourse," such as Deuteronomy and Jubilees). But he speaks in the conceptual space of Moses's authorial function as the authoritative prophet.[34]

In this sense, Hosea's Moses is not merely a figure in the past but is a discursive force in the present. I suggest that Hosea's Moses—as the source of Mosaic discourse—is a more apt focus for Freud's questions than his (and Sellin's) conjectural life of Moses. Guilt, remorse, anxiety, forgiveness, death, cathexis—all of these are expressed in the Mosaic discourse of Hosea and other classical prophets. It interpellates the people and shapes their moral consciousness. The force of this Mosaic discourse corresponds to what Freud calls the superego (*Über-Ich*), the agency "which confronts the rest of the ego in an observing, criticizing and prohibiting sense."[35] This is precisely the role of Mosaic discourse. When Freud writes, "the ego is apprehensive about risking the love of its supreme master; it feels his approval as liberation and satisfaction and his reproaches as pangs of conscience,"[36] this is precisely the discursive orientation of the book of Hosea and the effect of Mosaic prophecy.

When Hosea reports that God commanded him to marry a prostitute, to signify Israel's "whoring" after other gods, and to name his children "No Compassion" and "Not My People," his audience naturally feels guilt, pangs of conscience, anxiety, and remorse. When God changes the children's names to "Compassion" and "My People," the auditors naturally feel relief and cathexis (see Hosea 1–3). Freud's analytical categories are fruitful for the work of Hosea's Mosaic discourse. There is no need to posit a secret or repressed text. The Mosaic discourse is present in the plain sense of the biblical text.

Conclusions: Mosaic Discourse and Monotheism

FREUD'S THEORY THAT "Moses created the Jews"[37] rests on the untenable premise of the historical martyrdom of Moses, which was repressed in collective memory and returned to group consciousness in distorted form. As Assmann summarizes, "he identifies . . . Mosaic monotheism, as a neurotic compulsion centered on a complex of guilt."[38] Freud's historical conjectures are unwarranted. But his psychological categories may yet be fruitful for these issues if we reorient the analysis. The subject should not be the historical Moses, to which we have little or no access.[39] It should be to Mosaic discourse, to which we have ample access. As Assmann writes, "The truth can be found in the [biblical] texts themselves."[40] In so doing, we take the good doctor's own advice: "it is a good rule in the work of analysis to be content to explain what is actually before one and not to seek to explain what has *not* happened."[41]

Freud based his pseudohistory of Moses on Sellin's untenable analysis of Hosea. But if we take Hosea's Moses—not Freud's or Sellin's Moses—as our starting point, we may be able to advance Freud's project. I suggest that Mosaic discourse created the Jews. It was the pedagogue, or the collective superego, that molded an ancient tribal people into the Jewish people. Let me outline what the form of this neo- or post-Freudian argument might look like.

1. Mosaic discourse, that is, prophetic discourse, functions as a collective superego, an authoritative Mosaic voice that is over the self. As Hosea illustrates, Israel's response to Mosaic discourse constitutes the Jewish conscience, and its rejection of Mosaic discourse causes Jewish guilt.[42]

2. Mosaic discourse defines Israel as God's chosen people, which entails obeying Mosaic discourse. But since Israel rejects Mosaic discourse (see number 1), the doctrine of chosenness is a proximate cause of Jewish guilt. It is also, as Freud observes, a proximate cause of anti-Semitism, since it marks an ethnic

boundary between Jews and gentiles, which attracts the ani-
mus of "the narcissism of small differences" (*der Narzissmus der
kleinen Differenzen*).[43]

3. Mosaic discourse criticizes the practices of traditional Israelite
   religion and proclaims its laws and ethics as a substitute. This
   critique and revision of tradition constitutes what Freud calls
   "the advance of intellectuality" (*der Fortschritt in der Geistigkeit*)
   in Judaism.[44] It is also the intellectual-spiritual formation
   of monotheism. The internal arguments within Mosaic
   discourse—for example, the laws in Deuteronomy versus the
   laws in Exodus-Leviticus, or the theodicy of Isaiah versus
   Ezekiel—spur the advance of intellectuality into the postbiblical phenomenon of close textual interpretation and analysis.

4. Freudian discourse is a secular transformation of Mosaic
   discourse[45]—one of many such discursive transformations in
   the modern world.

The first three of these propositions are derivable from an
attentive reading of Hosea's Mosaic discourse, such as the following haunting text:

> When Ephraim multiplied altars for sin (offerings),
> they became for him altars of sinning.
> I wrote for him my multiple instructions,
> but they are regarded as strange things.
> They offer choice sacrifices,
> they eat flesh,
> but Yahweh does not accept them.
> Now He will remember their iniquity,
> and punish their sins;
> they shall return to Egypt. (Hosea 8:11–13)

These accusations and judgments—the people's apostasy, its
estrangement of the law, the proclamation of aniconic monotheism, the rejection of ritual practices, the emphasis on repetition
and remembrance, the return to bondage—are all exemplary
Freudian themes. Trauma and guilt, memory and anxiety, text

and transgression circulate in these prophetic indictments, creating the conditions of a complicated Jewish subjectivity, including the compulsion to engage with the text that creates these conditions. Mosaic discourse comprises all of these, not as latent but as manifest content.

A return to the biblical text holds promise for increasing our grasp on the problems Freud was compelled to face, including "how the Jews have come to be what they are," "why they have attracted this undying hatred," and "a theory of religion."[46] The answers Freud gave in his book are dubious and perhaps forgettable, but the questions he addressed remain pertinent and will not easily go away.

Notes

[1] Yosef H. Yerushalmi, *Freud's Moses: Judaism Terminable and Interminable* (New Haven, CT: Yale University Press, 1991), 2.

[2] William F. Albright, *From the Stone Age to Christianity: Monotheism and the Historical Process* (Baltimore: Johns Hopkins University Press, 1940), 75 (wording unchanged in the 1957 edition).

[3] William H. C. Propp, *Exodus 19–40*, Anchor Bible 2A (New York: Doubleday, 2006), 764.

[4] Jan Assmann, *Moses the Egyptian: The Memory of Egypt in Western Monotheism* (Cambridge, MA: Harvard University Press, 1997), 147.

[5] Freud to Zweig, September 30, 1934, *The Letters of Sigmund Freud and Arnold Zweig*, ed. Ernst L. Freud, trans. E. Robson-Scott and W. Robson-Scott (London: Hogarth, 1970), 102 = *Briefwechsel*, ed. Ernst L. Freud (Frankfurt am Main: Fischer, 1968), 91. This letter is often quoted in the literature; see Michel de Certeau, *The Writing of History*, trans. T. Conley (New York: Columbia University Press, 1988), 309–310; Yerushalmi, *Freud's Moses*, 16; Bluma Goldstein, *Reinscribing Moses: Heine, Kafka, Freud, and Schoenberg in a European Wilderness* (Cambridge, MA: Harvard University Press, 1992), 93, 96; Richard J. Bernstein, *Freud and the Legacy of Moses* (Cambridge: Cambridge University Press, 1998), 24–25.

[6] Jan Assmann, "Monotheism, Memory, and Trauma: Reflections on Freud's Book on Moses," in *Religion and Cultural Memory: Ten Studies*, trans. R. Livingstone (Stanford, CA: Stanford University Press, 2006), 51–52 (translation slightly adjusted).

7 This essay, "Wenn Moses ein Ägypter war . . . ," was first published in *Imago* 23 (1937), 387–419.

8 Sigmund Freud, *Moses and Monotheism*, in *The Standard Edition of the Complete Psychological Works of Sigmund Freud*, vol. 23, *1937–1939*, trans. and ed. James Strachey (London: Hogarth, 1964), 36 = Freud, *Der Mann Moses und die monotheistische Religion: Drei Abhandlungen* (Amsterdam: de Lange, 1939), 63–64. These sources are hereafter abbreviated *SE* and *MM*.

9 *SE*, 58 = *MM*, 104.

10 Jan Assmann, "Freud, Sellin, and the Murder of Moses," chapter 6 in this volume.

11 J. Philip Hyatt, "Freud on Moses and the Genesis of Monotheism," *Journal of Bible and Religion* 8 (1940), 88.

12 Salo Baron, review of *Moses and Monotheism*, *American Journal of Sociology* 45 (1939), 476.

13 *SE*, 17 = *MM*, 30. Freud previously used this metaphor in a letter to Zweig; see Yerushalmi, *Freud's Moses*, 21–22; Bernstein, *Freud*, 22–25.

14 *SE*, 88–89 = *MM*, 159–160.

15 Bernstein, *Freud*, 20; see also ibid., 127n16.

16 *SE*, 37 = *MM*, 64.

17 *SE*, 37 (translation slightly adjusted) = *MM*, 64–65.

18 Ernst Sellin, *Mose und seine Bedeutung für die israelitisch-jüdische Religionsgeschichte* (Leipzig: Deichert, 1922), 50–51. Sellin made other small changes in his subsequent treatments: idem, "Hosea und das Martyrium des Mose," *Zeitschrift für die Alttestamentliche Wissenschaft und die Kunde des Nachbiblischen Judentums* (1928): 26–32; idem, *Das Zwölfprophetenbuch*, 2nd ed. (Leipzig: Deichert, 1929), 120, 126–128.

19 See, e.g., Hans Walter Wolff, *Hosea*, Hermeneia (Philadelphia: Fortress, 1974), 222–224; Francis I. Andersen and David Noel Freedman, *Hosea*, Anchor Bible (Garden City, NY: Doubleday, 1980), 622, 626; Graham I. Davies, *Hosea*, New Century Bible (Grand Rapids, MI: Eerdmans, 1992), 284–285; Marvin A. Sweeney, *The Twelve Prophets*, vol. 1, *Hosea, Joel, Amos, Obadiah, Jonah*, Berit Olam (Collegeville, MN: Liturgical, 2000), 129.

20 The textual data and proposals are presented in Wolff, *Hosea*, 219; and astutely weighed by Davies, *Hosea*, 286.

21 The word רתת means "trembling, fear," but occurs only here in the Hebrew Bible. It is possibly a textual corruption. Sellin emends it to תרתי (my Law), relying on the Septuagint translation, δικαιώματα (statutes), which may reflect Hebrew תר(ו)ת.

22 Davies, *Hosea*, 284.

23 See note 11 above; see also the politely negative reviews by his German colleagues Paul Volz in *Theologische Literaturzeitung* 48 (1923), 433–435; Otto Procksch in *Theologisches Literaturblatt* 45 (1924), 69; and similarly Hermann Gunkel, "Mose," in *Die Religion in Geschichte und Gegenwart*, 2nd ed. (Tübingen: Mohr, 1930), 4.233: "The assertion of E. Sellin, that Moses had a martyr's death, is supported by doubtful interpretations and the rewriting of difficult prophetic texts, especially in Hosea, and remains in any case doubtful." See recently Ulrich Palmer, *Ernst Sellin— Alttestamentler und Archäologe. Mit einem Beitrag von Hermann Michael Niemann* (Frankfurt am Main: Lang, 2012), 135: "Sellin's book *Mose* caused quite a stir, but content-wise it was a . . . blunder."

24 André Caquot, "Presentation," in *The Seminar of Jacques Lacan: The Other Side of Psychoanalysis*, by Jacques Lacan, trans. R. Grigg (New York: Norton, 2007), 212.

25 Ernst Sellin, *Geschichte des israelitisch-jüdischen Volkes von den Anfängen bis zum babylonischen Exil* (Leipzig: Quelle and Meyer, 1924), 94.

26 Wolff, *Hosea*, 208.

27 Ibid., 216.

28 Edwin M. Good, "Hosea and the Jacob Tradition," *VT* 16 (1966), 147–149.

29 Ibid., 149.

30 Erhard Blum, "Hosea 12 und die Pentateuchüberlieferungen," in *Die Erzväter in der biblischen Tradition: Festschrift für Matthias Köckert*, ed. A. C. Hagedorn and H. Pfeiffer (Berlin: de Gruyter, 2009), 309–312.

31 Ibid., 310.

32 In light of this understanding, I cannot accept Arnold de Pury's proposal ("Osée 12 et ses implications pour le débat actuel sur le Pentateuque," in *Le Pentateuque: Débat et recherches*, ed. P. Haudebert [Paris: Cerf, 1992], 175–207) that Hosea's contrast between Jacob and Moses presents the two ancestral stories as rival legends of Israel's origin, based on two different conceptions of Israel's identity (viz. genealogical versus prophetic): "Hosea 12 . . . evokes two distinct traditions so as to oppose the one to the other. The patriarchal tradition is depreciated while the Mosaic tradition is valued. The addressees of the poem are themselves invited to decide between two legends of origin, to choose the one and reject the other" (206). See similarly Konrad Schmid, *Genesis and the Moses Story: Israel's Dual Origins in the Hebrew Bible*, trans. J. D. Nogalski (Winona Lake, IN: Eisenbrauns, 2010), 74–76 and references.

33 Hindy Najman, *Seconding Sinai: The Development of Mosaic Discourse in Second Temple Judaism* (Leiden: Brill, 2003), 13. I am using the term "Mosaic discourse" in a slightly different way than Najman does but am indebted to her discussion.

34 On the "author function," see Michel Foucault, "What Is an Author?," in *The Foucault Reader*, ed. P. Rabinow (New York: Pantheon, 1984), 101–120, esp. 107: "The author's name manifests the appearance of a certain discursive set and indicates the status of this discourse within a society and a culture." In Foucault's sense, Moses would be a legendary founder of a discursive practice (ibid., 113–117).

35 *SE*, 116 = *MM*, 207.

36 *SE*, 117 = *MM*, 207.

37 In the letter to Zweig, note 5 above; restated in *SE*, 106 = *MM*, 189.

38 Assmann, *Moses*, 166.

39 See Erhard Blum, "Der historische Mose und die Frühgeschichte Israels," *Hebrew Bible and Ancient Israel* 1 (2012), 37–63; Rudolf Smend, "Moses as a Historical Figure," in *"The Unconquered Land" and Other Old Testament Essays: Selected Studies by Rudolf Smend*, ed. E. Ball and M. Barker, trans. M. Kohl (Farnham, UK: Ashgate, 2013), 13–28; Ronald Hendel, *Remembering Abraham: Culture, Memory, and History in the Hebrew Bible* (New York: Oxford University Press, 2005), 67–71.

40 Assmann, "Monotheism," 51.

41 *SE*, 93 = *MM*, 167.

42 I am using "Jewish guilt" in a colloquial or Freudian sense, not in the traditional Christian meaning of Jewish guilt for deicide (Matthew 27:25, "His blood be on us and on our children"). The latter, of course, lies behind the problematic of *Totem and Taboo* and *Moses and Monotheism*.

43 Sigmund Freud, *Civilization and Its Discontents*, trans. and ed. James Strachey (New York: Norton, 1961), 72–73; cf. *SE*, 91 = *MM*, 163, on "the intolerance of groups . . . against small differences" (*die Intoleranz der Massen . . . gegen kleine Unterschiede*).

44 *SE*, 111–115 = *MM*, 197–204.

45 Cf. Yerushalmi, *Freud's Moses*, 99, where he attributes this to Freud's (unconscious?) intention: "you believed that psychoanalysis is itself a further, if not final, metamorphosed extension of Judaism, divested of its illusory religious forms."

46 See note 5 above.

Catherine Malabou

8 Is Psychic Phylogenesis Only a Phantasy? New Biological Developments in Trauma Inheritance

A fresh complication arises when we become aware of the probability that what may be operative in an individual's psychical life may include not only what he has experienced himself but also things that were innately present in him at his birth, elements with a phylogenetic origin—an archaic heritage. The questions then arise of what this consists in, what it contains and what is the evidence for it?
—Freud, *Moses and Monotheism* (98)

THE CONCLUSION OF the first part of the third essay of *Moses and Monotheism*, devoted to the issue of phylogenesis and transgenerational inheritance, is very striking.

Freud writes,

> On further reflection I must admit I have behaved for a long time as though the inheritance of memory-traces of the experience of our ancestors, independently of direct communication and of the influence of education by the setting of an example, were established beyond question. When I spoke of the survival of a tradition among a people or of the formation of a people's character,

I had mostly in mind an inherited tradition of this kind and not one transmitted by communication. . . . My position, no doubt, is made more difficult by the present attitude of biological science, which refuses to hear of the inheritance of acquired characters by succeeding generations. I must, however, in all modesty confess that nevertheless I cannot do without this factor in biological evolution. The same thing is not in question, indeed, in the two cases: in the one it is a matter of acquired characters which are hard to grasp, in the other of memory-traces of external events—something tangible, as it were. But it may be well that at the bottom we cannot imagine one without the other.

If we assume the survival of these memory-traces in the archaic heritage, we have bridged the gulf between individual and group psychology: we can deal with peoples as we do with an individual neurotic. Granted that at the time we have no stronger evidence for the presence of memory-traces in the archaic heritage than the residual phenomena of the work of analysis, which call for a phylogenetic derivation, yet this evidence seems to us strong enough to postulate that such is the fact. If it is not so, we shall not advance a step further along the path we entered on, either in analysis or in group psychology. The audacity cannot be avoided.[1]

This passage immediately resonates with a recent article published on 21 August 2015 in the *Guardian* and called "Study of Holocaust Survivors Finds Trauma Passed On to Children's Genes."[2] This article exposes the result of recent research on the part played by epigenetic inheritance in transgenerational trauma. The hypothesis of epigenetic trauma inheritance undoubtedly makes it possible to shed a new light on Freud's text by bringing together biological and psychic inheritance in a specific and promising way, thus opening unexplored paths for psychoanalysis. Such a thesis brings significant scientific confirmation of Freud's concept of phylogenesis. It confirms the possibility of transgenerational trauma inheritance. Children of psychically wounded people may suffer from stress or psychic trouble transmitted by their parents. In *Moses and Monotheism*, Freud is looking for an intermediary zone between the unpredictable dimension of history and the predictable dimension of biology, between absolute indeterminacy and total determinism. It seems that the existence of such a zone has been scientifically established today.

In a text from 2007, published in France and called "Phylogenesis and the Question of the Transgenerational," the psychoanalyst David Benhaïm declared that the disinterest of Freud's successors in the issue of phylogenesis has been practically total.[3] It seems there has been no other way, for a long time and until very recently, but to assimilate it with Lamarckism, as Freud himself admits it, that is, with the proven false idea of the inheritance and transmission of acquired characters. This explains why we find so few elaborations on it after Freud. Laplanche and Pontalis, for example, did not feel the need to create an entry for the term "phylogenesis" in their *Vocabulaire de la psychanalyse*. This, according to Benhaïm, was because they precisely doubted the accuracy of Freud's thesis on the matter.

Yet, as Benhaïm also argues, it is impossible to dismiss the phylogenetic argument without dismantling the whole psychoanalytic construction, as it constitutes a corner stone in Freud's approach to both the individual psyche and *Kultur*, or civilization. Freud defended the idea of phylogenesis all his life. It then seemed, for a long time, that the only solution for psychoanalysts was to consider it a helpful fantasy, something impossible to scientifically prove but endowed with a high heuristic and methodological value.

The theory of epigenetic inheritance precisely and currently allows us to put an end to such a hybrid and somehow monstrous status.

THE ARGUMENT OF phylogenesis, or phylogenetic inheritance, mainly appears in Freud's *Traumdeutung* (chap. 7), *An Outline of Psychoanalysis*, *Totem and Taboo*, and *Moses and Monotheism*. Let me first recall the content of Freud's thesis in general and the way it operates in *Moses* in particular.

The thesis consists in a twofold argument:

1. It first involves what Freud calls the "recapitulation" theory, according to which physical and psychic individual development (ontogenesis) recapitulates the whole physical and psychic evolution of the species (phylogenesis), so that a strict correspondence might be established between infancy and prehistory, for example, or between adulthood and civilization.

2. Such a correspondence—second-fold in the argument—is made possible because phylogenesis, also called "archaic heritage," "comprises not only dispositions but also subject matter—memory-traces of the experience of earlier generations" (*Moses*, 99). Archaic heritage is then both biological (instinctual dispositions and tendencies to repeat) and historical (memory-traces, remembrance of events). It not only comprises the biological "tendency . . . to enter particular lines of development," "such as are characteristic of all living organisms" (98), but also involves psychic traces. Without this interaction between the biological and the psychic operating at both the ontogenetic and phylogenetic levels, we would not be able to understand how complexes, such as the Oedipus complex, can be transmitted through generations or how the different phases of psychic development can be identical for each individual. Archaic heritage necessitates the coincidence or collaboration of something instinctual ("[Human] archaic heritage," Freud says, "corresponds to the instincts of animals even though it is different in its compass and contents"; 100) and of something symbolic, of automatic repetition and transmission of a meaningful psychic content by way of memory-traces. This coincidence or collaboration guarantees the paradoxical persistence, in all subjects, of a vestige that is not properly theirs because they have not experienced it directly but that at the same time constitutes them as subjects.

In *Archive Fever*, Derrida insists on the "irrepressible, that is to say, only suppressible and repressible, force and authority of this trans-generational memory," without which "there would no longer be an essential history of culture, there would no longer be any question of memory and of archive . . . , and one would no longer even understand how an ancestor can speak within us, nor what sense there might be in us to speak *to* him or her, to speak in such an *unheimlich,* 'uncanny' fashion, to his or her ghost. *With* it."[4] Derrida also declares that we cannot simply assimilate Freud's theory with a form of Lamarckism, and he affirms the necessity to "articulate the history of genetic programs and ciphers on all the symbolic and individual archives differently."[5] The imperative of such a "different" articulation nevertheless remains totally indeterminate, and Derrida leaves the question open. Benhaïm seems right, then, to characterize the Freudian thesis as a heuristic tool, which "helps us to conceptualize the subject's links with its ancestors" without being endowed with any objective or empirical status. It is, once again, a necessary "fantasy" (*la fantaisie phylogénétique*) or even a necessary "fiction."[6] Before starting to challenge such a reading, let us ask a few questions.

How is the issue of phylogenesis exposed and dealt with in *Moses and Monotheism*? What is the specificity of this text compared with others also defending psychic phylogenesis, such as *Totem and Taboo*?

AT THE END of the second essay of *Moses and Monotheism*, Freud states that the Bible and his own development at least coincide on one point, which is that Judaism lays its foundation on a fundamental duality. In the Bible, this duality lets itself split in three dichotomies (there are three "twos"): "Jewish history is familiar to us for its dualities: *two* groups of people who came together to form the nation, *two* kingdoms into which this nation fell apart, *two* gods' names in the documentary sources of the Bible" (*Moses,* 52). Let us recall that by two groups of people, we have to understand tribes from Egypt and tribes from the Midian area, Jews and Midianites; by two kingdoms, Judah and Israel; and by two gods, Yahve and Elohim.

Freud continues: "To these we have to add two fresh ones: the foundation of *two* religions—the first repressed by the second but nevertheless later emerging victoriously behind it, and *two* religious founders, who are both called by the same name of Moses and whose personalities we have to distinguish from each other" (*Moses*, 52). The two religions are those of Aten and Yahve; the two Moseses, Moses I and Moses II, are the Egyptian and the Midianite.

These dualities certainly do not contradict one another but actually constitute an identity, that of Jewish monotheism. If it is so important to add the two last ones, it is because an identity made of dualities is necessarily a result, a production, something that emerges out of a process, a very specific type of becoming, a type of becoming that Bruno Karsenti in his book *Moïse et l'idée de peuple* (Moses and the idea of people) calls "une répétition en devenir," a "repetition in progress":[7] Moses II becoming/reiterating/displacing Moses I, Yahve becoming/reiterating/displacing Aten. To such a becoming, Freud gives the name of latency. The identity proceeding from a series of dualities constitutes itself throughout a period of latency or what Freud also calls an "incubation period" ("a clear allusion to the pathology of infectious diseases," he says; *Moses*, 67), a long period during which identity seems to sleep and then appears, when it wakes up, as a "delayed effect" (*Moses*, 66).

This long period of latency—Freud proposes several hypotheses about its exact length—starts after Moses's murder and lasts until the Qades compromise, when, again, Moses I merged with Moses II, and Aten reappeared behind Jahve. This long moment of latency coincides with the formation of Jewish monotheism, which is also with the becoming Jewish of Moses himself.

Our problem appears at that point: "How are we to explain a delayed effect of this kind and where do we meet with a similar phenomenon?" Freud asks (*Moses*, 66). Here comes the psychic phylogenetic argument:

> The Mosaic religion [the religion of the first Moses] had not vanished without leaving a trace; some sort of memory of it had kept alive—a possibly obscured and distorted tradition. And it was this tradition of a great past which continued to operate (from the background, as it were), which gradually acquired more and more power over people's minds and which in the end succeeded in changing the god Yahweh into the Mosaic god and in the re-awakening into life the religion of Moses that had been introduced and then abandoned long centuries before. That a tradition thus sunk into oblivion should exercise such a powerful effect on the mental life of a people is an unfamiliar idea to us. We find ourselves here in the field of group psychology, where we do not feel at home. We shall look about for analogies, for facts that are at least of a similar nature, even though in different fields. And facts of that sort are, I believe, to be found. (70)

The analogy that Freud is making use of here is that of individual neurosis. A long development follows, explaining how a trauma, even if immediately repressed, leaves traces or "scars" in the psyche and how a neurosis is always produced by the return of the repressed, or the phenomenon of resurfacing. Such an analogy allows Freud to state that Jewish monotheism is the result of the initial trauma caused (1) by the murder of the primeval father and then by the murder of Moses I, (2) by the denial and repression of these deeds, and (3) by their final resurfacing: "Fate had brought the great deed and misdeed of primaeval days, the killing of the father, closer to the Jewish people by causing them to repeat it on the person of Moses, an outstanding father-figure. . . . To the suggestion that they should remember, which was made to them by the doctrine of Moses, they reacted, however, by disavowing their action; they remained halted at the recognition of the great father and thus blocked their access to the point from which Paul was later to start his continuation of the primal history" (89).

This slow, latent constitution of a tradition, this intermingling of preservation, forgetting, and reemergence, precisely leads Freud to interrogate, at the end of section 3 and in the passage I quoted to start with, the very possibility of transgenerational transmission, as it conjoins something comparable with "acquired characters" (*Moses*, 100) in the realm of biological development and memory-traces in the realm of psychic development.

The issue of a phylogenetic transmission of the parricide had been already elaborated and exposed in *Totem and Taboo*, and Freud refers several times to this book in *Moses and Monotheism* (see *Moses*, 81). As I mentioned earlier, though, there is something new in *Moses and Monotheism*, something different from *Totem and Taboo*, which constitutes the very singularity of the psychic phylogenetic argument developed in it and renders the question of archaic heritage even more complex and acute. The originality of the thesis pertains to the introduction of two elements: the notion of a "sliding 'complemental series,'" or else a *sliding scale*, between the traumatic and the nontraumatic in the etiology of trauma (73) and the notion of "historical truth" developed at the very end of the book.

Moses and Monotheism provides a more careful and thorough analysis of the specific modalities of archaic heritage than does *Totem and Taboo*. How, exactly, does such an inheritance proceed? How does it operate? The two notions of "complemental series" (*gleitende sog. Ergänzunßgsreihe—échelle mobile*, or *sliding scale*) and of "historical truth" appear in the wake of these questions. Exploring them will help us to bring to light the very specific type of transmission Freud has in mind here and will show that he was already, without knowing it, on his way to epigenetics. I start with "historical truth."

Archaic heritage is not comparable with any oral or written transmission. The passage I quoted to start with already taught us that archaic heritage is perfectly independent "of direct communication and of the influence of education by the setting of an example" (99), of any tradition "handed on from one generation to another by oral communication" (69). It has nothing to do with an oral tradition and is not reducible either to the sole transmission of a written document. It is not a myth, it is not a legend, it is not exactly a story. The father's murder and its repression are not transmitted like a legend or an epic (*Moses*, 68–71). I am referring here to the pages where Freud shows that what constitutes Mosaic religion as a tradition proper is inassimilable either with the "exceedingly rich store of tribal legends and hero-myths" of the Greeks (70) or with the "national epics" of Indians, Finns, or Germans (71). It is, once again, latency, with all its delayed effects, that determines the specific type of transmission we are looking for here. But how exactly do repetition, return, and traumatic revivification function in latency? How are we to characterize the systematicity of latent recurrence?

Here comes the answer: recurrence in latency is *historical*. In *Moses and Monotheism*, archaic heritage equates historical truth. Of course, "historical," here, does not mean historical, does not coincide with the usual definition of this term. Let us remember that Freud is looking for a type of transmission that situates itself in between biology and history. "Historical" designates one of the terms of this in-between only, not the in-between itself. Therefore, it is not a satisfactory word, and Freud makes use of it for want of a better one. My contention is that "epigenetic" is the missing term. Historical truth in reality means epigenetic truth.

"Historical" cannot mean historical because the event, here, the traumatic event, forgotten as well as remembered, with its uncertain chronology, is not exactly an event in the traditional sense of the term. And this because it is deprived of any contingency. A historical event, whatever its importance, even if fundamental, foundational, is by definition always contingent. It might as well not have occurred. The father's murder, with its religious implications, is on the contrary absolutely not contingent. It had to take place. How are we to understand its necessity, though? It cannot be a mechanistic, deterministic one; otherwise we could not call it historical. More precisely, and it is here also as if Freud were as anticipating the signification of this term, it cannot be *genetic*. The necessity of the inheritance we are looking for here is in part that of a program. In a certain sense, the traumatic event plays the part of a psychic genetic code. At the same time, this program is *from the outset* transcribed and expressed each time in a different way. This difference itself becomes inherited, so that the offspring are affected by both the trauma and its modifying reception. This means that the event, here, is not contingent but not mechanically determined either. Freud affirms that all individuals do not inherit the trauma in the same way. Here comes the sliding scale. Some individuals are very affected by the trauma, some others much less so. "We can easily arrive at the expedient of saying that something acts as a trauma in the case of one constitution but in the case of another would have no such effect" (*Moses*, 73). Certain facts act like traumas on certain individuals but remain effectless on others. Further, Freud reaffirms the fact that despite the dispositions to react similarly to "excitations, impressions and stimuli," "such as are characteristic of all living organisms" (98), there are dramatic differences among individuals regarding the way in which the trauma is received and repeated, that is, inherited. "The archaic heritage must include these distinctions; they represent what we recognize as the *constitutional* factor in the individual" (98).

Individual differences certainly do not constitute an objection to archaic heritage. On the contrary, they prove that the universality, identity, and similarity attached to the archaic do not doom individual psyches to just follow or obey the program without any variation, as if rigidly determined by its coding. "Our knowledge of the archaic heritage is not enlarged by the fact of this similarity" (98). Freud reminds us of the similarity and universality of linguistic symbolism as it appears in dreams (98) or of the similarity and universality of the Oedipal complex and so on. He then states that such a similarity and universality are undoubtable, and yet we have to understand that they are not exactly preformed. Language or complexes do not derive from any "thought-connections between ideas" (analogous to an "intellectual disposition"; 99). Individual variations are epigenetic transcriptions and expressions of the archaic and, in a certain sense, genetic trauma. Without them, the trauma itself could not be transmitted. Epigenetic variations, as differences within identity, constitute the conditions of possibility for latency, repetition, and transmission.

The sliding scale is this in-between zone that Freud is looking for between biology and history, between determinism and contingency. "We then have the conception of a sliding scale, a so-called complemental series," in which "a less of one factor is balanced by a more of the other" (73). This once again means that the process of inheritance has to allow for individual differences. As we said, some individuals are less traumatized than others. Some have not lived the trauma directly and just bear traces of it, some have experienced traumas in their lives that reactivate the initial one, others have no experience and no memory at all and seem unaffected by the trace, and so on. We then have to acknowledge the existence of a moving, fluid, open space, between the paradigmatic structure of the trauma (the murder and its religious signification—which is comparable to a genetic code, a psychic DNA so to speak), its universality, and the variability of individual constitutions. The sliding scale conjoins in its very name the plasticity (sliding) and the paradigmatic nature (scale) of its form. It is an instrument able to measure changes within a general pattern. Such a tool is at the heart of what Freud calls, improperly but so promisingly, the historical truth at work in and as the tradition of monotheism—an epigenetic, that is, nongenetic, truth.

The neologism "epigenetics" was created in 1940 by the British biologist Conrad Waddington. It refers to the branch of molecular biology that studies relations between genes and the individual features they produce, that is, the relation between genotype and phenotype—between the genetic code and the individual physical constitution and appearance. Reflecting with hindsight on the creation of this term, in 1968 Waddington commented, "Some years ago . . . I introduced the word 'epigenetics,' derived from the Aristotelian word 'epigenesis,' which had more or less passed into disuse, as a suitable name for the branch of biology which studies the causal interactions between genes and their products which bring the phenotype into being."[8] The adjective "epigenetic" thus refers to everything to do with this interaction and is concerned with the mechanisms of expression and transcription of the genetic code in the formation of the phenotype. Expression and transcription consist in the activation and inhibition of certain genes. Epigenetics thus studies the mechanisms that modify the function of genes by activating or deactivating them in the process of constituting the phenotype. Such modifications do not alter the DNA sequence itself; they are said to happen at the "surface" (*epi*) of the code, at the surface of the molecules—hence the name *epi*genetics.

With epigenetics, then, appears a space of biological negotiation, so to speak, between the code in its universality (genotype) and the individual differences produced by its transcription or expression (phenotype). The French geneticist François Jacob had already anticipated this when he wrote in his book *The Logic of Life: A History of Heredity*,

> The genetic programme is not rigidly laid down. Very often it only sets the limits of action by environment, or merely gives the organism the ability to react, the power to acquire some extra information which is not inborn. Phenomena such as regeneration or modifications produced in the individual by environment certainly indicate some degree of flexibility in the expression of the programme.[9]

This "flexibility" is precisely the object of epigenetics today. Epigenetic modifications depend on two types of causes: *internal* and *structural*, on the one hand; *environmental*, on the other. First, it is a matter of physical and chemical mechanisms (essentially pertaining to the RNA, nucleosome, methylation). Second, epigenetics also supplies genetic material with a means of reacting to the evolution of environmental conditions.

Let us come to the central point, which is the issue of inheritance. Epigenetic modifications have the particularity of being inheritable from one generation of a cell to the next. There is, therefore, a transmissible memory of the changes linked to environment. For example, while plants do not have a nervous system, they have the ability to memorize seasonal changes at the cellular level.[10] Among animals, reactions to environmental conditions are even greater. Laboratory studies of consanguine mice have recently shown that a change of diet had an influence on offspring. The fur color of the young—brown, yellow, or dappled gray—depends strictly on this change. When pregnant females are given certain food supplements,[11] the majority of their young develop brown fur. The young mice born of the control mice that did not receive these supplements have yellow or dappled fur. Unlike genetic heredity, epigenetic inheritance is reversible, meaning that it can cease at some point of the transmission chain. It is an actual inheritance nevertheless, and most geneticists now think that the behavior of genes can thus be modified by life experiences.[12]

In the fundamental text *Evolution in Four Dimensions*, Eva Jablonka and Marion J. Lamb acknowledge a certain return of Lamarckism. Epigenetic inheritance in a sense coincides with inheritance of acquired characters. They write, "Information transmitted through non-genetic inheritance systems is of real importance for understanding heredity and evolution."[13] Lamarckism is inevitable when it comes to *cultural* inheritance, which goes along with biological evolution. "The Lamarckian approach requires that

[we] treat inheritance as an aspect of the development not of just individuals, but of the social and cultural system."[14] We then have to understand that evolution and development do not follow a single direction but are a crossing point of several lines of transmission: genetic, epigenetic, behavioral, and symbolic.

UNTIL RECENTLY, RESEARCH on epigenetic inheritance has focused essentially on physical traits or characteristics, as we just saw with plants and animals. The issue, of course, is whether epigenetic transmission can also function at the psychic level. More and more studies are currently proving that such is the case. This new dimension of epigenetics was first brought to light by scientific research about the inheritance of stress. From there, something I would not hesitate to characterize as a new approach to trauma has progressively started to get elaborated. The article from the *Guardian* states, "If there's a transmitted effect of trauma, it would be in a stress-related gene that shapes the way we cope with our environment." Some studies have proposed a "connection between one generation's experience and the next. For example, girls born to Dutch women who were pregnant during a severe famine at the end of the Second World War had an above-average risk of developing schizophrenia. Likewise, another study has showed that men who smoked before puberty fathered heavier sons than those who smoked after." The article then moves to the very important work of Rachel Yehuda, a professor of psychiatry and neuroscience and director of the Traumatic Stress Studies Division at the Mount Sinai School of Medicine:

> The conclusion from a research team at New York's Mount Sinai hospital led by Rachel Yehuda stems from the genetic study of 32 Jewish men and women who had either been interned in a Nazi concentration camp, witnessed or experienced torture or who had had to hide during the second world war.
>
> They also analysed the genes of their children, who are known to have increased likelihood of stress disorders, and com-

pared the results with Jewish families who were living outside of Europe during the war. "The gene changes in the children could only be attributed to Holocaust exposure in the parents" said Yehuda.

She argues that "epigenetic changes stemming from the trauma suffered by Holocaust survivors are capable of being passed on to their children, the clearest sign yet that one person's life experience can affect subsequent generations." "'To our knowledge, this provides the first demonstration of transmission of pre-conception stress effects resulting in epigenetic changes in both the exposed parents and their offspring in humans,' said Yehuda, whose work was published in *Biological Psychiatry*."[15]

"Do Jews Carry Traumas in Our Genes?" is the title of another article, an interview of Yehuda. The title is misleading. The way in which journalists presents Yehuda's work might let us think that she is defending a theory of genetic determinism, as if something like a gene of trauma might exist. Yehuda is very clear nevertheless. Traumatic inheritance is epigenetic. What is an epigenetic change, then? the journalist asks. "Well, an epigenetic change occurs from the environment," Yehuda answers.

So there's something in the external environment that affects the internal environment, and before you know it a gene is functioning in a different way. Epigenetics has been something that cancer researchers studied for a long time because it helped explain how a dramatic change could occur in the environment of a person to cause a tumor. But it's become interesting now in neuroscience and mental health because it helps answer questions that have not been answered either by classic genetics or by stress theory. And those questions involve, "How do you create an enduring transformative change that isn't genetically programmed?"[16]

The idea of epigenetic inheritance is still controversial, as scientific convention states that genes contained in DNA are the only way to transmit biological information between generations. However, it becomes more and more obvious that our genes are modified by the environment, "through chemical tags that attach themselves to our DNA, switching genes on and off. . . . Whether the gene in question is switched on or off could have a tremendous impact on how much stress hormone is made and how we cope with stress." Yehuda declares, "It's a lot to wrap our heads around. It's certainly an opportunity to learn a lot of important things about how we adapt to our environment and how we might pass on environmental resilience." At this point, we find ourselves exactly at the crossing point, mentioned earlier, between biology and history. The epigenetic character of the impact of Holocaust survival on the next generation shows that intergenerational effects "are not just transmitted by social influences from the parents or regular genetic inheritance."[17]

In order to figure the relations between the genetic and the epigenetic, some scientists, such as Jablonka and Lamb, have used the metaphor of music and its instrumental performance:

> The transmission of information through the genetic system is analogous to the transmission of music through a written score, whereas transmitting information through non-genetic systems, which transmit phenotypes, is analogous to recording and broadcasting, through which particular interpretations of the score are reproduced. . . . What we are interested in now is how the two ways of transmitting music interact. Biologists take it for granted that changes made in genes will affect future generations, just as changes introduced into a score will affect future performances of the music. Rather less attention is given to the alternative possibility, which is that epigenetic variants may affect the generation and selection of genetic variation.[18]

Thomas Jenuwein, from the Max Planck Institute, for his part affirms,

The difference between genetics and epigenetics can probably be compared to the difference between writing and reading a book. Once a book is written, the text (the genes or DNA: stored information) will be the same in all the copies distributed to the interested audience. However, each individual reader of a given book may interpret the story differently, with varying emotions and projections as they continue to unfold the chapters. In a very similar manner, epigenetics would allow different interpretations of a fixed template (the book or genetic code) and result in different readings, dependent upon the variable conditions under which the template is interrogated.[19] (Cf. Freud, *Moses*, part 1: "In its implications the distortion of a text resembles a murder"; 43)

In the eloquently titled book *La fin du "tout génétique"?*, Henri Atlan notes the challenge to the "genetic paradigm." He writes, "The idea that 'everything is genetic' is starting to be seriously unsettled."[20] From that point on, a new model was established, "which renews interest in molecules that vector information that is not reducible to the information contained in the DNA structures alone." Atlan subsequently writes, "the idea that the totality or essential aspects of the development and functioning of living organisms is determined by a genetic program tends to be gradually replaced by a more complex model that is based on notions of interaction, reciprocal effects between the genetic, whose central role is not denied, and the epigenetic, whose importance we are gradually discovering."[21]

A new economy of inheritance currently emerges that situates itself at the very crossing between the biological and the symbolic, thus allowing for a new concept of *history* to be brought to light. History would designate not only a series of past events but also a specific type of biological inheritance. With this renewed version of phylogenesis, we are then moving from fantasy to reality.

In conclusion, I would like to insist on the fact that contrary to a widespread view, current biology—cellular biology and neurobiology, in particular—are able to bring confirmation of some of the major psychoanalytic theses. Epigenetics undoubtedly makes the idea of psychic phylogenesis sustainable and provides us with the concept of a deep interaction between the biological and the symbolic. We are now facing the emergence of a new chapter in the history of the archive and the transmission of traces—in which the biological, from the perspective of a renewed Lamarckism, plays a central role. The thesis of an epigenetic transmission of trauma is then replacing previous theories of either mysterious, purely psychic inheritance or, on the other hand, hardwired genetic heredity. To the extent that neuropsychoanalysis recognizes epigenetic inheritance as one of its core principles, it is in my opinion the strongest theoretical breakthrough susceptible to grant a future to Freud's thinking.

Some inevitable issues arise at this point. Among many characteristics of this future, one concerns the becoming of religion. What about the religious in the age of epigenetics? Is it not purely and simply suspended? In *Freud and the Non-European*, Edward Said follows this path when he praises Yerushalmi for his vision of Judaism as more a phylogenetic than a properly religious tradition. "Yerushalmi shrewdly points out that Freud seemed to have believed, perhaps following Lamarck, that 'the character traits embedded in the Jewish psyche are themselves transmitted phylogenetically and no longer require religion in order to be sustained. On such a final Lamarckian assumption even godless Jews like Freud inevitably inherit them and share them.'"[22] Such a desacralized vision of transmission is an anticipation of a new meaning of the death of God. God dies in the epigenetic transmission of his death, thus creating a space of indistinction between the sacred and the profane. Epigenetics suspends the religious meaning of the death of God by paradoxically objectively maintaining the trace of its traumatic consequences.

Let us go further in epigenetics and desacralization and raise an even more complex problem. Epigenetics never starts after genetics but always with it; genetics and epigenetics are strictly contemporaneous. Coming back to *Moses and Monotheism* and reading it through the epigenetics grid, we may affirm that all epochs, all steps in the constitution of monotheism and perhaps in the constitution of the sacred in general, are epigenetic transcriptions, that is, individual variations of a program. If such is the truth, then Egyptian monotheism, as well as Midianite monotheism and even the first primeval feast, are epigenetic versions of the trauma. This means that the trauma is always already a trace, a version. If such is the case, then religion is suspended right from the beginning, to the extent that it is reducible to phylogenetic traces with no origin proper. In that sense, Judaism loses its specificity and privilege. Said is right when he challenges Yerushalmi's claim that we just quoted. "On such a final Lamarckian assumption even godless Jews like Freud inevitably inherit and share [character traits]." But then Yerushalmi goes on to ascribe a kind of almost desperately providential leap to Freud that I find largely unwarranted. "If monotheism," he says, "was genetically Egyptian, it has been historically Jewish." He then adds—quoting Freud—that "it is honor enough for the Jewish people that it kept alive such a tradition and produced men who lent it their voice, even if the stimulus had first come from the outside, from a great stranger."[23]

With Said, even if differently, I claim the end of privileges. No tradition ever can be said to have been genetically monotheistic. The Egyptian moment, again, is already epigenetic. Inheritance always paradoxically proceeds from the outside of the program. This again means that there are no privileged moments in inheritance. The archaic is always already retranscribed, modified, and expressed, at its "surface" only perhaps but certainly deeply enough to plasticize its origin.

We can then ask ourselves what *Moses and Monotheism* becomes if we extend latency to time as a whole and if we are to consider that origin is already a variation. This leads me to a last remark, a more playful one, at least apparently. The end of privileges might also concern psychoanalysis itself. What if another latency, another repetition in progress, was preparing itself between the time when Freud wrote *Moses and Monotheism* and the current emergence of neuropsychoanalysis? What if a merging of Freud I with Freud II was secretly happening today? The use I have made of recent biological and neurobiological research in this chapter undoubtedly raises the question of a possible resurfacing of Freud's past as a neurologist. My contention is that Freud murdered this first identity in order to appear as the founder of a new discipline ("I will add the further comment that the psychical topography that I have developed here has nothing to do with the anatomy of the brain"; *Moses*, 97) and that the repressed past is now resurfacing. So in fact we would have three Freuds: the neurologist, the psychoanalyst, and the neuropsychoanalyst. Would we then be witnessing, with the emergence of neuropsychoanalysis, the end of a period of latency during which Freud II (the psychoanalyst) was secretly preparing his future merging with Freud III (the neuropsychoanalyst)? Mark Solms is not far from such a conclusion when he characterizes psychoanalysis as "a moment of transition" between Freud's beginning as a neurologist and the current state of neurobiology.[24] Are we at the end of such a moment of transition, when psychoanalysis appears as just an epigenetic version of phylogenesis?

Is current epigenetics definitely able to bring confirmation of Freud's thesis? We may wonder what "confirmation" means when it comes to the relationship between science and psychoanalysis. When "science" seems to be able to objectively prove some psychoanalytic assumptions, does it not always dismantle psychoanalysis itself? Can psychoanalysis remain what it is when it becomes "true"? Such is the question that has been haunting me since I have started researching the relationships between psychoanalysis and current neurobiology. Again, when science brings confirmation of psychoanalysis, does it not always mark the end of its reign by paradoxically bringing back the shadow of the sacrificed father—here something like the neural unconscious?

Moses I, Moses II, Freud I, Freud II, Freud III, neurobiology, psychoanalysis, neuropsychoanalysis: in any case and as always, as Karsenti rightly notes, "ce . . . qui devient répétition et rend la répétition répétable, c'est [toujours] un compromis": "what returns and makes repetition repeatable is always a compromise."[25]

Notes

[1] Sigmund Freud, *Moses and Monotheism*, trans. James Strachey, in *The Standard Edition of the Complete Psychological Works of Sigmund Freud*, vol. 23 (1937–1939), London: Vintage, 2001, 99–100 (part 3 trans. Katherine Jones for Hogarth Press). Hereafter cited parenthetically in the text.

[2] Helen Thompson, "Study of Holocaust Survivors Finds Trauma Passed On to Children's Genes," *Guardian*, 21 August 2015.

[3] David Benhaïm, "La phylogenèse et la question du transgénérationnel," *Le Divan Familial*, 2007/1 (no. 18), 11–25.

[4] Jacques Derrida, *Mal d'archive: Une impression freudienne*, Paris: Galilée, 1995, 59; translated by Eric Prenowitz as *Archive Fever: A Freudian Impression*, Chicago: University of Chicago Press, 1996, 35–36.

[5] Ibid., 58–59 (English ed., 35–36).

[6] Benhaïm, "La phylogenèse," 21–22 (my translation).

[7] Bruno Karsenti, *Moïse et l'idée de peuple: La vérité historique selon Freud*, Paris: Cerf, 2012, 112.

[8] Conrad Hal Waddington, "The Basic Ideas of Biology," in *Towards a Theoretical Biology*, vol. 1, *Prolegomena*, Edinburgh: Edinburgh University Press, 1968–1972, 9–10.

[9] François Jacob, *The Logic of Life: A History of Heredity*, trans. Betty E. Spillmann, New York: Pantheon, 1982, pp. 9–10.

[10] Research on certain types of cress have, for example, made it possible to show that being exposed to cold during the winter led to structural changes in the chromatin, which silenced the flowering genes. These genes are reactivated in the spring, when the longer and warmer days become suitable for reproduction. The environment may also provoke changes that have effects on future generations.

[11] Supplements rich in methyl, such as folic acid and vitamin B12.

[12] Cf. Mae-Wan Ho, *Living with the Fluid Genome*, London: Institute of Science in Society / Penang, Malaysia: Third World Network, 2003; and "Epigenetic Inheritance: 'What Genes Remember'?," *Prospect Magazine*, no. 146, May 2008.

[13] Eva Jablonka and Marion J. Lamb, *Evolution in Four Dimensions: Genetic, Epigenetic, Behavioral, and Symbolic Variation in the History of Life*, Cambridge, MA: MIT Press, 2005, 109.

[14] Ibid., 229.

[15] Thompson, "Study of Holocaust Survivors."

[16] David Samuels, "Do Jews Carry Trauma in Our Genes? A Conversation with Rachel Yehuda," *Tablet*, 11 December 2014.

[17] Thompson, "Study of Holocaust Survivors," citing Marcus Pembrey, emeritus professor of pediatric genetics at University College London.

[18] Jablonka and Lamb, *Evolution in Four Dimensions*, 245.

[19] Thomas Jenuwein, "Epigenetics," 2006, www.epigenome-noe.net. This site offers an excellent brochure that is very complete and clear on the definition and importance of epigenetics.

[20] Henri Atlan, *La fin du "tout génétique"? Vers de nouveaux paradigmes en biologie*, Paris, INRA Editions, 1999, 16.

[21] Ibid. See also "Épigénétique: L'hérédité au-delà des gènes," *La Recherche*, no. 463, April 2012, 38–54.

[22] Edward W. Said, *Freud and the Non-European*, London: Verso, 2003, 31.

[23] Quoted ibid.

[24] Mark Solms, *A Moment of Transition: Two Neuroscientific Articles by Freud*, London: Karnac Books, 1990.

[25] Karsenti, *Moïse et l'idée de people*, 112.

Gilad Sharvit

9 Moses and the Burning Bush: Leadership and Potentiality in the Bible

19 October. The essence of the Wandering in the Wilderness. A man who leads his people along this way with a shred (more is unthinkable) of consciousness of what is happening. He is on the track of Canaan all his life; it is incredible that he should see the land only when on the verge of death. This dying vision of it can only be intended to illustrate how incomplete a moment is human life, incomplete because a life like this could last forever and still be nothing but a moment. Moses fails to enter Canaan not because his life is too short but because it is a human life. This ending of the Pentateuch bears a resemblance to the final scene of L'Education sentimentale.

—Franz Kafka, *The Diaries*

Introduction

MOSES AND MONOTHEISM (1939) is a story about an absolute monarch. It is a tale about a powerful hero who was raised to greatness and destined to lead a nation. In Freud's version of the biblical narrative, Moses was an Egyptian prince who lived in the short period of monotheism during the reign of Akhenaten in

Egypt. The Egyptian monotheism ended shortly after the death of Akhenaten, but Moses was determined to maintain his religion and went on to invent a new people out of the Israelite slaves with the intention that they would worship his monotheistic God. The Bible centered on the exodus of the Jews from Egypt; however, Freud found that Moses's greatest challenge was not the Egyptian pharaoh but the weak minds of the Jewish slaves. His mission was to make the Israelites into a people, the Jewish people.

This chapter focuses on the portrayal of Moses as a tyrannical ruler in *Moses and Monotheism*. Moses, according to Freud, was an almighty and violent leader who subjugated the Israelite slaves thanks to his "decisiveness of thought, a strength of will, and an energy of action."[1] This depiction of Moses, however, essentially obscured the Bible's much more nuanced representation of Moses. In practice, Freud omitted the important, even defining event of the Burning Bush, when Moses was not domineering nor demanding but rather suffered under the imperious demands of God. In the story of the Burning Bush, Moses was a shepherd whom God coerced to go to Egypt, not a leader who coerced the Israelites to take on the monotheistic religion. My claim is that Freud's dismissal of this central element of the biblical narrative and his focus on the despotic nature of Moses suppressed a radical notion of freedom that defines Moses's struggle and captures the essence of his leadership. If Freud's Moses was a hero who condemned the Jewish people to repressions and restrictions, the Bible tells of an individual who fought to hold onto his freedom from the demands of divine law. My analysis of the interaction of Moses with God borrows several concepts from Giorgio Agamben's theory of impotentiality to argue that, contrary to the authoritarian Moses of Freud, the biblical Moses symbolizes the human struggle for impotentiality—for resistance to power and responsibility.

My argument engages with several disparate sources: the Bible, Freud's psychoanalytic theory, and Agamben's political and metaphysical works. My aim is to mine these texts for intellectual resources to think about the question of potentiality and identity. Most importantly, my argument suggests that Moses, and not Paul, should be reconsidered as the true and original hero of the impotentiality described by Agamben and that the scene of the Burning Bush is fundamentally a political narration of the basic human aspiration for freedom.

Freud's Moses: An Absolute Monarch

IN FREUD'S THEORY of the "Great Man," the Jewish people were created by an almighty sovereign. Moses had "great capacities, ambitiousness and energy."[2] He was "jealous, severe and ruthless" and had "an irascible nature" that tended to "[flare] up easily."[3] But most of all, Moses had the determination and inner conviction that were required for the submission of the Jewish slaves to the moral demands of monotheism—a religion that was based on repression and radical prohibitions. The restrictive nature of that new religion was not easy on the slaves and their sensual nature. "The harsh prohibition against making an image of any living or imagined creature" and the God that "even his name may not be spoken" were very different from their previous polytheistic system.[4] These prohibitions had to be violently imposed by a ruler with total domination.

In Freud's myth, the complete control of Moses over his people proved more than successful. His religion was "a rigid monotheism on the grand scale," one that "may have been even harsher" than the original monotheism in Egypt.[5] Indeed, the power and determination of Freud's Moses were so overwhelming that they reflected back on his people. Moses's domineering presence repressed the wishes of the Jewish people but also raised their self-esteem. The cruel demands for advances in intellectuality elevated the Jews from the nations around them and granted them a sense of "holiness."[6] It was Moses, their first leader, who

instilled in the Jews their eternal unshaken belief in their "superiority."[7]

There is no surprise, then, that Moses epitomized Freud's figure of the "Great Man" in human history.[8] Like Goethe, Leonardo
da Vinci, and Beethoven, Moses had a character that allowed him
to change the course of history:

> And now it may begin to dawn on us that all the character-
> istics with which we equipped the great man are paternal
> characteristics, and that the essence of great men for which
> we vainly searched lies in this conformity. *The decisiveness of
> thought, the strength of will, the energy of action* are part of the pic-
> ture of a father—but above all *the autonomy and independence* of
> the great man, *his divine unconcern which may grow into ruthless-
> ness*. One must admire him, one may trust him, but one cannot
> avoid being afraid of him too.[9]

Moses was able to control his people and to enslave them, to
remold their sensual nature into spiritual rationality, because he
had a "decisiveness of thought, a strength of will, and an energy
of action." Unlike his followers, Moses had a ruthless conviction
in a truth and the confidence and ability to realize his vision.
The effectiveness, the leadership, the absolute control made him
a suprahistorical figure.

Freud's focus in *Moses and Monotheism* on the role of the leader
in the life of a nation was partly based on his earlier *Group Psychology and the Analysis of the Ego* (1921), in which he famously argued
for an analogy between the leader and the figure of the father.
In *Moses and Monotheism*, that analogy was further developed to
explain the overwhelming control of Moses over his children, the
Israelites. Moses, Freud argued, coerced the slaves into the monotheistic religion like a father that educates his children: "there
is no doubt," Freud noted, "that it was a mighty prototype of a
father which, in the person of Moses, stooped to the poor Jewish
bondsmen to assure them that they were his dear children."[10]

The fatherly essence of Moses hinted at another father figure in Freud's theory, the one that inaugurated history. In *Totem and Taboo* (1913), Freud's famous depiction of the beginning of civilization and religion, there was also a "violent primal father," the ruler of the primal horde, who like Moses demanded unlimited obedience from his sons.[11] And like the Egyptian prince, the jealous primal father subjugated his sons, demanded they repress their wishes, and asked for their absolute obedience, "whose infringement was punished by death."[12] Moses, and the primal father before him, blocked the sun out: there was nothing they did not know, nothing they did not care about, nothing they did not demand. They both constituted an absolute and tyrannical presence in the lives of their children.[13]

The similarity between the Moses myth and the primal father uncovers a third and decisive dimension of Freud's Moses. In line with the transfiguration of the primal father into the first totem animal, Moses, the great man and father, was for all practical purposes also the Israelites' God. According to Freud, the impressive image of Moses invoked a divine presence. The Egyptian ruler was certainly much closer to a god than to the slaves he liberated from Egypt. This conflation was not uncommon in the ancient world, still under the impression of the totemic religious system, in which "kings have been treated in no way differently from gods."[14] But unlike other ancient rulers, Moses had a godlike personality.[15] In Freud's Feuerbachian myth, it was the individual Moses who granted his God his almighty power: "It was probably not easy for [the Jewish people] to distinguish the image of the man Moses from that of his God; and their feeling was right in this, for Moses may have introduced traits of his own personality into the character of his God—such as his wrathful temper and his relentlessness."[16]

Freud's Moses had no hesitations, no second thoughts, and no reservations. While the Greek gods suffered from inconsistencies and skepticism, Moses, the Jewish great man and godlike figure, was deliberate and accurate, clear and precise. Most of all, Moses had an "extraordinary effectiveness," which enabled him to "form a people out of random individuals and families, [to] stamp them with their definitive character and determine their fate for thousands of years."[17] In the end, it was not God but, rather, "this *one man Moses* who created the Jews."[18]

Moses and the Burning Bush

FREUD'S *MOSES AND MONOTHEISM* notoriously introduced an abundance of changes, shifts, and ruptures to the biblical narrative. The secret Egyptian identity of Moses and the myth of his death captured the imagination of most commentators. There is, however, another, fundamental episode in the life of the biblical Moses that Freud completely ignored: the story of Moses in front of the Burning Bush. This, I argue, was not an accidental forgetfulness.

In contrast to the idolizing portrayal of Moses, the divine leader and powerful ruler and father, the Burning Bush tells us of a different Moses, of a self-conscious and stubborn shepherd. Moses, the Bible tells us, was grazing Jethro's flocks in the desert when he came to the Mountain of God and saw a bush burned in a fire that was not consumed. However, when God called him from the fire and asked to bring the Israelites out of Egypt, Moses was not resolved but undecided and apparently fearful. His first reaction was not a reaction we can easily assign to a charismatic leader: Moses was not domineering or fatherly; instead, Moses insisted that he is "not eloquent" and "prayed" not to be the leader.[19] This is hardly a response Freud could have allowed his Moses, the primal father of the Jews.

In the original biblical narrative, Moses did not initiate or plan the liberation of the Jews from Egypt. It was the other way around: Moses tried to resist God's mission to liberate the Israelites. The biblical Moses resisted the position God has assigned him: five times he stubbornly challenged God's choice, and five times God answered, until, in the end, "the anger of the Lord was kindled against Moses."[20] Only then was Moses forced to obey God's will. The Bible tells us nothing of Moses's last words before God. In the end, he just "went and returned to Jethro his father in law."[21]

Freud's Moses, the great man who subjugated the Jewish mob, was according to the biblical narrator hesitant, uncertain—reluctant to agree to the ultimate demand of God's calling. He worked hard to make God's decision inoperative, to live outside the rule of God. In that, Moses was very different from Abraham, the one who obeyed his God without hesitation. There was no refusal, not even discussion, when God asked Abraham to leave his homeland and emigrate to the Promised Land. There was no refusal even when the obedient Abraham was asked to sacrifice his son, only an unbounded faith that "God will provide."[22]

Moses's reluctant surrender to God's calling, however, was not the end of the story. The events following the scene of the Burning Bush hint at an ongoing struggle, one that highlights the deep meaning of Moses's position toward the absolute rule of God. On his way to Egypt and accompanied by his wife, Zipporah, Moses faced once again the fury of God. In this second round of instructions to Moses on the road to Egypt, God's monologue was suddenly interrupted in a scene that reveals the true essence of Moses's earlier surrender: "And it came to pass by the way in the inn, that the lord met him, and sought to kill him."[23] The Bible says nothing of the reasons for God's violence. And while the Jewish Midrash usually focuses on Zipporah's reaction to claim that God's fury originated from the fact that Moses's son was still uncircumcised, I suggest that it is also feasible to assume that Moses on his way was still struggling with God. Despite his previous obedience, Moses could have expressed one last time, his wish not to lead. This time, God was very clear in his reaction: he sought to "kill" him. Only a heroic act of Zipporah, who understood the full ramifications of the continuous struggle, saved Moses: "Then Zipporah took a sharp stone, and cut off the foreskin of her son, and cast it at his feet, and said, Surely a bloody husband art thou to me."[24] God's wish to kill Moses was outmaneuvered by a bloody violence inflicted on the body of the son of Moses. Instead of Moses's death, Zipporah circumcised his son as a symbol of radical submission. The fact that Zipporah, immediately after the circumcision, "cast [the foreskin] at [Moses's] feet" hints at Moses's responsibility, maybe even at the symbolic castration of Moses himself. Zipporah's quick response, I argue, manifested a latent meaning of circumcision, one that Freud picked up easily: "Circumcision is the symbolic substitute for the castration which the primal father once inflicted upon his sons in the plenitude of his absolute power, and whoever accepted that symbol was showing by it that he was prepared to submit to the father's will, even if it imposed the most painful sacrifice on him."[25] The act was a symbol of marking of the power of the sovereign on the body of his subjects. From an individual outside the control of God, from a person with a potentiality not-to-be, Moses became a body, a *bare life*. If, in Freud's myth, it was Moses who inflicted his power on his people, in the Bible, it was God whose demand for obedience was expressed through the subjugation of the body of Moses and his son. This act, this marking on the body, finally committed Moses to the rule of God.

Freud, I argue, upended the biblical narrative. The story of the biblical Moses offers an archetypal story of one's potential *not* to lead, *not* to accept an offer, *not* to cooperate. In *Moses and Monotheism*, in considerable divergence from the Bible, the hero was the one who demanded, the one who compelled his people. Moses was the one who tore the Jewish people away from their previous lives. Freud applied the biblical narrative in inverted form. In the Bible, it was not only the Jews but also their leader who was forced to obey. Moses, and not only his people, was deprived of the opportunity to resist. In Freud's myth, on the other hand,

Moses invented the Jewish people *and* their God. There was nothing to be asked of Moses, no one to demand he go back to Egypt. It was Moses's plan through and through. Freud's Moses could have been subjugated to no one, not even to God. He was the one who circumcised them all.[26]

Freud, Agamben, and Impotentiality

WHAT IS THE core of Moses's refusal? Why did he insistently disobey? One can argue that Moses's refusal is only a natural response of a timid shepherd that should not reflect on his character. Buber, in his *Moses* (1946), explains that Moses's "smallness" compared to the vast task could have only led to such a reaction. This resistance belonged in that sense "to the most intimate experience of the prophetic man."[27] As Ilana Pardes rightly points out, Abraham's reaction was exceptional: divine missions were actually often refused in the Bible. All who were commanded attempted to escape in one way or the other:

> Divine love is as strong as death. . . . No one who is asked to be a divine agent can escape God. It is a tyrannical offer one cannot refuse. Moses, who tries to convince God in the initiatory scene by the burning bush that he is not meant for the mission, is one such case. Jeremiah, who claims that he is but a na'ar (child or youth) and cannot deliver the Word, is another relevant example, not to mention Jonah, who runs off to the vast sea in an unsuccessful attempt to hide from God.[28]

Pardes importantly elaborates on another reason for the attempts of escape. There was, she claims, a "tyrannical" nature to the offer. There was something unbearable in the divine love that was "as strong as death." It was irreparably oppressive. I would like to pursue this reading to argue that Moses was not merely afraid. He was certainly anxious and fearful to face God, but Moses was also very strong and impressive in his negotiations with God. Moses did not run away to the sea. Moses fought back.

His fight, nonetheless, expressed a very different set of character traits and a different political position. The Moses who faced the Burning Bush was not domineering and controlling but defiant and strong-minded. My reading of the Burning Bush noted anxiety and fear. However, my argument suggests that Moses was as afraid as he was confident; he was anxious but also daring. Moses fought not to control others but to stay outside God's control. His struggle was not to force the Jewish people into submission but to resist the complete domination of God.

In the following, I aim to reframe the reluctance of Moses vis-à-vis Agamben's theory of impotentiality. I claim that the resistance of Moses to God's command manifested his qualities as a leader and symbolized a basic human struggle: to make the demands of the law inoperative. Moses's reaction, in my reading, manifests a powerful image of the basic, most human fight, to escape the inescapable request of the ultimate monarch.

Agamben's concept of potentiality/impotentiality is based on Aristotle's theory of potentiality in book 9 of *Metaphysics*.[29] Aristotle opens his discussion of potentiality by differentiating between two kinds of potentialities: The first, which he terms "generic potentiality," refers to the potential to know or do something unknown or never before experienced. The second is the potential to actualize an existing knowledge or ability. In the first, there is a change, an alteration—the individual learns something. In the second, there is no alteration: it applies to a musician who already knows how to play music. Aristotle and Agamben are interested in the second kind, in which the person has a potential "thanks to a *hexis*, a 'having,' on the basis of which he can also not bring his knowledge into actuality (*mē energein*) by not making a work."[30] At this point, we should note that the biblical drama of Moses portrays a story of a leader who refuses to lead. Moses had a *hexis*: God did not bestow on Moses the qualities of a leader—Moses was a leader all on his own. The Bible hints at that by commenting on the reasons for his finding the Burning Bush:

"He *led* [וַיִּנְהַג] the flock to the backside of the desert, and came to the mountain of God."[31] Moses *led* the sheep in the desert, the Bible insists, the same way he will *lead* the people of Israel in the desert. This distinction, of the shepherd as a leader, is intensified by the identification of God as the ultimate shepherd in Psalms: "The lord is my shepherd; I shall not want."[32] Thus, Moses's resistance to God's command does not address his leadership traits: Moses is concerned that the Jewish people will not believe him or that he will not be understood, but nowhere is his inability to lead his people mentioned.

The "red thread" running through Agamben's thinking on potentiality is Aristotle's criticism of the Megarians' claim that "all potentiality exists only in actuality."[33] Instead of a theory of potentiality that always passes into actuality, and in that sense is not different from actuality, Aristotle and Agamben aimed to formulate a theory of potentiality that is independent, and in fact constitutive of, actuality. In Agamben's discussion of Aristotle's analysis of the faculty of vision in *De anima*, he elaborated on such a concept. To think of the potentiality to see, Agamben argued with Aristotle, one has to consider the possibility of not-seeing. Otherwise, all potentiality will always realize itself into actuality, and there will be no real potentiality (to see). Accordingly, the potentiality of vision is not the potentiality to see (light) but the potentiality not to see (or to see darkness). People can see because "they have the *potential* not to see, the *possibility of privation*."[34] For that reason, all potentialities, like the potential to be a poet or a shepherd, are defined not by one's ability to act but rather as a *"relation to one's own incapacity."*[35] Any and all capacities are thus dependent on their privation. Otherwise, they would become static, unchanging, and, according to Agamben, also inhuman.

The interpretation of the scene of the Burning Bush via Agamben suggests that Moses battled for the same impotentiality. To explain, let us note that in the Bible, Moses was a leader, a shepherd, who was forced to lead the Israelites, forced to fully actualize his potential. Moses was capable to lead, but he was also forced to lead. This would suggest a paradox: the divine calling, that radical and absolute demand, not only forced Moses to the rule of divine law but strangely deprived Moses of his potentiality to lead by *requiring* him to lead. Moses, however, needed the possibility not to be the leader, so he could "accumulate and freely master [his] own capacities, to transform them into 'faculties.'"[36] *His resistance was an act of a leader who fights for his potentiality not-to-lead*:

> Those who are separated from what they can do, can, however, still resist; they can still not do. Those who are separated from their own impotentiality lose, on the other hand, first of all the capacity to resist. And just as it is only the burning awareness of what we cannot be that guarantees the truth of who we are, so it is the only lucid vision of what we cannot, or can not, do that gives consistency to our action.[37]

In Agamben's theory of potentiality, the measure of what someone can do is defined not solely by his actions but by his relation to his possibility *not* to do. Moses's resistance to God's command was not a simple refusal of someone who wished to be left alone, incapable to act, or afraid of the mission: Moses needed the vision of what he could not do, in order to become the leader he was. He resisted because he needed a truth of who he was that was different from God's definition. He needed to refuse, and here it gets tricky, to be able to comply. To be the Jewish leader, Moses had to fight against the commandment to lead the Jewish people.

Moses's speech impediment illustrates, in my reading, his position in front of the law. However, first, let us note that according to Freud in *Moses and Monotheism*, Moses's stammer is meant "to present a lively picture of the great man."[38] Freud's Moses was the ruler who could not speak the language of his people. The stammer signified his ability to take over and tame a different nation. Moses was so dominant that he was able to cross over the border of language. Nothing stopped him. This stammer, interestingly, indicates something completely different from the perspective of the theory of potentiality. My claim is that Moses's stammer should be associated with "infancy," a term Agamben develops in his early *Infancy and History* (1993) to designate a "'wordless' experience in the literal sense of the term."[39] In *Idea of Prose* (1995), Agamben elaborated on this experience, claiming that an infant is still "so little specialized, and so totipotent that it rejects any specific destiny and any determined environment."[40] The infant is outside of language and for that reason is able to enjoy an "openness," a carelessness that the speaking adult lacks. The infant's wordless experience grants him or her an indeterminacy and thus a freedom from biopolitical power.

I argue above that Moses's reluctance was a fearful reaction, but nevertheless illustrated his qualities as a leader. I argue likewise that Moses's speech impediment does not mark a weakness but rather is a symbol of infancy: it manifests his struggle to retain his potentiality, an "openness" to undetermined experience. The stammer symbolizes Moses's resistance to God. It is a sign of Moses's wish to retain his impotentiality, as an "authentic recalling of humanity."[41] Freud converted the stammer into an image of a powerful leader. His Moses was able to move beyond his weakness and to control the Jewish people. The biblical Moses of impotentiality, on the other hand, insisted on retaining his stammer. His stammer grounded the possibility for self-definition beyond the rule of law and language.

Thinking through Foucault's model of biopolitics, Agamben's theory of potentiality redefined the relations of the individual with the political. For Agamben, the political was a realm of certainties, of absolute definitions, that completely determines the subject. His radical notion of potentiality, as constitutive of actuality, was aimed at rethinking that relation: "Every human power is *adynamia*, impotentiality; every human potentiality is in relation to its own privation. . . . *Other living beings are capable only of their specific potentiality; they can only do this or that. But human beings are the animals who are capable of their own impotentiality. The greatness of human potentiality is measured by the abyss of human impotentiality."*[42] While animals are defined by their actuality, by the concrete manifestation of their nature, humans are able to evade that fate, by sustaining the freedom not to choose this way or the other. Fire, Agamben tells us, can only burn; humans can choose not to. Fire is always actual and thus always the same. Humans have the possibility not to be and thus a potential to change, a potential for freedom. To put it in Heideggerian terms, the suspension of actualization renders the individual a way out of the order of things, a negativity that defines humanity. Moses's struggle accordingly symbolizes the fundamental human struggle: Moses fought not only for his potentiality to lead but for his freedom.[43] Moses resisted so that he could be free, that is, "to be capable of one's own impotentiality, to be in relation to one's own privation."[44] His struggle was not a struggle to have the power to decide this or that or to refuse to do this or that. In *resisting*, the biblical Moses *was* free. In *resisting*, Moses was *human*.

Freud completely missed that as he portrayed a father figure who dominated his people. In Freud's liberal theory of freedom, it was only the primal father and Moses after him who were truly free, since freedom was granted only to those who were outside societal repression.[45] Moses was free because he was the ruler, the father. And freedom was enjoyed only by the very few in every society—those figures of the law who were above the law. The Burning Bush, I suggest, hints at a different political theory: Moses was not above the law but before the law, and his fight against the divine command, the reality of resistance, granted him his humanity, his freedom, his leadership. His struggle with God was not accidental but imperative: it signaled his humanity and grounded his heroic character. Moses was the great man, but not because of his coercive nature: he was the first to struggle for his potentiality, for his humanity.

Freud was unable to integrate the story of the Burning Bush with his image of the fatherly Moses because he identified fear and undecidedness that were unfit for his powerful hero. In my reading, however, Moses was a hero of a different kind. In *Moses and Monotheism*, Moses was the father of the Jews and was their god; in the story of the Burning Bush, Moses was the first hero of potentiality. Like Bartleby the scrivener in Herman Melville's novella, whose only reply, "I would prefer not to," signified, per Agamben, "a complete or perfect potentiality,"[46] Moses refused to cooperate with the demands of the political. Moses, too, "preferred not to," and impassively took up a resistant position in the face of God. The Freudian Moses was the hero of the sovereign ban; the biblical Moses was a hero of potentiality. There could have been no greater distance between them.

Moses, no doubt, was also different from Bartleby. Moses was, after all, God's "servant . . . who is faithful in all mine house."[47] Remarkably, the ambiguity of the scene of the circumcision of Moses's son allowed for more than one interpretation.[48] Circumcision was not only a mark of sovereign power; it was also a symbol of the covenant with God. The Bible, I would argue, leaves it to the reader to decide if Moses accepted an offer or was condemned to obey—if Moses was humanly free or divinely coerced. Regardless of either interpretation, Moses's loyalty was certainly not a slavery. His insistence and his struggle to resist God and for potentiality were still manifested throughout the biblical story. His style of leadership was indeed unmatched. In that sense, Kafka is perhaps a better literary antecedent to Moses's potentiality than Melville is. Kafka's famous diary entry on the "essence of the Wandering in the Wilderness" provides a future of potentiality to Moses. For Kafka, Moses was a paradigmatic symbol of humanity for exactly the same reasons that the scene of the Burning Bush portrayed: In Kafka's version, Moses presented "how incomplete a moment is human life." His Moses was fragile, ambivalent, and uncertain. Human life was incomplete, and Moses's wandering illustrated the impossibility of a destiny, far from the despotic and confident hero of Freud.

Eventually, the potential not-to-be and the disobedient fight for impotentiality maybe even saved the Jewish people. Confronted with the divine wrath after the incident of the Golden Calf, when God asked to "consume" the corrupted people, Moses struggled, once again, for a change of heart.[49] This time, this crucial time, God indeed repented.

Notes

I wish to deeply thank Karen S. Feldman, Eyal Bassan, Joseph Albernaz, and Ilana Pardes for their wonderful suggestions and insightful comments. Epigraph: Kafka, F., *The Diaries, 1910–1923*, trans. Greenberg, M., with the cooperation of Arendt, H., ed. Brod, M. (New York: Schocken Books, 1948–49), 393–394.

[1] Sigmund Freud, *Moses and Monotheism: Three Essays*, in *The Standard Edition of the Complete Psychological Works of Sigmund Freud*, vol. 23, trans. and ed. James Strachey (London: Hogarth, 1953 [1939]), 109. Hereafter the *Standard Edition* is abbreviated *SE*, followed by volume number.

[2] Freud, *Moses and Monotheism*, 32.

[3] Ibid., 33, 36.

[4] Ibid., 18.

[5] Ibid., 18, 47.

[6] Ibid., 106.

[7] Ibid.

[8] In the Great Man versus *Zeitgeist* debate over the actual impact we can assign to the "hero" in historical events, Freud interestingly chose no sides, assessing that "there is room in principle for both." Ibid., 107. Freud was willing to acknowledge the material conditions that prepared the way for the Egyptian monotheism, while his analysis of the establishment of the Jewish religion and the unification of the Jewish people was exclusively focused on the role of Moses.

[9] Ibid., 109–110 (emphasis added).

[10] Ibid., 110.

[11] Sigmund Freud, *Totem and Taboo*, in *SE* 13, 142.

[12] Freud, *Moses and Monotheism*, 83.

13 Jacques Lacan famously built on these relations between Moses and the primal father to develop his later theory of the Symbolic, the Imaginary, and the Real father. Jacques Lacan, "The Other Side of Psychoanalysis 1970," trans. Russell Grigg, in *The Seminars of Jacques Lacan*, vol. 17 (New York: Norton, 2007), 102–140.

14 Freud, *Moses and Monotheism*, 112.

15 See also Ruth HaCohen, "Psychoanalysis and the Music of Charisma in the Moseses of Freud and Schönberg," in *New Perspectives on Freud's "Moses and Monotheism*," ed. Ruth Ginsburg and Ilana Pardes (Tübingen: Niemeyer, 2006).

16 Freud, *Moses and Monotheism*, 110.

17 Ibid., 107.

18 Ibid., 106. Freud's fascination with the despotic image of Moses probably had biographical reasons. The powerful father of the Jews portrayed a counterimage to Freud's father, the "unheroic" Jacob. Moses, the father of all the Jews, was the hero that the true father of Freud could have never been. In the following, I aim to focus on the theoretical implications of that narrow image. See also Marianne Krüll, *Freud and His Father*, trans. Arnold J. Pomerans (New York: Norton, 1986); Emmanuel Rice, *Freud and Moses: The Long Journey Home* (Albany: State University of New York Press, 1990); and Yosef H. Yerushalmi, *Freud's Moses: Judaism Terminable and Interminable* (New Haven, CT: Yale University Press, 1991), 73–74. In Bluma Goldstein's *Reinscribing Moses* (1992), Moses highlighted Freud's unconscious need for rescuing. Freud's attraction to Moses expressed his fears regarding anti-Semitic violence. Moses was a violent and domineering hero, who captivated Freud thanks to "his superiority, his individuality, and uniqueness, and his power." He embodied an imaginary answer to a real and concrete violent danger: his unrestrained powers promised to suppress not only the Jews but, more importantly, the anti-Semitic mob. Bluma Goldstein, *Reinscribing Moses: Heine, Kafka, Freud, and Schoenberg in a European Wilderness* (Cambridge, MA: Harvard University Press, 1992), 111.

19 Exodus 4:10, 13.

20 Exodus 4:14.

21 Exodus 4:18.

22 Genesis 22:8. My reading here follows on Søren Kierkegaard's argument in *Fear and Trembling*, ed. C. Stephen Evans and Sylvia Walsh, trans. Sylvia Walsh (Cambridge: Cambridge University Press, 2006).

23 Exodus 4:24.

24 Exodus 4:25.

25 Freud, *Moses and Monotheism*, 122.

26 Not accidentally, in Freud's only reference to the scene of Zipporah's circumcision of Moses's son, he was very quick to dismiss it as "distortions." Ibid., 26.

27 Martin Buber, *Moses: The Revelation and the Covenant* (New York: Harper, 1958), 47.

28 Ilana Pardes, *The Biography of Ancient Israel: National Narratives in the Bible* (Berkeley: University of California Press, 2000), 83.

29 Aristotle, *Metaphysics Theta*, trans. and commentary Stephen Makin (Oxford: Oxford University Press, 2006).

30 Giorgio Agamben, "On Potentiality," in *Potentialities: Collected Essays in Philosophy*, ed. and trans. Daniel Heller-Roazen (Stanford, CA: Stanford University Press, 1999), 179.

31 Exodus 3:11 (emphasis added).

32 Psalms 23:1.

33 Agamben, "On Potentiality," 180.

34 Ibid., 181 (emphasis in original).

35 Ibid., 182 (emphasis in original). Impotentiality (*impotenza*), in that sense, was different from inability: it is a potentiality not to be that grounds any potentiality to be.

36 Giorgio Agamben, *Nudities*, trans. David Kishik and Stefan Pedatella (Stanford, CA: Stanford University Press, 2011), 44.

37 Ibid., 45.

38 Ibid., 33.

39 Giorgio Agamben, *Infancy and History*, trans. Liz Heron (New York: Verso, 1993), 47.

40 Unlike animals—that also have no language but are defined by their natural/genetic predispositions and thus "attend only to the law"—the infant is in a "condition of being able to pay attention precisely to what is not written, to somatic possibilities that are arbitrary and uncodified." Giorgio Agamben, *Idea of Prose*, trans. Michael Sullivan and Sam Whitsitt (Albany: State University of New York Press, 1995), 96.

41 Ibid., 96.

42 Agamben, "On Potentiality," 182 (emphasis in original). The move for actuality is now perceived as a second negation of potentiality, yet one that "preserves itself." Actuality becomes potentiality to a second degree: "What is truly potential is thus what has exhausted all its impotentiality in bringing it wholly into the act as such." Ibid., 183.

43 The authoritative political system, by defining the individual in all respects, forces us to live in absolute actuality of our powers and capa-

bilities and as such denies us the freedom not to choose. The law, which radically defines the individual, thus brings about a reality of bare life. In Agamben's political philosophy, however, the solution cannot be found simply in more possibilities. Absolute freedom that modern democracy promises is also problematic. While human beings are defined by their potentiality not to do, the overabundance of possibilities in modernity deprives the individual of any meaningful connection with what we cannot do. Democracy blinds the individual with all the potential to do and by that conceals the political operation that manufactures those possibilities. Only radical passivity, the resort to impotentiality, can be used against such a system. See Agamben, *Nudities*, §5.

44 Agamben, "On Potentiality," 183.

45 Sigmund Freud, *Civilization and Its Discontents*, in *SE* 21, 115.

46 Giorgio Agamben, "Bartleby," in *Potentialities: Collected Essays in Philosophy*, ed. and trans. Daniel Heller-Roazen (Stanford, CA: Stanford University Press, 1999), 246–247.

47 Numbers 12:7.

48 In fact, the move from Moses's struggle for his potentiality to his position as the ultimate sovereign later involves only a rearticulation of his relation to impotentiality and actuality and signals the fact that "at the limit, pure potentiality and pure actuality are indistinguishable, and the sovereign is precisely this zone of indistinction." Giorgio Agamben, *Homo Sacer: Sovereign Power and Bare Life*, trans. Daniel Heller-Roazen (Stanford, CA: Stanford University Press, 1998), 47. In the chapter "Potentiality and the Law," Agamben claims that to understand the sovereign ban, we need to see how even sovereignty relates to the potentiality not to be: "For the sovereign ban, which applies to the exception in no longer applying, corresponds to the structure of potentiality, which maintains itself in relation to actuality precisely through its ability not to be." Ibid., 46. For more on the relation of theology and governance in Agamben's work, see Giorgio Agamben, *The Kingdom and the Glory: For a Theological Genealogy of Economy and Government*, trans. Lorenzo Chiesa (Stanford, CA: Stanford University Press, 2011).

49 Exodus 32:10.

Contributors

Jan Assmann is Professor Emeritus of Egyptology at the University of Heidelberg and Honorary Professor of Cultural Theory at the University of Constance. His books in English translation include *Moses the Egyptian: The Memory of Egypt in Western Monotheism* (1997); *The Price of Monotheism* (2010); *Cultural Memory and Early Civilization: Writing, Remembrance, and Political Imagination* (2011); and *From Akhenaten to Moses: Ancient Egypt and Religious Change* (2014). *The Invention of Religion: Faith and Covenant in the Book of Exodus* will appear in 2018.

Richard J. Bernstein is Vera List Professor of Philosophy at the New School for Social Research. He is the author of *Praxis and Action: Contemporary Philosophies of Human Activity* (1971); *Beyond Objectivism and Relativism: Science, Hermeneutics, and Praxis* (1983); *Hannah Arendt and the Jewish Question* (1996); *Moses and Monotheism: Freud and the Legacy of Moses* (1998); *The Abuse of Evil: The Corruption of Politics and Religion since 9/11* (2006); and *The Pragmatic Turn* (2010).

Karen S. Feldman is Associate Professor of German at the University of California, Berkeley. She is the author of *Binding Words: Conscience and Rhetoric in Hobbes, Hegel and Heidegger* (2007). Recent publications have appeared in *Philosophy and Rhetoric, MLN, PMLA,* and *Germanic Studies.*

Willi Goetschel is Professor of German and Philosophy at the University of Toronto. He is the author of *Constituting Critique: Kant's Writing as Critical Praxis* (1994); *Spinoza's Modernity: Mendelssohn, Lessing, and Heine* (2004); and *The Discipline of Philosophy and the Invention of Modern Jewish Thought* (2012).

Ronald Hendel is Norma and Sam Dabby Professor of Hebrew Bible and Jewish Studies in the Department of Near Eastern Studies at UC Berkeley. His books include *The Text of Genesis 1–11: Textual Studies and Critical Edition* (1998); *Remembering Abraham: Culture, History, and Memory in the Hebrew Bible* (2005); *Reading Genesis: Ten Methods* (editor and contributor, 2010); and *The Book of Genesis: A Biography* (2013).

Catherine Malabou is Professor at the Centre for Research in Modern European Philosophy at Kingston University (UK) and Professor of Comparative Literature at the University of California, Irvine. Her recent books in English include *The Heidegger Change: On the Fantastic in Philosophy* (2011); *The New Wounded: From Neurosis to Brain Damage* (2012); *Ontology of the Accident: An Essay on Destructive Plasticity* (2012); *Self and Emotional Life: Philosophy, Psychoanalysis, and Neuroscience* (with Adrian Johnston, 2013); *Before Tomorrow: Epigenesis and Rationality* (2016).

Gabriele Schwab is Chancellor's Professor of Comparative Literature at UC Irvine. She is the author of *Subjects without Selves: Transitional Texts in Modern Fiction* (1994); *The Mirror and the Killer-Queen: Otherness in Literary Language* (1996); *Haunting Legacies: Vio-*

lent Histories and Transgenerational Trauma (2010); and *Imaginary Ethnographies: Literature, Culture, Subjectivity* (2012). She also edited the volume *Derrida, Deleuze, Psychoanalysis* (2007).

Yael Segalovitz is a fellow of the Townsend Center for the Humanities and a Posen fellow. She is a PhD candidate in the Department of Comparative Literature at the University of California, Berkeley. Her dissertation, "New Criticism, Int.," explores the global circulation of New Criticism. She is the translator of Clarice Lispector's *A via crucis do corpo into Hebrew* (2016). Her poetry translations into English have appeared in *Mantis*, *Two-Lines*, and *T-joLT*.

Gilad Sharvit is a Townsend fellow at the Townsend Center for the Humanities at the University of California, Berkeley. He was a Diller postdoctoral fellow at the Center for Jewish Studies at the University of California, Berkeley (2014–2016). His recent publications have appeared in the *Journal of Modern Jewish Studies*, *Idealistic Studies*, and *Journal of Austrian Studies*.

Joel Whitebook is former director of the Psychoanalytic Studies Program at the Institute for Comparative Literature and Society and a faculty member at the Center for Psychoanalytic Training and Research at Columbia University. He is the author of *Perversion and Utopia: A Study in Psychoanalysis and Critical Theory* (1995) and is currently working on an intellectual biography of Freud.

Index

42; explanations Freud suggests for, 33–34, 48–49, 52, 140, 158; failure to terminate, 40; Freud's fear of Nazis and need for rescuing, 215n18; Freud's foreseeing of Nazis and, 1–2; Freud's hope that reason will triumph over irrationality of, 40; *Geistigkeit* and, 47; Nazi violence, Freud's reaction to, 17; psychological roots of, 2; as undying hatred of the Jews, 2, 19, 27–28, 31–33, 35, 42, 140, 158; Zweig's attempt to explain in Germany, 22n1

Aram, 166–169

archaic heritage, 180, 184–185. *See also* transgenerational transmission

archive. *See* Derrida, Jacques; historiography, criticism of; history

Aristotle: on epigenesis, 188; on potentiality, 208–209; works: *De anima*, 209; *Metaphysics*, 208

Armstrong, Richard, 63n30

Asiya (mother of Moses in Qur'an), 90

Assmann, Jan, 20–21, 138; on Axial Age relating to Akhenaten's and Moses's monotheism, 49; on ban on graven images, 31; on Christianity in Freud's affirmation of patriarchy, 55; on cultural memory, 37, 40, 43–44n10; on Exodus myth, 45n19; on Freud's presentation of evidence, 99, 159; on "mnemohistory" in pattern of trauma–latency–return, 37; on Mosaic monotheism, 171; on *Moses and Monotheism*'s depiction of Freud's obsession, 158; on Moses's story and normative inversions, 91, 105n10; on revolutionary vs. evolutionary

monotheism, 44n18; on Sellin's theory of murder of Moses, 20–21, 144–154, 160–161; on violence's relationship with *Fortschritt in der Geistigkeit*, 35; on violence's relationship with religion and monotheism, 44–45n19; works: *The Invention of Religion*, 156n14; *Moses the Egyptian*, 15–16, 38; *The Price of Monotheism*, 25n36, 38–39

Assyrians, 149, 168

Aten religion, 4, 29, 39, 67, 93, 142, 182

atheism, 39, 53, 100, 102

Atlan, Henri: *La fin du "tout génétique"?*, 193

Aton (Egyptian god), 93, 105n17

attention: deliberate attention, 114, 131; "evenly suspended attention," 20, 109, 113–115, 117, 121, 123, 128, 131, 132n9, 136n56; free association technique and mobile attention, 115–116, 121, 123, 125–126; in New Critics' method, 111–113, 134n19

Aufklärung, 54

Augustine, 152

Axial Age, 49–50

Baal Peor, 144, 152, 164

Babylonians, 79, 149

Bakan, David, 22n5

Baltzer, Klaus, 147

Baron, Salo, 23–24n23, 110, 118, 161

Beethoven, Ludwig, 122, 202

belonging and exile, 20, 87–107; brother horde and, 91, 92, 105n11; Freud dying in exile, 101; historical truth vs. belonging, 102–103; imperialism and monotheism, 94–95, 104n7, 106n19; mirroring ancient hero legends, 89; monotheism as counterreligion to polytheism, 92–93; Moses as abandoned child, 87–89, 103, 104n4; Moses's biblical story of, 87–91; Moses's need to flee Egypt after committing murder, 97; psychoanalytic reading of historical archive and, 96–104; Roma story of Moses and, 90–91

Benhaïm, David: "Phylogenesis and the Question of the Transgenerational," 179, 181

Benjamin, Walter, 20, 42, 55

ben Zakkai, Jochanan, 31

Bernstein, Richard J., 19, 27, 54, 161–162; *Freud and the Legacy of Moses*, 13–14, 19, 30–31, 62n4

Bible: Deuteronomistic history of punishment of Israelites in, 148–150; on Moses's death, 146; *The Philippson Bible*, 58; ten, use of number in, 151. *See also* Hosea

Biblical citations: Acts 7:52–53, 147; Deuteronomy, 148, 170; Exodus, 88, 149; Exodus 1–15, 155n5; Exodus 2, 104n4; Exodus 3:11, 216n31; Exodus 4:10, 215n19; Exodus 4:13, 215n19; Exodus 4:14, 215n20; Exodus 4:18, 215n21; Exodus 4:24, 215n23; Exodus 4:25, 215n24; Exodus 14, 149–150; Exodus 32:10, 217n49; Genesis 22:8, 215n22; Genesis 31:47, 169; Hosea 1–3, 170; Hosea 1:4, 164; Hosea 2:10, 164; Hosea 2:18, 164; Hosea 4:2, 164; Hosea 5:13, 168; Hosea 6:8–9, 164; Hosea 7:7, 164; Hosea 7:11, 168; Hosea 8:11–13, 172; Hosea 9:7, 162, 165; Hosea 9:7–8, 164; Hosea 9:10, 164; Hosea 11f., 165; Hosea 12, 166, 169, 175n32; Hosea 12:2, 168; Hosea 12:3, 166; Hosea 12:13–14, 166; Hosea 12:15, 164, 165; Hosea 12:15a, 162–164; Hosea 12:15b, 162–164; Hosea 13, 164–167, 169; Hosea 13:1, 162–164; Hosea 14, 166–168; Isaiah 7, 168; Isaiah 52–53, 147; 2 Isaiah, 165; Jeremiah, 148; Joshua, 148; Jubilees, 170; Judges, 148; Kings, 148; 2 Kings 16, 168; Luke 13:34, 147; Matthew 23:37, 147; Matthew 27:25, 176n42; Numbers, 149; Numbers 12:3, 165; Numbers 14:22–23, 151; Numbers 14:30, 151; Numbers 14:33, 151; Numbers 25:1–3, 164; Numbers 25:3–5, 144; Psalms 22:2, 106n30; Psalms 23:1, 216n32; Psalms 106, 153; Samuel, 148

Bion, Wilfred, 128, 136n56

biopolitics, model of, 211

bisexuality, 59, 63n35

Bithiah (Egyptian princess who rescues Moses), 88–89, 90

Bloom, Harold, 83

Blum, Erhard, 169

Bollas, Christopher, 136n56; *The Infinite Question*, 127–128; "Unconscious Perception," 108, 110

Börne, Ludwig, 72

Boyarin, Daniel: *Unheroic Conduct*, 17–18

Breasted, James Henry: *The History of Egypt*, 59–60

brother horde, 91, 92, 105n11

Buber, Martin, 85n15; *Moses*, 12, 207

Buddha, 49

Burning Bush, 21, 200, 204–207, 209, 213

Caleb, 143

Canaan, 143, 147, 150, 153, 199

Caquot, André, 165

Caruth, Cathy, 23n20, 108

Catholicism, 2–3, 28, 87

Chasseguet-Smirgel, Janine, 58

Christ. *See* Jesus Christ

Christian, Barbara, 132n7

The Interpretation of Dreams, 67,
115, 127, 137n64; *Jokes and Their
Relation to the Unconscious*, 67–68;
Leonardo, 59, 63n35; *An Outline of
Psychoanalysis*, 179; "Project for a
Scientific Psychology," 137n64;
"Recommendations to Physicians
Practicing Psycho-Analysis,"
113, 120, 124, 127–128, 137n64;
Totem and Taboo, 4–6, 8–9, 23n14,
24n25, 27–30, 32, 53, 54, 92,
104n6, 129, 138, 139, 161, 179,
184, 203; *Traumdeutung*, 179;
"Two Encyclopedia Articles,"
117, 119, 127. *See also Moses and
Monotheism*

Galileo Galilei, 71
Gaskill, Nicholas, 112, 134n19,
134n30
Gay, Peter, 108
Geistigkeit, 19, 30–31, 42, 46–64;
Bernstein on, 54; *Fortschritt in
der Geistigkeit*, 19, 32, 34–35, 42,
45n19, 54; Freud identifying
as fundamental value of
Jewish people, 47; instinctual
renunciations required in
Judaism and, 50, 52–53, 57,
60; maternal role and, 51, 55,
57; monotheism and, 49, 55;
patriarchy and, 47, 50–51, 56–58
gender politics: of Moses's biblical
story, 90, 104n7; of readers,
135n39; of Woolf's *To the
Lighthouse*, 131
genetics: contemporaneous with
epigenetics, 195; modifications
caused by environmental factors,
190–193, 197n10. *See also* DNA
Gilman, Sander: *Moses and
Monotheism*, 18
Goethe, Johann Wolfgang von, 3,
20, 122, 123, 149, 154, 202; on
murder of Moses in "Israel in der
Wüste," 143–144

Goetschel, Willi, 19, 65, 86nn21–22
Golden Calf, 52, 88, 105n15, 150,
152, 214. *See also* idolatry
Goldstein, Bluma: *Reinscribing Moses*,
16–17, 215n18
Good, Edwin, 168
Greeks, 57, 81–82, 203
Grubrich-Simitis, Ilse, 23n11, 25n38,
51, 56, 109
Guattari, Félix, 120, 127, 136n55
guilt, feelings of, 5, 20, 145–146,
159, 163–165, 171–172, 176n42.
See also latency period; return of
the repressed
Gunkel, Hermann, 175n23

Hegel, Georg Wilhelm Friedrich, 78
Heidegger, Martin, 212
Heine, Heinrich, 3, 19, 66–86;
"dead Maria" motif of, 77–78;
on dynamics of history, 72–73;
Freud's relationship with, 66–68,
78, 82–83; on history as reality,
74–78; Jewish identity of, 66; on
Marengo battlegrounds, 76–77;
on messianism and history,
19, 69–72; on monotheism's
genesis and its resonances
to Freud's thinking, 78–83;
on poet's mission, 74–75;
works: "Confessions," 80–82;
"Disputation," 78; "Hebrew
Melodies" from *Romanzero*, 76,
78; *Ludwig Börne: A Memorial*,
70–73; Messiah in Golden
Chains story, 70–73; "The New
Israelite Hospital in Hamburg,"
84n3; *On Poland*, 71–72; *On the
History of Religion and Philosophy
in Germany*, 75, 78–83; *Pictures
of Travel* installment ("From
Munich to Genoa"), 74–78; *Rabbi
of Bacherach*, 75
Heine, Solomon, 84n3
Hendel, Ronald, 21, 157
hermeneutics, 20, 108–137. *See also*

literary analysis of *Moses and Monotheism*

hero legends, 3–4, 89, 185

historiography, criticism of, 1, 8–9, 14, 102

history: biblical history, 149; defined by moment of afterward, 73; encrypted histories containing historical truth, 103, 106n31; Freud's depth-psychological approach to, 68–69, 96–104, 141; Freud's turning Sellin's hypothesis into historical research, 162; Heine on dynamics of, 72–73; "historical," definition of, 185; modern theory of, 23n14, 23n20; pseudo-history of *Moses and Monotheism*, 157–159, 166, 171

Hoffmann, E. T. A.: "The Sand Man," 110

homosexuality, 18, 59

Horkheimer, Max, 53, 56

Hosea, 21, 159–176; illuminating Freud's claim that "Moses created the Jews," 159; Mosaic discourse and, 169–173; as Mosaic prophet, 169; Moses's death not covered in, 5, 144, 165; Moses's one reference by name in, 166; poetics of juxtaposition in, 167–168. *See also* Biblical citations

Hurston, Zora Neale, 105n9

Hyatt, Philip, 161, 165

idolatry, ban on graven images, 30–31, 49, 50, 54, 88, 142, 201

Ikhnaton, 93

Imago (journal), 2, 28, 118

impotentiality, 21, 200, 207–214, 216n35; animals and, 212, 216n40; infancy and, 211, 216n40; Moses's stammer and, 210–211; Moses's struggle for his potentiality, 217n48

infancy, 180, 211, 216n40; abandoned male infant myths, 89

instinct: archaic heritage and, 180; death-instinct, 10; instinctual renunciations required in Judaism, 50, 52–53, 57, 60

intellectuality, 35–36, 40, 42, 142, 158, 172, 201

intergenerational transmission. *See* transgenerational transmission

International Psychoanalytic Congress (Paris 1938), 22n3, 30, 46

Islam, 44n11, 104n6, 143

Israel, establishment of, 95

Israelites: conversion to Egyptian monotheism, 4–6; God's punishment for disobedience of, 148–150; killing of prophets and opposing the law, 147–149; latency period to assuage guilt of Moses's murder, 9; poor self-representation in Exodus story, 152–153; "sick theology" as result of sin of killing Moses and forsaking monotheism, 145–146; true history of not told, 7; wandering and murmuring in the wilderness, 143, 144, 146, 149–153, 213. *See also* murder of Moses; prophets

Jablonka, Eva and Marion J. Lamb: *Evolution in Four Dimensions*, 189, 192

Jacob, 166–169, 175n32

Jacob, François: *The Logic of Life: A History of Heredity*, 188

Jahve (as warrior god), 93–94, 105n17

Jameson, Frederic, 127, 136n55

Jaspers, Karl, 49

Jensen, Wilhelm: *Gradiva*, 109

Jenuwein, Thomas, 192–193

Jeremiah, 49, 148, 207

Jesus Christ: abandoned child/son analogy with, 106n30; killing of, as return of the repressed for the

Jews, 98, 101; passion narrative's roots in Jewish tradition, 154; as successor to Moses, 32, 147, 154, 165

Jewish identity, 25n39; assimilation, 13; of Freud, 13, 16, 30, 53, 67, 99–100, 106n23, 157

Jews: covenant with God, 21, 45n19, 150, 152, 213; ethical narcissism of, 141–142; Freud explaing character of, 140; Gypsies as enemies of, 90–91; manliness and, 82; Mosaic discourse as responsible for creation of, 159; Moses as embodiment of tragic history of, 89; survival of, 33–34, 82, 140. *See also* anti-Semitism; Israelites; Judaism

Jochebed (Hebrew slave mother of Moses), 88, 90

Jones, Katherine, 30

Joshua, 143

Judaism: abstraction of God as greatest accomplishment of, 49–50, 52, 55; Christianity's relationship to, 83; constructed from merger of two Moses figures, 93–94; Freud's view of, under Nazis, 100; iconoclasm in, 55; Jewish exceptionalism, 19; modern secular Judaism, 13, 25n40; monotheism as Jewish tradition, 195; patricide as seminal event according to Freud, 92; unconscious guilt in, 104n6. *See also* Jews; monotheism

Jung, Carl, 52, 101

Kafka, Franz, 55, 213–214; *The Diaries*, 199

Karsenti, Bruno: *Moïse et l'idée de peuple*, 182, 197

Kierkegaard, Søren, 215n22

King, Martin Luther, Jr., 105n9

Klein, Melanie, 52

Kristeva, Julia, 130

Kronfeld, Chana, 109, 132n7

Laban (Jacob's uncle), 167, 169

Lacan, Jacques, 215n13

Lamarckism and neo-Lamarckism, 1, 11, 13, 14, 21, 24n29, 179, 181, 189–190, 195

Lamb, Marion J. *See* Jablonka, Eva and Marion J. Lamb

Laplanche, Jean and Jean-Bertrand Pontalis: *Vocabulaire de la psychanalyse*, 36, 179

latency period: Assmann on, 37, 43–44n10; Bernstein's focus on Freud's treatment of, 14; duration of, 182; recurrence in latency as historical, 185; role in Jewish history, according to Freud, 9, 29, 93, 98, 138–139, 182, 185

leadership role of Moses, 21, 199–217; Bible's more nuanced depiction of Moses, 200; Burning Bush incident and, 21, 200, 204–207, 209, 213; Freud's focus on despotic nature of Moses, 200, 201–204, 215n18; impotentiality and, 21, 200, 207–214; Kafka's portrayal of Moses, 199, 213

Lentricchia, Frank and Andrew DuBois (eds.): *Close Reading: The Reader*, 112

Leonard, Miriam, 81, 86n27

Leonardo da Vinci, 122, 123, 202

Levy-Valensi, Eliane Amado, 22n5

Librandi-Rocha, Marília, 135n40

Lippit, Akira, 100

Lispector, Clarice, 131

literary analysis of *Moses and Monotheism*, 20, 108–137; close reading and New Critics' approach to critical theory, 110–114, 116, 127, 131–132, 132–133n10, 133nn13–14; creative mind-set employed in, 125–126; desert-like experience of reading, 122–123; "evenly suspended attention" as approach of psychoanalysis and, 20, 109, 113–115, 117, 121, 123, 128, 131, 132n9, 136n56; "Freudian reading," understanding of, 130–131; loosening of readers' critical faculties, 124–125; mobile attention in terms of reader-text relations, 115–116, 121, 123, 125–126; potentiality and fulfillment in text-reader relationship, 116; reading and listening, affinity of, 135n40; the unconscious as participant in reading, 119–120; unedited appearance of *Moses* and free association, 117–118; as work "alien" to its own author, 125

Luke, 147, 148

Maciejewski, Franz, 25n38
Malabou, Catherine, 21, 177
Mann, Thomas, 6
masculinity and androcentrism, 17–18, 47, 50, 56–61
maternal relationship, 47–48, 51, 56–57; Freud's need to suppress, 61; "phallic mother" figure, 59
matriarchy, 61, 92
Melville, Herman: "Bartleby, the Scrivener," 213
memory: cultural memory, 37, 40, 43–44n10; inheritance of, 11–12; of Moses's religion among the Israelites, 145; unconscious memory, 119, 121, 128. *See also* return of the repressed; transgenerational transmission
Mendelssohn, Moses, 53–54
Messiah and messianism, 19, 32, 69–73
Messiah in Golden Chains story (Heine's retelling), 70–73, 83
Meyer, Ed, 104n4
Michelangelo's Moses sculpture, 16
Midianites, 95, 144, 182, 195; Moses as, 93–94, 182

Midrash, 71, 85n15, 88, 148, 205
Miriam, 150
misogyny, 47, 58, 61
Mollins, Mattheu, 134–135n33
monotheism: anti-Semitism linked to, 49; as counterreligion, 15, 37, 52, 92–93, 201; dematerialization and abstraction as part of, 49–50, 52; Egyptian rejection of, 52; Egyptian roots of, 4–5, 15, 52, 93, 138; evolutionary monotheism, 44n18; Freud on historical truth at work in, 187; Freud on neurosis aspect of, 142, 154, 171, 183; Freud on "two monotheisms," 44n11, 93–94, 181–182; imperialism and, 94–95, 104n7, 106n19; Moses's role in continuing Egyptian version of, 6, 29, 92, 138, 201–204; revolutionary monotheism, 37–39, 44, 44n18; Syrian monotheism, importation from, 106n21; violence associated with, 25n36, 35, 39, 44–45n19
Mosaic discourse, 169–173, 175n33, 176n34; "advance of intellectuality" and, 172; anti-Semitism arising from, 171–172; Freudian discourse as secular transformation of, 172; Hosea's poetry as, 169–170; Mosaic distinction, 15, 31, 37–38, 45, 45n19; responsible for creation of Jews, 159, 171
Moses: African American culture's use of Moses story, 105n9; as aristocratic Egyptian, 3–4, 15–16, 18, 29–31, 54, 89, 91, 96, 104n4, 116, 138, 199; attributing his own traits to God, 17; biblical story of, 87–91, 200, 204–207, 209–210; as creator of the Jews, 13, 29, 31, 42, 92–93, 142, 171, 200, 207; in debate over essence of Judaism, 15; etymology of name, 3; as first

Messiah, 83; Freud's identifying with, 51–52, 97, 100, 215n18; Freud's portrayal of, 17, 43n9, 54, 91, 200–204; Freud's two religious founders with same name of Moses, 182; as God figure to Israelites, 203; as Great Man, 17, 122–123, 201–203, 210, 212, 214n8; Heine's portrayal of, 80–83; in Hosea, 166; Kafka's portrayal of, 199, 213; King, analogy to, 105n9; masculinity of, 57; Michelangelo's sculpture of, 16; Midianite Moses vs. Egyptian Moses, 93–94, 182; miracles performed by, 90–91, 150; mirroring ancient hero legends, 4, 89; mystery of historical figure's true life, 146; as primal father figure, 203; Roma tradition and, 90–91; Wiesel's portrayal of, 89. *See also* belonging and exile; leadership role of Moses; murder of Moses

Mosès, Stéphane, 85n7

Moses and Monotheism (Freud): biographical nature attributed to, 16; Burning Bush omission in, 204–207; circumstances surrounding writing of, effects of, 108–109; continued relevance due to complex concerns of, 158, 173; critical reception of publication of, 12–15, 23–24n23, 157; "Der Fortschritt in der Geistigkeit," 30–31, 46–47; as "haunted work," 100; idiosyncratic nature of, 65, 108, 116; increased relevance of, 106n22; as masterpiece of psychoanalysis, 7, 96–104; as opportunity for Freud to reflect on his life work, 6–7; original title of *The Man Moses, an Historical Novel*, 158; Part I: "Moses, an Egyptian," 3–4, 28, 68–69, 116,

193; Part II: "If Moses was an Egyptian," 4–6, 28–29, 66–67, 116, 160–162, 181–182; Part III: "Moses, His People and Monotheistic Religion," 6–9, 22n3, 28, 30, 124–125, 161, 177–178; as pseudo-history, 157–159, 166, 171; publication of separate parts and of book in full, 28; repetitiveness of, 6, 12, 108, 110, 116, 118; Said viewing as critique of Zionism, 95, 106n23; topics covered in, 1–2, 29, 138–139, 202; tradition and history as focus of, 68–69; Yerushalmi misreading, 41–43. *See also* literary analysis of *Moses and Monotheism*

Mount Nebo as site of Moses's death, 47, 152, 156n15

Mozart, Wolfgang, 6

murder: Moses committing, 97; of primal father, 32–33; of prophets, 147

murder of Moses: anticipating martyrdom of Christ, 32, 98, 101, 165; contemporary interest in Freud's theory of, 25n36; Goethe on, 143–144; guilt after, 5, 9, 101; Israelites reacting to Moses's repressive religious tenets by killing, 51–52, 105n15, 138; latency period to assuage guilt of, 9; polytheism, return to after, 29, 39; psychoanalytical approach to, 96–97; return of repressed memory and acceptance of monotheism, 5–6, 29, 31–; second Moses after killing of first Moses, 6, 9–10, 182; Sellin as influencing Freud's theory of, 5, 20–21, 144–154, 160–166; "sick theology" as result of, 145–146; textual murders of Moses, 97–98, 101–102. *See also* transgenerational transmission

Mut (Egyptian deity), 59

Monotheism as masterpiece of, 7, 96–104; reading *Moses and Monotheism* through lens of, 109; of religions, 10; as successor of religion, 39, 42, 101; Yerushalmi on, 53. *See also* attention; free association

Qumran, 148

Rachel (wife of Jacob), 167
racism, 17–18
Rank, Otto, 52; *The Myth of the Birth of the Hero*, 3–4
reason and rationality: as characteristics of Jewish people, 6, 12, 25n40, 36, 39; Freud's challenge to historical constructions based on, 69; Freud's opposition to irrationality, 40, 42. *See also* intellectuality
Red Sea, dividing of, 150
religion: belief vs. disbelief in, 143, 149, 151, 154; compulsive power of, 40; idolatrous nature of, 54; Nazi persecution of, 34; as neurosis (in Freud's view), 129, 139, 142, 149, 154, 171, 183; origins of, 1, 18, 32, 158; phylogenetic traces of, 195; psychoanalytic theory of, 10, 129–130, 141; violence associated with, 25n36, 35, 44–45n19. *See also* Aten religion; Christianity; Islam; Judaism; monotheism
repetition, 33, 68, 72, 97, 108, 131, 172. *See also Moses and Monotheism*
repression, 41. *See also* return of the repressed
resistance, 52, 148, 200, 204, 206–208, 210–213
return of the repressed: Assmann on, 37, 41; current outbreaks of anti-Semitism as, 40–41; as entry to new theory of history, 23n20;

Jewish identity and, 13; killing of Jesus and, 98; original Mosaic religion based on, 10, 29–30, 32, 41, 98, 139, 140, 145, 183; violence and, 35; World War I soldiers experiencing, 10. *See also* transgenerational transmission
Rice, Emmanuel, 25–26n40
Richards, I. A., 133n13
Rieff, Philip, 43n9
Robert, Marthe: *From Oedipus to Moses*, 16, 25n40
Roith, Estelle, 61
Roma, origin of, 90–91

Said, Edward, 95, 100, 101; *Freud and the Non-European*, 6–7, 14–15, 106n22, 194–195
Sammons, Jeffrey, 85n14
Schäfer, Peter, 24n27
Schiller, Friedrich, 3, 15, 126
Schmid, Konrad, 175n32
Schmidt, Pater Wilhelm, 2, 28
Schmitt, Carl, 33
Schoenberg, Arnold, 48
Scholem, Gershom, 55, 85n15
Schwab, Gabriele, 19–20, 87
Schwartz, Lawrence H., 133n13
Sedgwick, Eve Kosofsky, 110, 132–133n10
Segalovitz, Yael, 20, 108
Seleucids, 149
Sellin, Ernst, 93; Christian roots of theories of, 165; confusing Ephraim with Moses, 163; criticism of his theory of Moses's death, 161, 165–166, 175n23; Hosea interpretation by, 170–171; influence on Freud's theory of Moses murder, 5, 20–21, 144–154, 159, 160–166; *Mose und seine Bedeutung für die israelitisch-jüdische Religionsgeschichte* [*Moses and His Meaning for the History of Israelite-Jewish Religion*], 5, 144, 159, 175n23

sensual enjoyment, renunciation of, 5–6, 12, 50–51, 52, 56, 60, 201
sexuality, 17–18, 47–48, 59. *See also* bisexuality; femininity; gender politics; homosexuality; masculinity
Shakespeare, William: *Hamlet*, 109–110
Sharvit, Gilad, 1, 21, 199
Shittîm, 144, 152
Shorske, Carl, 57–61
Simon, Ernst, 85n15
Sinai covenant. *See* covenant with God
sin and transgression, 165, 173. *See also* transgenerational transmission
Sinnlichkeit, 50–51, 55, 57, 60
Slavet, Eliza, 24n28
Socrates, 49
Solms, Mark, 196
Sophocles: *Oedipus Rex*, 109
Spencer, John, 15
Spinoza, Baruch, 67
spirituality: carnality vs., 55; Christian, 55; of Jewish people, 12, 13; progress in spirituality of intellectuality, 45, 172; psychoanalysis and, 130
Steck, Odil Hannes, 148–149, 154
Steinberg, Michael, 25n40
Stephen, 147
Strachey, James (trans.): *The Standard Edition of the Complete Psychological Works of Sigmund Freud*, 30, 46
"Study of Holocaust Survivors Finds Trauma Passed On to Children's Genes" (*Guardian* article 2015), 178, 190
suffering servant tradition, 147, 154, 165
superego, 21, 43n9, 170, 171
Syria, importation of monotheism from, 106n21
Syro-Ephraimite war (735–732 BCE), 168

Tacitus, 105n10
Talmud, 71, 148
telephone metaphor, 119–121, 137n64
Ten Commandments, 88, 151; ban on graven images, 30–31, 49, 50, 54, 88, 142; no other gods before YHWH, 152
Thotmes III (Egyptian pharaoh), 94
Titus Vespasian, 70
Tiy (Queen), 60–61
tolerance, loss of, 33, 93, 103
Tong, Diane: *Gypsy Folktales*, 90–91
Torah, 31, 141
tradition: Bernstein and Derrida on Freud's treatment of, 14; as difference between written record and oral transmission, 7, 185; Freud's depth-psychological approach to, 68–69, 84; intergenerational transmission and, 184; revelations of oral tradition as more reliable than formal historical records, 8, 14
transference, 20, 90, 92, 94, 97, 99–101, 127
transgenerational transmission, 11–12, 13, 21, 40, 92, 177–198; archaic heritage distinguished from oral or written transmission, 184–185; epigenetic variations as conditions of possibility for, 187–194; Freud considering Jewish character traits as more phylogenetic than religious, 194; genetic modifications caused by environmental factors, 190–193, 197n10; of historical erasures and symbolic murders, 102; of Holocaust survivors' trauma, 178–179, 190–191; irrepressible of transgenerational memory, 180–181; of Jewish guilt, 176n42; memory traces of archaic heritage, 180,

184; Moses as carrier of, 89; recapitulation theory, 180; Sellin and Steck on, 148–149; sliding scale of inheriting the trauma determined by constitutional factors of individuals, 186–187; studies showing evidence of, 190–191; YHWH sentencing Israelites to punishment for 40 years, 151

trauma: Assmann on, 37; childhood traumas, effect on adult persons, 11; as connection to earlier history, 23n20; in Freud's childhood, 56–57; in Freud's works, 10; Hosea making explicit theme of, 165; inheritance of memory and, 11–12; latency period following, 9; Mosaic trauma vs. historical traumas at time of establishment of biblical canon, 20; neo-Lamarckism and, 11; psychic genetic code created by traumatic event, 186; religion as response to, 10. *See also* murder of Moses; return of the repressed; transgenerational transmission

truth: belonging vs. historical truth, 102; in Freud's recasting of Moses story, 98; historical truth at end of *Moses and Monotheism*, 184, 187; Moses's conviction of, 202

Turel, Adrien, 74, 85n16

the unconscious: definitions of, 120; Freud attempting to explain, 128; guilt in Judaism and, 104n6; Heine and, 67; power of, 36; in reading of *Moses and Monotheism*, 119–120; telephone metaphor and, 119–121, 137n64

unconscious memory, 119, 121, 128

Untermeyer, Louis, 67

violence, 15, 17, 20; continual opposition to, 42; of monotheism,

25n36, 35, 39, 44–45n19; reactionary violence, 36, 40–42. *See also* anti-Semitism

Volz, Paul, 175n23

Waddington, Conrad, 188

Walzer, Michael, 153

Weizman, Eyal, 99

Whitebook, Joel, 19, 46, 61n1

Wiesel, Elie, 89

Wimsatt, William, 134n30

Wolff, Hans Walter, 166, 168

Woolf, Virginia: *To the Lighthouse*, 130–131

Yahweh (YHWH): anger toward and punishing Israelites, 148–151; compared to Allah, 44n11; dual gods of Yahve and Elohim, 182; as Mosaic god, 39, 145; as pagan god, 5; saving the Israelites, 150; as warrior god, 93–94

Yehuda, Rachel, 190–192

Yerushalmi, Yosef Hayim: on biblical scholars' opinion of *Moses and Monotheism*, 157; on fate of religion, 41; on Freud's ambivalence about his Jewishness, 16, 53; *Freud's Moses*, 13–15, 24nn28–29, 25n39; on monotheism as Jewish tradition, 195; on psychoanalysis as metamorphosed extension of Judaism, 176n45; on return of the repressed, 29; on Said's categorizing Judaism as phylogenetic instead of as proper religious tradition, 194, 195

Zimri, 144, 152

Zionism, 95, 106n23

Zipporah, 144, 205–206, 216n26

Zweig, Arnold, 1–3; attempt to explain anti-Semitism, 22n1; *Bilanz*, 2; Freud correspondence with, 27–28, 31, 140, 158, 161–162